Every Cloud Has A Silver Lining Or Does It?

Ann Murdock

with Robert MacGowan

Shankhouse Books

First Edition 2017

Edited by R MacGowan
Cover design by R&B MacGowan

Made from renewable resources by

Shankhouse Books©

20 Allonby Mews, Shankhouse, Cramlington, Northumberland NE23 3BJ, UK.
Tel: 01670 207703

Order this book at Amazon or any major online retailer

'Every Cloud Has A Silver Lining, Or Does It?'

ISBN: 978-0-244-90063-2

ACKNOWLEDGEMENTS

I'd like to thank my three sons: Craig, Darren and Wayne, for not giving up on me and providing me with the determination to write this autobiography. You will always be the shining lights in my life.

I want to offer a very special thank you to Rob MacGowan for his patience and dedication. Without his expert help and guidance this book would not exist.

Many thanks also to Rob's wife, Beverley, for her understanding and support, and for listening to my story when we first met in November 2016.

DEDICATIONS

This book is dedicated to my beloved parents, Charles & Jessie Chambers, who gave me the best possible start in life and also a set of values to live by, which eventually saw me through very difficult times.

They taught us right from wrong,
And kept our family strong.
When cancer took Mam away,
Dad died a little, that day.
He couldn't live without his wife,
And time inevitably, took his life.
I love them both in every way,
For they made me, who I am today.

Ann Murdock

Chapter One

How it all began

I know a lot of people don't believe in destiny or fate, but over the years I believe my life has been ruled or at least led by it. My mother and father met in 1944, during the Second World War, and the way they met couldn't have been anything other than fate, I believe. My mother, or Mam as we affectionately called her, was a 'Lancashire lass' born in Blackburn in 1923, and both her parents were deaf. Grandma Ann was born deaf, while Grandad Walter's hearing didn't abandon him until he was seven. Both grandparents were brought up in institutions for the deaf, so I suppose they actually met by a twist of cruel fate.

Mam, christened Jessie, often told us over the years about how strict her parents were, probably due their upbringing which I believe was quite Victorian in nature. They were both members of the Salvation Army, which did a lot of valuable work before and during the war, and has continued to do so ever since.

Mam was one of five siblings - two sisters and two brothers, but both brothers sadly died in their teens so I never knew either of them. My dad was born in the small fishing town of Whitehaven in Cumbria, or Cumberland as it was back then, and came from a large family. His parents: Grandma Emily and Grandad Isaac Chambers; known to everyone as Emily May and Ike, had a large family of thirteen: five boys and eight girls.

Emily May was a Roman Catholic but had her first child 'out of wedlock' as they said in those days. Consequently they weren't allowed to marry in church so got hitched in the Salvation Army Meeting Hall. Grandma admired the work that the Army did so much that eventually, she became a Salvation Army Officer; proud to wear the uniform and bonnet out on weekend collections around local pubs. Mam said Grandma was a smart, good-looking lady.

She was also well loved by everyone who knew her, and someone the neighbours called for help to deliver babies, or lay people out when they died, and various other difficult duties. Nothing was ever too much to ask of her and both sets of grandparents were respected figures in their communities.

Mam loved talking about the years when she was growing up into a teenager during the war years. With her friend, Dorothy Brown, she attended Salvation Army rallies that often took place in Whitehaven, and that was where they met Emily May. They chatted together and Emily commented that they were both good-looking girls. During morning tea one day, they noticed that Emily wore a photograph on each lapel, of two handsome young men in uniform. Dorothy asked Emily, with a big grin, who the two young soldiers were. Emily pointed to one and said that was her eldest son, Tom, but that he was taken and soon to be wed. The other was her second eldest, Charlie, who everyone called 'Chuck.'

'They're away in the forces but they'll be home soon, I hope, and Chuck's still available,' Emily said, smiling at Dorothy. 'He's in the navy, would you like to write to him?'

Dorothy pulled a face and said, 'Write? Oh, no thanks, he's nice but I couldn't be bothered with all that fuss.'

Mam was standing beside her and liked the look of the man in the picture, so said, 'I wouldn't mind writing to him.'

Mam felt that Emily would've preferred it to be Dorothy, but she gave her the address anyway, and that was how my mother and father started writing to each other. Mam met him off his train when he returned home, and Dad always said that he fell in love with her at Barrow-in-Furness railway station, the first time they met - and he'd loved her ever since. He said she looked like a little lost soul, standing there waiting for him, and he knew straight away that she was the one for him.

They married in Blackburn on 10th August 1946, straight after the war ended, and then moved to Whitehaven where they lived with Grandma Chambers until they got a house of their own. Mam was pregnant right away and on 3rd July 1947, my sister Dorothy May was born. She was named after my grandma and my mother's sister, and having a newborn baby helped them get a council-house. Grandma's house was too small anyway and soon they were given one of the little pre-fabs that were built to house the thousands of homecoming soldiers and their new families, who would no longer put up with privately-owned, over-priced hovels.

They wanted more than one child and Albert Edward was born on 12th January 1950. Fifteen months later, on 4th April

1951, Mam had another baby boy, Charles Henry; named after Dad. Things were different back then; neighbours and family looked out for each other so they had a lot of help providing for their new brood.

Dad went back to mining at the local pit, which wasn't great for his health. He had a long-term chest problem and with pit conditions so bad at the time, was forced to leave in late '51. Phase 2 of the Windscale nuclear reactor site opened just afterwards, in '52, and was just down the west coast from us near Seascale. Dad was fortunate enough to get a job which didn't aggravate his chest there, but the ailment didn't disappear and he always had health problems. They never stopped him going to work though, which was now so much easier than being a miner, and he hardly ever even took a day off.

Later in life we realized how fortunate we'd been, when we heard about all the problems that many families had, and are still having perhaps even more so nowadays. We had a great upbringing and each one of us children was loved immensely. The pre-fabrication was our first home but we soon needed something bigger, and there was a new estate called Mirehouse being built nearby to the south of the town. Mam and Dad applied for one of these properties and soon heard that they'd been successful, and very soon would be moving to Whinlatter Road.

Chapter Two

New house - new baby

When they got the keys to the new house everyone was so excited, and were all moved in by Christmas 1953. The family loved Christmas and this one was to be extra special, as they celebrated it in their new home. Mam and Dad had been thinking about more children, maybe after another year or two, but in February 1954 they found she was already pregnant again. Dad was over the moon though Mam told me later that they'd been using protection at the time, but it obviously hadn't worked. So the forthcoming baby wasn't planned but maybe fate took a hand again?

Mam had never experienced any difficulty carrying her babies, not until now that is, but this one seemed to give her quite a few problems and every month there was fear that she might lose the pregnancy. She was told to rest but trying to rest with a seven, four and three year-old running around the house was quite impossible. Dad helped out as much as he could when he wasn't at work and some of the neighbours chipped in as well, but Mam gradually felt worse and on one occasion, went into town for some essentials and woke up in a shop doorway after fainting. She came round sitting on a stool with people fussing over her and no idea where she was.

As the pregnancy progressed she was told not to do anything at all but sit with her feet up. Only Dorothy was at school at the time and there weren't any affordable local nurseries back in the 50s, so Mam found taking it easy very difficult indeed whilst still having to look after the two boys. She was a fighter though and carried on as best she could, despite being told that this pregnancy was not good for her health, which worried her even more.

All her three children so far had been born at home, and she chose to have this one there too. Grandma had delivered the first three with no problem, so told Dad to call her when the new baby was ready to arrive. The date she'd been given was 15th September 1954 and Grandma came to see her that day.

'Well Jessie,' she said. 'You know I'm away for a break in Blackpool tomorrow, so let's hope the baby arrives today or waits until I get back.'

Three days later on Saturday morning, 18th September, Mam woke up feeling a little more uncomfortable than usual. Dad told her to stay in bed and he would get the kids up and dressed. Not long after lunch Mam asked him to call the midwife, knowing it was time and that Grandma was still away in Blackpool. Mam was getting a lot of pains but they weren't helping the baby to come. The midwife wrapped a double pillowcase tight around Mam's stomach, which seemed to have the desired effect. At 7.30pm she gave birth to another baby girl - I arrived weighing 8 pounds 12 ounces, with dark curly hair. Mam said I was beautiful but mothers always think their babies are, don't they?

The midwife called Dad up from the lounge to let him know everything was alright, and then the whole family came in to see Mam and welcome me into the world. When he looked in my cot, Dad said, 'You better take her back, she has dark hair and must be the milkman's baby.'

Mam looked up in despair and cried, 'Chuck, don't you dare say that!'

'Only teasing love,' he replied. 'Look, she has my curls!'

My brother Albert said, 'We wanted a baby brother, but she's a girl so she can go straight back where she came from!'

Dorothy said very little and Charlie nothing at all. He was very shy. Dad put the children to bed, made Mam a warm drink and came back upstairs to sit with her. He leaned over to kiss her and said, 'Thank you Jessie for another daughter, she's beautiful and now our family's complete.'

She felt one of Dad's teardrops fall on her cheek, and pulled away. 'What's wrong, Chuck?' she whispered.

'I never told you,' he answered. 'But all this time your health's been seriously at risk. I was told months ago that you could lose the baby at any time, and that if you did get to full term, it could be a choice between you or the baby.'

Poor Dad had kept this to himself for so long so as not to worry Mam. She said, 'Well we're both fine now,' and took hold of his hand. 'And you didn't even have to choose.'

He smiled and said, 'How lucky we are. Look at her, she's so beautiful.'

Chapter Three

Grandma comes to stay

My maternal grandparents often came over from Blackburn to Whitehaven for holidays but in 1956, Grandad became very ill, and sadly died. I never knew him as I was far too young, but Mam told us stories about him all through our young lives. After his funeral everything was arranged for Grandma to come and live with us, and she stayed until she also died, though many years later.

The year that Grandma came to us, she bought me a baby doll called Susie for Christmas. I still have her today, a little bit worse for wear, but Susie sits on my bed along with another two dolls and she's my favourite. I have lots of memories of growing up and the majority of them are wonderful, and most have Susie in there with me somewhere. Wherever I went she came too, and Mam said I wouldn't go anywhere without her.

One day we were returning home from visiting relatives in Blackburn, by train which is how we always travelled, and along the way had to change at Preston. When we pulled in the connection for Whitehaven was already waiting, as the train from Blackburn was running late. Mam took hold of my hand as we had to be quick and run to another platform, and somewhere in my memory I can actually see this vision as I write: I remember running and suddenly we stopped because the guard from the train was shouting after us. When I look round he was calling, 'Your little girl has left her dolly,' and he was waving Susie.

I was always wary of strangers, especially men, but that day I ran back quickly and grabbed Susie. Mam was shouting, 'Thank you,' as we ran to catch the train.

It was one of Mam's favourite tales and she often talked to me about it. She thought it was so funny as all the way back on the train I was saying to my doll, 'What would I have done without you Susie? I'm so sorry I forgot you.'

Mam said that there would've been no way to console me if the guard hadn't found her in time, and I never left her behind again.

We never had much money but enjoyed lots of lovely times together and were a strong, united family. I've always been grateful to my parents for the wonderful childhood they provided for me and my brothers and sister.

As my grandma was deaf, I learnt from an early age how to communicate with her by signing, and could soon sign the full alphabet with my hands. Grandma loved telling her friends how clever I was and would get me to show them what I could do. With Grandma and four children in the house, there really was never a dull moment.

She was a member of the Deaf Society and met lots of different people at the meetings. I was a very shy child and never took kindly to strangers, and Mam said that if anyone even spoke to me when I was a toddler, I'd cry. But I loved to show off so would always perform my signing skills when Grandma asked me to. I also liked singing as a child and still do today, and loved copying singers on the wireless, mainly because I was often told that I was really good at it. Despite my early shyness I've always preferred to be around people in my adult life, and am happy to speak with anyone; even strangers. How things can change.

Chapter Four

Things are about to change

I used to dream a lot and even have nightmares, and think I must have had a very vivid imagination. The shadows in my bedroom were always people that were there to hurt me, at least that's what I imagined, and my brothers didn't help. I know I was a pest and always wanted to do whatever they were doing, so they once locked me in the wardrobe! They had a Morse code toy with a little light bulb that flashed on and off, and the only way you could see it was in complete darkness. One day when I'd asked so many times if I could play with them, they coaxed me into the wardrobe then locked me in and took off!

Mam said I was always crying about something or other, and it must have been a nightmare for her with the four of us to cope with. There was always some drama or crisis on the horizon. One or other of us was always landing up at the hospital – usually one of the lads after some calamity, but on the whole there were lots of good times as well.

One of the things I remember most, was during the summer

holidays one year when Mam was changing the beds and I was busy playing with my dolls on mine. I had so many and Mam asked me to move them while she stripped the sheets. As I was doing so she said to me, 'Mammy is going to have a baby.'

I was only eight and looked up at her to reply, 'No, you're not!'

'Yes I am, love,' she said softly. 'After Christmas you'll have a new brother or sister.'

I didn't want a brother or sister and ran downstairs in distress. My sister, Dorothy had a job by then and her wage was a good help, Mam said. She was excited about the new baby though the lads didn't seem really bothered. There were so many times when Mam wasn't very well - she was now over forty and this would be her fifth child! She was advised to take lots of rest like she tried to whilst carrying me.

I didn't really understand why but apparently, Mam was advised not to have any more children after me, so it was another big worry for both her and Dad. He worked shifts and whenever he was on nights, Mam would get Dorothy to sleep with her just in case anything went wrong. I hated this more than anything because we normally shared a room and I felt lonely and abandoned, and took every last one of my dolls to bed with me. I'd obviously taken a dislike to this baby before it was even born, which would be soon enough regardless of my thoughts on the matter, and it was to change so much in my life. With Mam being over forty years old, she needed to have an operation to allow the birth and was in hospital for six weeks. I can remember going to see her and standing outside under her window while she waved to me because I wasn't allowed in.

On 18th April 1963 my baby brother, Brian was born. I can remember us all getting ready to go see Mam and the new baby in hospital. There were so many different rules and regulations back in the sixties, and one of them was that you had to be twelve to go into the maternity ward. My brothers were twelve and eleven and both looked old enough, but I was only eight.

Dad couldn't leave me at home with anyone that day so I went along, but wasn't allowed on the ward, and didn't my brothers tease me about that! I had to stand by the door but at least Mam waved to me. She knew how unhappy I was being left out, so asked if she and the baby could go to a parents' room. The nurses agreed and I met my new brother. Back then, hospitals didn't always consider the feelings of other family members so much. Nowadays, mothers are sent home so quickly after having their babies, there's not always time for visitors! Eventually she came home with the new addition to our family. The baby took up a lot of her time but life carried on, and everything went alright until 1965:

At school we had a nurse who we called 'Nitty Nora - The Nit Explorer'. I think she was a health visitor for other schools too. Around Easter time that year she came to our house, and after a while Mam called me down and said, 'Would you like to go on a little holiday, Ann?'

I looked at them both. 'A holiday?'

'Uh-hum, with some other little girls your age, it'll be such fun.'

Mam smiled encouragingly, and Nora said she would call back later after we'd discussed it. I was ten at the time and would be going into the last year of junior school the following term. I don't know if I was happy about going away on my own or not, but knew they'd never make me do anything awful that I didn't want to, and after we talked more about the holiday it began to sound quite exciting.

13

Nora the nit nurse thought it would be good for Mam to have some respite care after the traumatic birth, and had found a free vacancy for me at a place called The Sunshine Home. Apparently this place was at Allonby, between Maryport and Silloth on the south shore of the Solway Firth.

Chapter Five

First time away from home

Mam's respite was to be during the school summer holidays for two weeks, and after we both agreed that I should go, it was all arranged. I was given a small suitcase and saved up my pocket money. Relatives gave me extra money to take and it was all very exciting – but also quite daunting. I had never been anywhere without my parents before and I was really quite nervous.

The time arrived for me to leave for The Sunshine Home, and Mam took me on the bus down to Flat Walks Clinic, from where the minibus would pick me up. I remember sitting on the bench beside Mam when some other girls arrived. They looked about the same age as me if a little taller, but they smiled and I smiled back. The bus arrived and we all got on board, and I watched through the window as Mam waved goodbye. We stopped to pick some other girls up at Workington and Maryport, heading north up the coast towards Scotland.

I can't actually remember speaking to anyone all the way there and the journey seemed to take forever, but probably wasn't as long as I thought. It was only about 20 miles to The Sunshine Home which was an old, Victorian-style house obviously owned by wealthy people years ago. The bus pulled up outside the main gate and we were greeted by a very large lady, who was also quite intimidating. She led us into a big room that looked like a play area, but with chairs in rows and a table at the front. The large lady stood beside the table and told us all to take a seat. I sat beside a girl whose name I can't remember now, but we smiled and I thought - I bet she feels as scared as I do.

The lady then started to tell us what we had to do which was: when our names were called go up to the front with our suitcases. There were twelve of us altogether and eventually my name was called. I walked up to the table and put my case upon it. The lady opened it and took out my toiletries and purse. She then opened the purse, counted out the money and noted the amount beside my name on her list, and told me to sit back down.

We were split into two groups of six and each group was designated a dormitory. I was one of the last two girls assigned to a dormitory with only five beds, only one of which was left. Luckily, I was about an inch taller than the other girl so got the last bed, and unfortunately she was put into a nearby room with only babies' cots. I didn't envy the night's sleep that poor girl was likely to get.

That night we were given a meal, but I don't remember much about it because we'd been told that we were 'to be bathed' afterwards and the thought of that was preying on my mind. After eating we were instructed to strip down to our knickers, and stand in line to await our turns at the bathtubs. I felt embarrassed and degraded, but that's what happened and we all did exactly as we were told.

There were two bathtubs on either side of a large washroom, and one by one we got into the same, lukewarm water that the person before us had left behind. We were washed down quickly and then told to get dressed for bed. Before being allowed into the dormitories though, we were told to go back into a smaller bathroom and clean our teeth. We were then given one last chance to go to the toilet, before being marched off in line to our dorms for the night.

There were bars across the windows and not long after we were all under the sheets, we heard the door being locked from the outside. It felt like being in a prison cell with bars across the windows and the doors locked, and looking back now I shudder to think what might have happened if a fire had broken out! I don't think our health & safety was deemed very important in those hopefully bygone days, at least not at the scary Sunshine Home.

We did have fun that night though strangely enough; talking to each other and telling stories in the dark. I didn't think I'd sleep very well or even at all afterwards, but I did and woke up next morning with the sun shining. So the first night didn't turn out too badly after all and there was some sunshine at the home. One of the girls tried the door and it was already unlocked, so someone must have opened it before we woke up, and a nice young woman came in and advised us all to go to the bathroom, to get washed and dressed before coming down for breakfast.

When we entered the dining room however, we were told we had to polish the floor before we could have any breakfast. We had to get down on our hand and knees and polish the whole area, which was huge!

'What kind of holiday is this?' one girl said and we all laughed.

For breakfast we had a choice of white or brown toast with butter, jam or marmalade. It certainly wasn't the Ritz Hotel, that's for sure, but it was free so I should appreciate it, Mam had said. After breakfast we were told we could go into Allonby and were given some of our money back. I bought a post- card to send home.

When we got back it started to rain and we were all locked up in the playroom. I began talking with the girl that had no bed the previous night, and she said it was awful having to sleep in a cot in a room with all the younger kids. The rain eventually stopped and we were allowed to go outside and I said to the others, 'I'm going to write a post-card and tell my parents I want to come home.'

One of the girls said, 'They'll read what you've written and won't send it.'

'That's terrible,' I said. 'So what should I do then?'

'You should write it. The post-box is just outside the gate so we'll keep watch while you sneak out and put it in.'

I felt so afraid, like I was doing something really bad, and scribbled something like: Mam and Dad, I want to come home, please can someone come and collect me very soon?

While they all watched in case someone discovered my plot, I quickly sneaked outside the gate to post my card. My heart was thumping so hard and if someone had put a hand on my shoulder, I think I'd have died of fright! Thankfully no one saw me or appeared to suspect anything later.

Chapter Six

Great escapes

There were two girls at Sunshine Home who lived in Maryport, just a few miles down the B5300 coast road. Both decided to run away back home one evening, so again we all kept watch while they sneaked out of the gate and made their escape. I thought they were so brave and could never have done anything like that. It was teatime before they were eventually missed, and the police were called, so right after tea we were all sent up to our dormitories and told to stay there.

From our room we could see right across the open sea to the Isle of Man, and as daylight faded, blue flashing police-car lights came through the darkness towards us. Downstairs we could hear deep voices and listened to the girls' alarmed parents, who'd just been informed of their daughters' disappearance. Thankfully they were both found quite quickly and went straight back home to their families.

That night the young cot girl was brought into our dormitory as now there were two spare beds! We all laughed and talked about everything that had happened that day. I never mentioned my postcard again but wondered if Mam & Dad would receive it the following day, or ever?

Next morning I was given a new job, which was to help clean the bedrooms with a lovely girl who was in charge of such matters. She wasn't like the matron lady and we laughed all the time. We heard the phone ringing and then I heard my name being called from the hallway below, 'Ann, your mother's on the telephone, would you like to say Hello?'

I ran downstairs and soon as I heard Mam's voice, I cried out to her, 'Mam, I want to come home right away, I don't like it here, it's scary.'

The matron snatched the phone back, covered the mouthpiece with her hand and snarled at me, 'Get back up those stairs this instant!'

I was scared of her retribution now and burst into tears. The matron called for the girl I was working with, who then returned and told me to go to my dormitory and keep very quiet until I was called for. Now I was really scared as I awaited my punishment.

I sat alone in the dorm for an eternity and my nervousness increased by the minute. I wondered how long I'd be kept prisoner there, as I realised my parents couldn't collect me because neither could drive and there wouldn't be any buses at that time of night. I went to the window and looked out towards freedom, and wished I'd made a run for it with the Maryport girls.

An hour or so later I was still there and nodding off to sleep, when I saw a dark figure walking up the path to the front door. I heard the heavy knocker and then the matron shouting at somebody, before everything went quiet. I got up quietly to listen at the door, but was terrified when my name was called out by the matron. She sounded calm and calculated and I wondered what horror awaited me as I opened the dormitory door and headed for the stairs. When I reached the head of the staircase I stopped in amazement at what I saw waiting for me below. It was my wonderful, fantastic dad and I ran down straight into his arms. He hugged me and exchanged some words with the matron as he led me to the door. I don't know what was said; I just remember getting into a car that was waiting outside for us.

My mother worked for Eric, landlord of the local pub where we lived, and he told her to make the call earlier that night. Apparently when she received my postcard she was shocked by what I'd written, as it was just scribbled as if in panic and she was really worried about me. When she finished speaking to me on the phone she was crying, and Eric offered to drive Dad through to collect me. All the way back I sat close to my dad in the back of the car. I'd been so scared they would make me stay, and was telling him and Eric what it was like. They laughed all the way home and Eric said, 'Sounds like a bloody concentration camp not a holiday home.'

Mam was so annoyed with Nitty Nora, and said she would ask her what on earth she was thinking about, sending me to a place like that. Some of my cousins went there every year but their home life can't have been as good as mine, because they couldn't understand why I didn't like it! Sunshine Home wasn't very sunny at all to me and I hoped that I was never ever sent back there.

Good old Dad, Eric, and the Royal Mail!

After the summer holidays I went to the High School, which I really enjoyed although I couldn't spell and hated English lessons. I could put words together in my head alright, just not so well on paper. I always did well in maths and arithmetic though, and made lots of new friends. I met one of my best friends ever at High School. She was called Christine and we were friends all the way through until the day I left, which happened in quite an unusual way.

Charles & Jessie Chambers – my parents – 10th August 1946

Ann & Charles Henry Chambers

Albert Edward, Ann, & Charles Henry Chambers

Chapter Seven

Another change on the horizon

The sun was shining brightly through my bedroom window, and as I awoke I could hear blackbirds singing outside. Down in the kitchen I could hear Mam tinkering about; she was always up and about well before us, making sure the house was warm and cosy for the family coming down as she did all through our school days. It was the last day before the Easter break, with two weeks holiday. It was also a non-uniform day, so we could go to school in everyday clothes instead of our usual kit, though I can't say I was over-excited about that.

I'd chosen my little mint-green skirt, a white blouse and nice cardigan just in case I felt the March cold. It was my fourth year at Overend Secondary Modern School; a year which passed by quickly even though occasionally, time seemed to take forever dragging past. But generally I had a very good school life; I enjoyed most of it and learned a lot from my teachers.

I'd been lucky enough not to have any bad reports, and I didn't dare get into much trouble either as Mam would've killed me. I didn't only respect my parents, but because of them I respected myself too, and didn't want to be in the small group that was always sitting outside the headmaster's office, waiting for some punishment to be meted out. Then again I didn't know what their home lives were like; maybe they had awful circumstances to live with and maybe getting into constant trouble was their way of asking for help? Whitehaven was a place of high unemployment after the EU killed off the UK fishing industry, so who knows the truth about such things?

As I lay awake thinking in bed, I suddenly heard Mam call to Brian and me that it was time to get up. I heard my little brother jump out of bed and run quickly to the toilet, and then downstairs. I knew he would be sitting on the floor right in front of the fire to keep warm. Nobody I knew had central-heating back in those days. Not long before I would've raced him down and we'd fight over the warmest spot, but this morning I had other things to think about.

Whilst getting dressed after washing I thought about my best friend, Christine and wondered what she'd be wearing that day? I knew she'd look great; like a model usually, and turned to my reflection in the mirror - it'll have to do, I decided.

'Good morning, love,' Mam greeted me as I entered the kitchen for tea and toast. Toast always smells so delicious in the mornings, to me. It's always been the aroma of love and comfort and there were always plenty of both in our house. Sometimes though, toast brought back feelings of dread about Allonby's Sunshine Home – because it was usually burnt and the sun didn't shine for me!

'Last day today love, for two weeks,' Mam added as I burnt my lip with hot tea.

'Yeah, I'm looking forward to the break,' I replied, licking my lip, and went to sit at the table.

Last day of term was always easy. I knew we'd be doing very little so I could have a long chat and a good laugh with Chris. It felt strange that morning, standing out in the crisp air waiting dutifully for the school bus to arrive, as if I was waiting for more than transport to come my way. When I got off at the other end, I saw Chris watching for me, and she looked amazing as I knew she would. She came straight over and said, 'Hi Ann, you look nice.'

That's what Mam had just said – nice, but not amazing like Chris. We linked arms and went into the hall for the last assembly of term. It was really loud and noisy but as soon as the teachers entered the room there was silence. I believe that back then there was a lot more respect for teachers and elders amongst children than there is today; far fewer silly rules, and I personally think it was so much better that way.

Mr Smith, our headmaster, stood up to tell us all that today was the last day of term and there was no more school for two weeks. He also announced that there were some pupils leaving that day; that he would like to wish then all the very best for the future, and hoped they all found the careers they wished for. Suddenly, from nowhere, that strange bus-stop feeling came back and with it - the firm knowledge I wanted to leave school that very day as well! I realized in an instant that I'd had enough of schooling, was bored to tears with it and needed to get out into the real world.

Chris was chatting away non-stop but I was miles away in my imagination. I couldn't get this new thought out of my head and just before the bell sounded for lunch, decided to go and see the headmaster about it. This kind of instant action was not like me at all. I'd never been impulsive before. It was like someone or something was driving me along, and maybe that something was fate again?

I knocked on the head's door and entered his office, heart pounding in my chest as he asked, 'Can I help you?'

'Yes sir,' I replied. 'I'd like to leave school today.'

He looked up from whatever it was he was doing and frowned at me. 'Do you have a job to go to?'

'No sir,' I answered.

'Well if you don't get one very soon, I'll expect to see you back here after the holidays.'

I gave him my name, left his office and headed towards the canteen. Did that really happen, I thought. Did I really just go into the headmaster's office and tell him I wanted to leave school today? The answer was – yes!

Chapter Eight

New friends and new horizons

Chris was mortified when I told her I was leaving school for good, and had already told the headmaster.

'Why would you do that?' she asked.

'I just need to,' I replied. 'I want to get a job and work.'

'Yeah but next year we'll be prefects and we're staying on to get good grades, and then get a better job or if we do really well at our school work, we could even go to university.'

Chris was lovely and I know she meant well, but I didn't want to go to university - I wanted to work alongside real people like my parents and earn money now. She was so nice and I loved her as my friend, but I knew we'd soon go our separate ways and I'd miss her terribly.

School always finished early on the last day of term, and Chris always waited at the stop with me until I caught my bus. She lived just a five-minute walk from the school so was never in a rush. I gave her a hug and as I was leaving she called out, 'See you after Easter.'

I smiled and waved but already knew that she wouldn't, at least not at school. I'd made a decision and knew that this was the last day of my official education. As the bus set off I suddenly thought about my parents - what if they say I have to go back to school?

At home we sat down to our usual fish & chips Friday tea, but they didn't look as appetizing as usual because I was nervous. We weren't Catholics but always had fish on Fridays, mainly because my uncle still worked on the boats and had lots of fresh catch left over at the end of the week. I decided not to prolong matters and announced outright, 'I er, I've spoken to Mr Smith, the headmaster, and told him I wanted to leave school for good, today.'

Dad said, 'Really?'

'Uh-hum.' I answered nervously.

'What will you do then?

'I want to look for a job while I'm off during the holidays,' I replied.

Dad said the same as Mr Smith, 'Well if you don't get one it's back to school I'm afraid, young lady.'

Chris was my best friend at school but at home it was Lynda. She lived straight across the road from me, and we'd been friends since infants' school. She didn't go to the same senior school as me; she went to the Catholic school but at home we were always together.

Later that night I told Lynda and her parents about my plans and they were surprised. Lynda was really clever; quite a brain box in fact and was always reading something or other. I used to sleep at her house sometimes and when I fell asleep she'd be reading, and when I woke up she was still reading! She used to laugh when I asked if she'd been reading all night.

'No,' she'd say, 'Just most of it!'

Lynda was twelve months younger than me but seemed so much older, or at least wiser.

Her mother asked, 'Why do you want to leave so early, Ann?'

'I'd like to get a job,' I told her.

'Oh, well I think they're taking people on at Woolworths,' she said, about the big shop where she worked. 'I'll put a word in for you, if you like?'

'Oh, yes please, that'd be great.'

'I'd like to leave school too you know,' Lynda said later. 'But they'd never let me.'

'Yeah, that makes sense because you're so brainy and will easily get good exam results,' I told her.

She just shrugged and frowned.

Next morning when I came downstairs, our house was empty. My sister, Dorothy was married now with two girls of her own, and lived up in Carlisle. I was godmother to them both and loved them dearly. Both my brothers were out at work; Dad too no doubt but where was Mam and Brian? I heard voices outside and realised Mam was talking to our next-door neighbour, Gladys. Brian was in the garden playing with her son and daughter.

'Your mother was telling me you're looking for a job,' Gladys said over the fence when I poked my head out the back door.

'Oh, er, yes I am, Gladys.'

'Well I'll ask at the place I work if you like? They always need people.'

'Oh thank you. That's really nice of you,' I replied.

They carried on chatting and I went back inside to get some breakfast. Gladys worked in an office in town and I wondered whether I'd like that kind of environment, but it was kind of her to think about me, so I decided to go for the interview if I was offered one. I wasn't at all sure that would happen though, and put it from my mind, until Monday evening when Gladys called in and asked to speak to me:

'Ann, can you come down to the office tomorrow for an interview?'

Wow, I thought, that was quick! It will probably sound very strange to most people nowadays, but back then jobs were 'ten a penny' as the saying went, even in West Cumberland!

'Thank you ever so much, Gladys,' I replied enthusiastically.

'If you get there for one-thirty and ask for personnel, they'll be expecting you.'

I had very mixed emotions and was excited, scared and very nervous all at once. Thinking back now about how young I was at the time, Chris was probably right that I should've gone back to school and carried on with my education. Mam understood me though and was delighted with the opportunity.

'See I told you not to worry and something would come up soon enough,' she said with a smile.

Next day my head was in a spin and suddenly, I wasn't so sure that this was what I wanted. It was kind of Gladys to get me the interview, but I was worried that I might not be able to do the job. I wasn't stupid and could leave most people in my class behind when it came to maths, but English wasn't my best subject. But I told myself to stop worrying and that what will be, will be, and once again I'd leave my future to fate

Hope I don't look as distraught as I'm feeling, I thought as I waited outside the interview room, but in my mind I just could not picture myself working in this type of environment. It was so quiet and serious. Nobody even spoke never mind laughed, and when I was called through it was in an actual whisper.

Mam was waiting for me when I returned home, and asked how it went. I shrugged my shoulders – 'I've never had an interview before so don't really know, but I'm not over-optimistic.'

I was right not to be and soon found out that I wasn't going to be offered the job. Again I felt mixed emotions and a little disappointed, but quietly relieved as well. Mam said, 'Don't worry about it love, what's meant for you will never pass you by.'

I was happy to believe that fate had decided I wasn't meant to work in an office, and the very same day Lynda's mother told me I had an interview at Woolworths on Friday the same week. I had to ask for personnel - the same as I did three days before.

I knew Woolworths wasn't as highly-rated as Gladys' office job, but I felt sure that I could do it well enough and would probably be happier there. I knew plenty of people got stuck in jobs they didn't like and thought what a miserable life that must be.

Lynda came with me and chatted with her mother while I was being interviewed. This time I felt more confident because I'd been told I'd have to do an arithmetic test, so hoped I could make a better impression than I had at my last interview. I was taken upstairs, asked a few questions about myself and given a few simple sums to do, and a few minutes later was told the job was mine if I wanted it!

I did, and had to be there for 8.30am two days later on Monday morning, and felt like I'd won first prize in a very big raffle. I went back downstairs and found Lynda with her mother, and they both knew the result without even asking.

'I can see by your smile that you must've got the job?' Lynda's mum asked.

'Yes I did, and thank you so much for arranging it for me. I start on Monday!'

I felt sure on that last day at school, when Chris and I hugged and said goodbye - that I would never return. Rightly or wrongly and for better or worse - I was right.

Chapter Nine

Working for a living

Mam was delighted when I arrived home with a big smile and told her I got the job at Woolworths.

'Well done,' she said. 'So that's your school days over then?'

I nodded and said, 'I'll miss Chris though.'

'You can still see her.'

'Yes, I suppose so,' I replied.

'Things change in life, love. You meet new people and then before you know it, old friends are gone, sometimes forever, sometimes not.'

'But I know I'll never forget Chris,' I said, and to this day I never have.

The weekend passed quickly and on Sunday night I decided to go to bed quite early, with my 8.30 start on Monday and a whole new adventure in front of me. I was excited but still very nervous, though I knew Lynda's mother would be there and another neighbour, Jean, who also worked at Woolworths with her daughter Pam, so I least there would be some familiar faces around.

As always, Mam was up early on Monday and soon let me know it was time to be out of bed. I was already awake so washed and dressed straight away and went downstairs. She could see I was nervous and said, 'Don't worry darling, you'll be fine,'

'I know, Mam,' I smiled at her. 'It's just so different. It's a whole new, unknown world.'

Our parents were always supportive and no matter what happened I knew they would stand by me, so what could really go that wrong? Mam said she'd pay my bus fares to and from work, and we agreed that I would give her £2 from my first wage of £4.11shillings. It doesn't seem much now but it wasn't too bad at the time, in fact I think Woolworths paid quite good rates relatively speaking, and we were both happy with our arrangement.

We got our wages handed to us in cash, in a little brown envelope with our names on the front, and I'd never had so much money at one time. I had to work what they called a week in lieu, which actually meant in arrears, so my first week was paid at the end of the second. Also, I had to work twelve months before I got paid for any holidays, but working life in general still seemed so much better than it often is now. Maybe because people seemed to be valued more, and were at least names on a sheet, not just numbers.

When I first started my new job I probably only looked about twelve years old. The bus stop wasn't far down the road and Mam waved me off that morning. Heather, Jean and Pam were all standing at the stop, and Jean said, 'Good morning, young Ann, how are you this fine day?'

'Nervous,' I replied. 'But really looking forward to it.'

I didn't speak much on that first journey to work, I was too busy concentrating on what was to come, but we all got off the bus and walked down the street together into the shop. They were laughing and joking amongst themselves, because it was just an ordinary day for them. There was one door open at the end of the store for the staff, who all seemed to be arriving at the same time. Everyone seemed really nice and either said Hello, or smiled at me. So far so good, I thought; they all seemed a happy lot and I hoped I could fit in well.

The shop didn't open to the public until 9.30am one Monday every month, for staff training and my first day happened to be that Monday. So those who weren't being trained all had to wait in the canteen. My neighbours introduced me to the rest of the staff as a new starter, and everyone clapped which I found just a little embarrassing.

Eventually I was taken by personnel to get my uniform, and meet the lady I'd be working with. Her name was Eileen and she was very tall. She towered above me and was loud but also nice, and straightforward as well, and I knew we'd get on alright.

It was all very new and different from anything I'd known before. I had quite long hair and had to tie it up when working with food, so I plaited it into pig tails and then I did look young; like a cute little schoolgirl, my colleagues said.

I was put on the bread counter and never knew there were so many different varieties of the stuff, which was piled so high around me I could hardly see the customers. I asked poor Eileen a hundred times that day: 'How much is Sunblest White? How much are Bloomers? And how much is Nimble Brown again?'

She knew all the prices and told me not to worry - I'd soon get to know them all as well. We had to remember them all because there were no barcodes to do it automatically then, and we also had to add the costs up in our heads because there were only so many tills. It was before decimalization in 1970/71, so everything was worked out in good old pounds, shillings and pence.

Most of the loaf prices were around two shillings; there were 12 pennies in each shilling, and 20 shillings in a pound. The maths never bothered me; I could add up really quickly in my head, and each day found that I was remembering more and more. Before I'd been there a week I hardly had to ask any prices, and was feeling really good about myself and my new job. Then we were told all the bread prices where to go up the following day so I'd have to learn them all again! But I fit in well and coped with whatever I was asked to do.

Eileen took me under her wing and never let anyone pick on me. She was still loud but the other girls told me her bark was worse than her bite, and they were all good friends and colleagues. She was always making me laugh but took no nonsense from anyone, and ran the delivery men around in a merry dance if they didn't toe the line, but I'm sure they loved her flirty banter.

I soon got to know all our regular customers, some of whom would ask for certain things to be kept aside for them as they worked until late afternoon. There was even a book of special orders for the weekend. Bread was a staple in most peoples' diets and we sold a large amount every day, the majority going before each lunch time. The same customers always came in regardless of the weather to get their fresh, daily supply, and the counter was always busy until about 2.30 in the afternoon. After that it would usually be much quieter.

I was starting to really like my job and was secretly glad I hadn't got the one at the office. The customers got to know me and were soon calling me by name, and I was as happy as I think I'd ever been. The morning bread deliveries used to arrive before the shop opened, and after I'd worked there a few weeks was asked if I'd like to start earlier and finish sooner. I agreed and every day from Monday to Saturday, I had to be at work from 7.30am to finish at 4pm. I had each Wednesday off, and a lunch-break of one hour from 12noon 'til 1pm. I still like this hour for my lunch after all these years - old habits die hard.

I became really good friends with a girl called Evelyn, who'd started work at Woollies a few weeks before me, after coming to Cumbria to live with her grandparents. I didn't ask why but her father was in the army and they'd lived all over the world at different times. The family included Evelyn, her mother and father, three sisters and a brother. Evelyn's birthday was in August and she was near enough the same age as me. She worked on the grocery counter with Jean, our supervisor and one of my neighbours. Her sister June worked at Woolworths too, in another department.

Evelyn and I soon became inseparable and started staying over at each other's houses. After a while she had to sleep at her aunt Jenny's house, because of overcrowding at her gran's. Jenny was married to Albert; a name made popular by Queen Victoria's German husband, and there were still a lot of Alberts about in the 50s and even 60s. They had one daughter, Michelle, but Evelyn still ate all her meals at Grandma's. I loved going to both places because they were all such lovely people and treated me like one of their own.

Jenny and Albert, or Tabby as he was known, were in their early twenties and still very much like teenagers, so we always had fun when I stayed there. My parents also loved Evelyn who was like another sister to me, and although sadly I don't see a lot of her nowadays, we still keep in touch. Like my mother often said - things keep changing. I love meeting new people and finding friends, but have always hated leaving the old ones behind. That's life, I suppose.

Evelyn (left) and me on Woolworths roof, 1971

My niece, Pauline and me

Evelyn and me at home

Chapter Ten

Sweet sixteen

Evelyn and I had lots of good times and when it was her sixteenth birthday I stayed at her aunt's. We went to a pub that night called the Hope Inn, at Harris Moor. A few of us got together and walked all the way as there wasn't a bus route, and I had a couple of lagers with lemonade. We were all under-age and I know for sure that none of us looked old enough, but it didn't seem to be an issue and none of the bar staff said a word to us.

We were very well-behaved though and sat listening intently to the new juke box, and I first heard a very teenage song that became one of my all-time favourites: *Leader of the Pack* by the Shangri Las, who were also one of the first all-girl groups. The song was about motor-bikers and a little rebellious I suppose, but I don't know if liking it was related to anything other than the fact that I was simply enjoying my youth. It was 1970 and the whole world seemed to be rebelling against something or other.

We were all so young and innocent, chattering and laughing, and it was a wonderful night. We made the two miles home before it got dark, and never found it a problem walking to wherever we needed to be, whatever the weather.

My sixteenth birthday was also a day to remember – I'd become quite friendly with one of delivery lads who worked for *Mothers Pride*. His name was Marshall and he had a really good sense of humour. He was a bit older than me and Evelyn and was married with two little daughters, but was always flirting with anyone around including me. Eileen flirted with all the drivers but something about the way he talked to me always made me blush – I was so young and innocent.

That year my birthday was on a Wednesday which was still my day off, but I'd arranged to meet Evelyn during her lunch break and spent the whole hour chatting with her. After Evelyn went back to work I went to say hello to Eileen, just as Marshall arrived with a delivery.

The afternoon drivers came right into the shop to check if there was any bread that hadn't sold, and if so they'd reload and take it to other stores as fresh deliveries. Marshall came straight in and stood right beside me, and started chatting. My face turned bright crimson. I knew he was just larking about but I hated blushing and Eileen never missed a thing.

'Why you are blushing, Ann?' she asked, but I was too embarrassed to speak.

'What are you saying to her, Marshall?' she switched her enquiries. 'I think you better just leave her alone.'

'I was only asking her why she was all dressed with nowhere to go,' he answered.

'She has Wednesdays off and it's her birthday today,' Eileen replied.

'Oh, Happy Birthday,' he said. 'How old are you?'

'She's sixteen,' Eileen replied loudly, making sure he heard very clearly.

'Oh well, think I'll be off now,' I said, and as I turned to go

Marshall actually winked at me!

I walked slowly off, feeling a little clumsy, and turned to wave at Eileen. 'See you tomorrow,' I said.

She smiled and waved back.

When I arrived home that day I was feeling a little overwhelmed by everything that was happening to me. I had to admit that I found Marshall very handsome, but knew that I shouldn't because of his wife and family. I also cringed at the thought of what my parents would say if they knew about my friendship with a married man, but didn't dwell too long on that subject – it was way too scary!

Chapter Eleven

Dangerous days

Seven years earlier in December 1963, a brand new pub had opened up on the site of an old trailer park, down the coast at Nethertown, south west of Egremont. It was built from asbestos sheeting, which nobody knew was dangerous at the time, or if they did they didn't tell us, with timber cladding over the top. But it had proper central heating and live music, with big-name bands coming from places like Liverpool, which was just becoming world-famous because of The Beatles! It was called the Tow Bar Inn and soon became the most popular night-life venue in the whole area, and definitely the place to be at weekends, and remained so for years to come.

It had all kinds of things going on, including mid-week bingo for older generations, but at weekends it had dancing until 11.30pm! Entry started off at 5-shillings, or five-bob as most folk said, on Saturdays but was a bit cheaper on Sunday.

I'd heard about the place, everybody had by the time I started work, but never been there. Out of the blue one day Evelyn asked if I'd go there with her, the coming Sunday night, but by now the Tow Bar had a kind of nightclub reputation at weekends, and I wasn't sure my parents would let me go. I was working full time, contributing to the family income and supposed to be growing up, but they were still very protective and a little old fashioned in that way. Evelyn was going to stay with us at the weekend if I was allowed to go, even though I hadn't plucked up the courage to ask yet, because it was much easier to get from my house to the bus station and from there to the Tow Bar, which was a good few miles away from Whitehaven.

Eventually I did ask, without mentioning the nightclub bit, and was really surprised when they both said I could go. Mam said, 'I don't suppose you can take any harm, and your brother Albert will be there as well, so I'll tell him to keep an eye on you.'

'Oh great,' I whispered to myself. 'That's all I need - big brother watching over me!' But I still couldn't wait to get back to work on Thursday and tell Evelyn the good news!

We were both excited and chattered continuously about very little else. On Saturday I went into work at 7.30 as always, and finished at 4.00. I went over to the groceries section to tell Evelyn I'd see her later at home, after she finished.

Evelyn had stayed over many times and thought of our house as more like a second home, and even called my parents Mam and Dad! She never took anything for granted though and all my family loved her. I finished my tea before Evelyn even got home, but reliable Mam had her hers all ready for when she arrived.

I really liked it when Evelyn stayed at our house. We were more than friends because she was more like a sister to me than my real sister, and I realised all the little things I'd missed out on. Dorothy was so much older than me that we were never close, in fact we were more like strangers and she hated having to take me anywhere with her. Sometimes Mam used to make her hold me by the hand when I was little, and told her she was in charge of looking after me.

Dorothy obviously saw me as a chore and a burden to her before I was even five years old, and because of that probably started to dislike me as a person. As soon as Mam was out of sight many times, Dorothy would let go of my hand and push me away. I thought she'd rather hold a stranger by the hand than me. I wondered if siblings ever truly liked each other until they were older, and wiser, and had left petty jealousies far behind.

When Sunday evening finally rolled around and it was time to get ready to go out, we both chose tiny black mini-skirts with short tank-tops over tight white blouses, and white tights with high platform shoes to finish off the ensemble. I thought Evelyn looked amazing and she said I did too.

So off we went to catch the local bus into town, from where we'd get the special express coach laid on by the Tow Bar in the evenings. Evelyn was chatting to some friends and I was watching for the bus, which soon trundled along and we all rushed aboard to grab a seat. The old bus engine was very noisy and combined with everybody yelling and chattering, I didn't realise that someone was shouting at us. Everyone went quiet and looked round to see who the coach driver was shouting at, and all eyes seemed to be on Evelyn and me. As we gawped back and wondered what was going on, the driver shouted again, 'Hey Miss Woolworths!'

As I looked towards the front of the bus I saw a familiar face smiling at me through the rear view mirror. My own face immediately blushed crimson with embarrassment as I recognised Marshall, and even more so when he gave me one of his suggestive, flirty winks. I smiled shyly in return but then turned away and started chatting to Evelyn.

'Who's that?' she asked, noticing my red face.

'Oh, it's just the guy who drives the Mother's Pride van.' I answered nonchalantly.

'Aww, that's sweet of him,' she laughed, and we carried on chatting.

The journey seemed to go on forever with Marshall watching me every second in the rear-view, and it's a wonder he didn't crash the bus and kill us all before we got halfway there! When he finally stopped at the Tow Bar and I was walking past him to get off, he said, 'Happy Birthday, Miss Woolworths.'

I smiled politely but carried on without pausing or even turning towards him.

It was a great night in the Tow Bar. The music was loud and everyone was noisy, buzzing and full of life. We got a stamp-pass on our hands and there were infra-blue lights shining and flashing everywhere. Our blouses looked like an advert for *Persil* – whiter than white! I kept an eye out for Albert but never saw him until much later on, and he didn't show much interest in what I was doing, which was mainly dancing around my new handbag with Evelyn. We were drinking *Merry-Down* cider because it was cheap and sweet, but it was stronger than we realised. It definitely did made us merry but the next day we certainly felt down, so hence the name maybe?

As I came back from the ladies I noticed Marshall making his way through the bar. He saw me, came straight over and I wasn't sure what to do, but he stopped me and said, 'Hello, can I have a birthday kiss?'

I stuttered some unintelligible excuse, turned tail and ran back to my seat with Evelyn. After that I kept seeing him all night, always looking at me but I tried to avoid his stare. I didn't feel very well as the night wore on, and figured the cider must have gone to my head. I wasn't used to drinking alcohol and went outside for some fresh air. I sat on the low wall near the entrance but soon heard Evelyn calling to me, 'Come on Ann, or we'll miss the bus.'

'Okay, I'm coming,' I drawled, not realising how late it was.

As I climbed up the bus steps, Marshall was sitting in the driver's seat looking straight at me. He didn't smile for once and I felt somehow guilty. He was connected to work and I didn't want to fall out with him because of that, but what did he expect from me?

As I got to the top of the steps he looked away, out of the front windscreen. He seemed hurt and for some reason I felt really sorry for disappointing him. Before I turned right, into the bus, I leaned over and gave him a quick kiss on the cheek, then went and sat down with Evelyn.

When we got off the bus I was careful not to even look in Marshall's direction. He never said anything and I tottered down the steps into the road as daintily as I could. We had a long walk home, at the dead of night and loaded with booze, but being in any danger never even crossed our minds. The world and even West Cumbria seemed a much safer place in those days, and soon we were tucked up fast asleep in bed. Mam popped her head around the door to wish us good-night before we nodded off, and probably couldn't sleep before being sure we were both home safe and sound.

Chapter Twelve

Close encounters

Next morning I had a terrible hangover but knew I couldn't take time off work. It was self-inflicted anyway Dad said, so I rolled out of bed and managed to get myself dressed and off to work. I really didn't feel too well but Evelyn wasn't as bad – maybe she was more experienced with the Merry-Down?

Mid-morning I had to go to the loo. There was a steep flight of stone steps at the back of the store, leading up to the canteen and staff toilets. Esther the cleaner was out there, just finishing swilling them down and as I clambered up towards the toilets, gripping the handrail with both hands, I threw up all over the clean steps. I couldn't apologise enough, even though I still felt sick and had a banging headache, but Esther just laughed anyway.

Miss Singleton who worked in personnel, came out the door at the top of the steps right at the wrong moment. She saw what happened and immediately told me to go straight home. Miss, or Ma Singleton as we called her behind her back, seemed to be the most miserable of people usually, but I'm sure I saw a little smile cross her face, when she realised I was suffering from a self-inflicted hangover at the age of sixteen!

I got my things and told Evelyn and Eileen I had to go home, and in one way I was relieved that I didn't have to face Marshall during his afternoon visit. Mam was surprised to see me but knew right away I wasn't well. I took myself back off to bed and slept until the next day. I've never been able to drink Merry-Down since, and even thinking about it makes me feel queasy. Ah, the excitement of youth and growing into adulthood!

Next day I felt much better and got up early for work. I was worried that I might have ruined my reputation a bit with the hangover episode, and that bothered me because I did not want to lose my job or spoil my prospects. It wasn't a job I'd dreamed about exactly, and as I was good at maths I'd always had the idea of working in a bank. But surprisingly, I found shop work really interesting. I was definitely a people-person and got to know all our customers individually, and the majority of them were always pleasant in return. As most places there were the odd nasty ones too, but on the whole it was a healthy, rewarding occupation.

Nothing seemed to have changed though, everybody was just as they had been before my Monday mishap, and I carried on with my work cheerfully, feeling relieved. I'd even forgotten about kissing Marshall, though the embarrassment came flooding back when I remembered at about 2pm, as I happened to look out of the window and saw his big Mother's Pride van parking up outside.

I couldn't see Marshall and wondered if he'd changed routes to avoid me, so I carried on with my work but then heard his voice and turned to see him talking to Eileen.

'Won't be a minute, Eileen,' I mumbled, heading outside

and noting how clean the stone steps were on my way to the loo.

'You be careful out there,' she said with a smile. 'Esther's just finished the steps.'

I knew Marshall had seen me and was hoping he'd be gone by the time I got back. I dallied as long as I dared in the loo but when I emerged he hadn't left. They were still talking and I slunk past them with my head down, hoping I wouldn't be noticed so I could hide myself away behind the *Hovis*, but Eileen chirped up, 'What's wrong with you, then?'

My face burned but I managed to squeak, 'Nothing, just catching up with my work after yesterday.'

'Hope your big night out taught you a big lesson then?' she laughed.

I paused for a split second, turned to look right at Marshall and replied, 'Yes, I think it did.'

He didn't say anything, and I was thankful because I was still embarrassed about getting drunk and kissing him on the bus.

Although we never drank Merry-Down ever again, the Tow Bar was the best night-life place in our area at the time, and Evelyn and me started to go there every week. Marshall always drove the bus there and back - it was obviously a handy part-time earner for him and his family, and one day he had them all in the bus with him. The girls were two little beauties and so was his very young wife.

Over time I resumed a platonic friendship with Marshall and on our way home from the Tow Bar on his bus one night, he told Evelyn and me to stay on board until everybody else got off. I was a bit worried about what he'd got planned, but he saved us a very long walk in the dark and the rain, by driving us all the way home to the house! He did it every week after that, and one night parked up on the road outside the house because we were still busy talking. After that he parked up every time and we all just sat and talked for hours about all kinds of stuff.

One night after Evelyn got off the bus and went into the house for a pee, Marshall went down to the back of the bus and said, 'Come and have a look at this, Ann.'

'Have a look at what?' I asked.

'Come and see.'

I was nervous but walked slowly along the aisle towards him, and he pulled me down onto the long back seat. My heart was pounding as he put his arms around me and gave me a passionate kiss on the lips. I hadn't really had any boyfriends before, and his kiss was very different to those few I'd ever experienced. It made me feel wanted and desired, and like a woman, but I knew he was far too experienced for me and I knew it was wrong, because he was married and had two little girls who loved and depended on him. Thankfully Evelyn poked her head around the door and said, 'Come on Ann or I'm off home. You've got the key and I need the loo, and it's starting to rain!'

Marshall didn't take us home very often after that night, and I never let anything such thing happen ever again. He was very nice and I was excited by his passion for me, but I could never allow myself to get involved with him as anything but a friend and work associate. So thank you Evelyn for returning just at the right time.

Chapter Thirteen

The party

Evelyn and I still carried on going to the Tow Bar every Sunday night, and I still saw Marshall from time to time when he drove us back to Whitehaven. I also spoke to him most days in the store but I think he'd given up the chase by then, which made me feel a little sad in one way, though relieved most of all.

I never thought I was very pretty, not like some girls who to me always seemed amazing. But looking back over the years and the pictures that were taken of me, I don't think I was too bad. I was only 5feet 2inches tall and weighed about seven and half stone, with long brown hair. I was a happy-go-lucky teenager and always had a bright smile on my face, and could talk to just about anybody.

I'd been working at Woollies for a few months and was content with my role as shop assistant. I loved meeting all the new people who came in, and chatting to all the regular customers who knew me quite well by then. I was part of the team at world-famous F.W. Woolworths, in their Whitehaven branch. I felt quite proud of myself and loved the team-spirit feeling.

Christmas was coming and the shop looked fabulous with all the decorations in place. Christmassy songs played all day, which drove most of the other girls crazy but I liked them. They reminded me of my happy childhood and I sang along merrily to most of them. Even today I still like all the Christmas songs, even the new ones, and still hum along secretly to them.

Christmas was a time to look forward to and remember afterwards at home, when we were kids. My parents always made it a special time for us. I can recall Mam getting annoyed with Dad because she was fed up with him making a mess all over the house, putting the decorations up. But she was always delighted with the outcome when he'd finished, even though she had to clear the mess away every time.

Like a lot of people back in the seventies and every other decade, we didn't have much money to spare but we had plenty of things much more valuable - our house was always filled with love and laughter. All my friends and my siblings' friends, and lots of neighbours came along to our house at Christmas, and they were always made very welcome.

All Woollies' employees were invited to the work's Christmas Party, and could also tickets for family members. It was to be at the big Cumbrian Ballroom in Workington, a few miles up the coast on the road to Maryport. Free transport was laid on for everyone, and all tickets were free for staff.

Evelyn and I went shopping to get new dresses for the big night. I often wonder how we managed financially, as my wage had increased but was still only £4.11s, and I gave Mam £2 of that for my keep. She did pay for my bus fares and lunches, but what I had left over seems such a tiny amount now. Obviously it bought a lot more back then than it could now.

After a lengthy perusal I ended up buying a lacy, trouser and dress sort of thing that was all white and really pretty. My old friend Lynda was also going to the party, as her mother bought her a family-member ticket, and she got a dress that was similar to mine but in pale yellow. I bought Mam and Dad tickets so they could enjoy a good night out together at Christmas time, after doing so much for others.

At work everyone was talking about the party, even our under-manager, Martin who usually maintained a professional distance from us lowly shop girls. He had a pretty wife like Marshall and most of the other young girls thought he was a bit of a heart-throb. The older women said he was a ladies' man and were wary of him, but I could see how he could be popular with the opposite sex.

The day of the party came around, and we were all getting a little excited about what promised to be a brilliant night. I had my hair done by our next door neighbour, in loose ringlets which hung right down my back. I liked it but wasn't very impressed with my outfit when I tried it on again. I thought it made me look fat; don't us females so often think that? But when I came downstairs Mam said I looked beautiful. She was always telling me that but she would, wouldn't she, being my mother? I thought I was okay but not beautiful.

The party was excellent with really nice food, good company and the music was a mixture for all generations. I loved to dance; don't all girls, so as soon as the music started I was straight up there on the floor with my friends. After a couple of modern numbers the music switched to a ballroom waltz, so we went to sit down. Before I reached my seat though, Martin grabbed me by the hand and pulled me back onto the dance-floor.

'Oh,' I said in surprise. 'I haven't done any ballroom dancing since junior school!'

'That's okay,' he replied, spreading both hands in the air like a magician conjuring up a parrot from nowhere. 'I'll lead you.'

I tried to protest but in a second we were off and dancing! All eyes in the whole room were on us, because of who he was and because he was married. I felt embarrassed but also kind of honoured that the under-manager had chosen me to dance with. I looked around for his wife, who was watching us intently, and instantly felt very sorry for her. I know that if he'd been my husband and left me sitting there like that, I'd have been very angry and probably jealous. I avoided all eye-contact with either her or her errant husband, but must admit that I enjoyed those few brief moments of local celebrity. Afterwards, I sat down quickly knowing I'd be the talk of the store the following day.

I was a bit wary on the way to work next morning, but thankfully no-one even mentioned my brief twirl in the spotlight. Christmas was always a busy period, and we held a special day for disabled people with their carers, to come in and do their shopping in a less crowded environment. It was always on a Sunday when we'd otherwise be closed, and we let other shoppers in too because there was plenty of room and the staff were in anyway. It was a successful day from the start and the shop became quite busy later in the morning. Of course we were paid overtime for working Sunday, so that was a nice little bonus as well.

I met Evelyn's father for the first time over the holiday period. He'd been in the army most of his life and was very strict. I understood then why Evelyn loved my own father so much. Her mum and other relatives seemed fine though, especially Jenny and Tabby. Her mum and siblings still lived with their grandparents but there was still no room for Evelyn, who I'm sure must have felt a bit left out in the cold. Jen and Tabby were only a few years older than us but their little daughter Michelle, was growing fast.

I spent a lot of time at their home and slept over often. That same Christmas, her cousin Albert decided to have a party at his place and made some cocktails. They tasted lovely but were apparently very potent, and I'm pretty sure he purposely tried to get me drunk that night. Unfortunately he succeeded quite easily. I can remember going upstairs to the toilet and feeling very peculiar, quite early in the evening. Evelyn came up to check I was alright and we started laughing and joking together, probably too loudly, and when we came down Albert asked if I wanted to go outside for some fresh air.

Albert was quite an okay bloke, though quite a big-head if I remember rightly, but I said yes anyway to be polite. As the night air hit me the drink went right to my head, then straight down to my legs and I became very wobbly. Whatever his intentions were I hoped he hadn't planned this, because the street seemed to spin around like nothing I'd ever experienced. I knew I was going to be sick, and was up against the wall, and next thing I remember is Albert carrying me back into the house. I recall slurring to Evelyn's aunt that I was sorry for making such a fool of myself, and she made me a sweet cup of tea to make me feel better. It made me worse - a lot worse! So they dragged me back to Jenny's house and Evelyn put me straight to bed.

Next morning was Sunday, thankfully, as I felt like I was dying a slow and horrible death and certainly not fit for work. I never drank another cup of sweet tea again, and even steered clear of home-made cocktails for a good while. I was definitely a lightweight when it came to drinking, but I was young and decided I'd just have to try harder!

Tabby and Jen laughed at the state I was in that night. I was disappointed with myself but didn't want to admit it. Jenny said, 'I bet you won't do that again in a hurry?'

I replied, 'No, I'll take it slower next time.'

Then they really laughed.

Chapter Fourteen

First love

After Christmas things went straight back to normal, and very soon we were looking forward to spring and better weather. One Thursday afternoon I was covering for Jill on the fruit and veg counter, while she had her lunch. I was still in charge of the bread mountain and had to keep running from one counter to the other, although bread sales did calm down pretty soon. Most customers came in early to get their bread while it was still fresh.

When Jill came back things were quiet and I drifted off into a daydream, thinking about the coming weekend, when I noticed a young man walking up and down the street outside and looking in through the window. I realised he was looking at me and then I recognised him - it was Peter, my friend Lynda's childhood sweetheart all through the juniors and well into High School.

He realised I'd seen him so hesitated, then came inside and started talking to me. We chatted about school days for about thirty minutes, during which time I only sold two thin white-sliced, when right out of the blue he said, 'Any chance I could take you out, Ann?'

I was surprised but had known him for years, always liked him as a person and thought he must be lonely, and decided to accept his offer.

'Erm, alright,' I answered.

'No idea what's on but fancy going to the pictures tonight?

'Er, okay, that would be nice.'

'Okay, see you tonight, I'll call round for you about seven?'

'Alright, I'll see you then.'

I really was surprised that he'd asked me out; he always seemed so taken with Lynda and had never shown any interest at all in me. I couldn't wait to get home and tell Mam I was going out on a date with Peter, as she'd also known him for years and liked him.

It was quite a warm night, not really spring yet but the weather was definitely improving. I was ready early and sat near my bedroom window waiting for Peter to arrive. When I saw him come around the corner, I skipped down the stairs and shouted, 'Bye, see you later,' to everybody.

Mam shouted back, 'Bye, love. Have a nice night and I'll see you later.'

As I went outside Peter was halfway along the road, and as he got closer I could see how tall he'd grown. I hadn't really noticed earlier, in the shop. He smiled and waved when he saw me, and I smiled back.

'Should we walk?' he asked.

I said, 'Yes I like walking, when the weather's nice of course.'

'Sure you wouldn't prefer the bus?'

'No, not tonight,' I answered, a fleeting picture of Marshall scurrying across my mind. 'Buses often make me queasy.'

We never stopped talking after that. We talked and laughed all the way into the town and when we got to the pictures he said, 'Fancy some popcorn?'

'No thanks,' I answered. I was always careful what I ate, thinking I was never my ideal weight.

I can't remember what film was showing that night but we didn't see much of it anyway. Peter made it very clear that he wasn't just with me because of loneliness, and we kissed and cuddled all the way through it! A girl from work was sitting with her new boyfriend a few seats away, and next day she said, 'Enjoy the picture last night?'

I said, 'Didn't see much of it.'

She laughed and said, 'I didn't see much of it either, I was too busy watching you two!'

We both laughed at that.

When Peter and me came out of the pictures we set off strolling back to my house. We weren't chatting and laughing though like we were on the way there. We were both quiet and kind of, thoughtful. I was beginning to wonder if he'd gone off me already, when all of a sudden he stopped and put a hand on my arm. I thought he was going to say he didn't want to walk all the way with me, and was bracing myself to be cool about it. He looked me straight in the eye and I think my chin wobbled slightly. But he said quietly, 'I think I love you, Ann.'

I was absolutely shocked. 'Don't be silly,' I said. 'We've only had one date, well almost!'

'It might sound silly but I'll prove it to you.'

'Will you?'

'Yes, I'll prove that I love you.'

I'm not quite sure what happened that night, but something special did. Whether he did love me or not, I didn't know at that point, but I soon fell head over heels in love with him, and from that day forward we were inseparable.

Chapter Fifteen

First passion

The days flew past, turned into weeks and months and my happiness just grew and grew. I'd never known anything like it and wanted it to last for ever. Peter and I had been an item for what seemed like half a lifetime. I loved him so much and he often said he truly loved me. Mam was happy because I'd settled down a lot and she always knew where I was at night. Peter and me still went to the pictures every week and actually watched the films, or at least some of them, and then we'd always go back to his house. I was just like part of their family by then and we all got along well. I talked a lot with his mum, Kathy, his sister and younger brothers.

One night we'd been to visit Peter's aunt in Workington. She's Kathy's sister and I really got on well with her too. We were sitting on the sofa and she was teasing Peter. I think he was her favourite nephew, as he'd lived with her and her family before Kathy met and married Hans, a Danish bloke who worked on the fishing boats. She obviously knew Peter and I were really happy together and with a little glint in her eye, she looked at us both and said, 'So when are you two getting hitched then?'

We had talked about getting engaged, though not until I was eighteen the following September, but we'd never told anybody of our plans so we both started giggling like kids and never answered. Later, as we were getting ready to leave and catch the bus back to Peter's, she gave him a kiss and a hug and said, 'Well hurry up and get it arranged, you two. I love a family wedding and make sure you let me know first so I can get a new hat.'

We sat at the back of the bus, kissing and cuddling all the way home. I snuggled up to him and knew he was my whole world now. I felt safe and warm with him, and was sure that nothing could ever spoil us as a couple, or our happiness together. When we arrived Kathy asked, 'How is she then? I haven't seen her for weeks.'

Peter said, 'She's fine and asked about you as well.'

When she went through to the kitchen to make us some tea, I followed and said, 'I really like your sister, she's so nice and you're both very much alike.'

Suddenly we heard the front door opening and in came Hans, Kathy's husband who'd been away at sea for weeks. He'd then gone back over to Denmark to see his family for a week, and was just home that night.

'Good trip Hans?' Peter asked him. 'Catch many fish?'

Kathy and I carried tea and biscuits through and after Peter's young brothers and sister had theirs, they finished watching their television programme and went off to bed. It was only about 10.30 but Hans was very tired, so got up and said, 'Goodnight, Ann,' and nodded to Peter.

Kathy washed the cups and then poked her head around the door, 'Goodnight you two love-birds, see you both tomorrow.'

'Goodnight Kathy,' I replied.

They never usually went to bed so early but Hans was obviously tired, and having been away so long they'd probably missed being close to each other. It was a terrible thing to think, but I couldn't help pondering just how easy it would be for Hans to have another wife in Denmark! Maybe elsewhere too – a wife in very port as the saying goes!

We never usually got much chance to be on our own either, so Peter switched the light off and we snuggled down on the sofa to watch television. We were soon kissing and cuddling again but this time it was definitely more passionate than usual, and if getting carried away feels like floating on air, then that's what we were doing.

In the months we'd been together Peter had never tried anything really sexual before now, but we were never on our own long enough so the opportunity never arose. My heart was beating fast and opposing thoughts were swirling around in my head: If I let this happen and my parents find out they will not be pleased, but I was with the man I loved desperately and wanted him to have every part of me.

Peter was very gentle and considerate and kept pausing to ask, 'Are you alright, Ann?'

'Yes, I'm okay,' I answered between deep breaths.

I loved him so much and knew he loved me, and it seemed like the normal thing to do - the thing that all lovers do. I was desperate to keep him happy so he wouldn't want anyone else, and I so wished us to be happy together for the rest of our lives. What could be wrong with that? Nothing at all I decided and so – we did it. Right there and then and it was wonderful!

Afterwards we stayed together on the sofa, and suddenly a light went on upstairs. We heard Peter's mother get up and go into the bathroom, and that's when reality hit me. A few minutes before it felt like we were floating on a wave of love and passion, and there was only us in our own little world. But there were five other people upstairs and not much soundproofing between us. We stayed silent until she got back into bed, then Peter whispered, 'Do you want to go home?'

'I think so,' I answered, collecting myself and my clothes.

We sneaked out quietly and he walked me home. My mind was racing with mixed emotions and as we turned into my street, I held his arm tight and looked up into his eyes and said softly, 'Peter.'

'Yes, Ann?'

'You know that I love you, don't you?'

'Well I hope you do,' he answered.

'So what if...if...?'

'If what?'

'Well, what if I'm pregnant?'

He went very quiet for a few seconds until we reached my door, then gave a kind of shrug and said, 'You're always worrying about something, Ann.'

'Am I?' I said, quite surprised.

He laughed, kissed me on the cheek and said, 'Goodnight little worrier, I'll see you tomorrow.'

I smiled and nodded. 'Okay, goodnight.'

He was right though, I was worried. We were both still teenagers and suddenly, the wonderful feeling of being young and free with the whole world at our feet, had gone in a flash. Fear and dread of making major mistakes had taken its place.

As I opened the front door Mam called out, 'Are you alright, love?'

Why is she asking me that? I wondered immediately, a little panic rising in my heart, but then I remembered that she always did. I looked into her bedroom as she was obviously awake, and her light was on. I said, 'Goodnight Mam, see you in the morning.'

As I lay awake in bed, the last few hours of my life swamped my thoughts. Surely I should be happy making love to the man I want to be with forever, and even having his baby? So why did I feel the way I did? Why was I so scared of the future and what it might bring? Eventually I tried to resign myself to fate, remembering Mam telling me so often, 'What will be - will be.'

Chapter Sixteen

Broken heart

I heard Mam calling, 'Ann, are you up yet? You'll be late for work.'

I must have fallen asleep at some point but it didn't feel like I had. I was still really tired and as I crawled out of bed Mam was padding around on the landing, carrying washing and old socks and she shouted through, 'We're all going to Blackpool in July, and Dad wondered if you and Peter would like to come with us?'

'Blackpool?'

'Yes, Blackpool.'

'Mm that might be alright, I'll ask him tonight when he comes over.'

Peter came round about seven as usual, and we sat in the kitchen playing *Maggie May* on my little pink record player. He loved Rod Stewart.

'What would you think about a break in Blackpool in July?' I asked him.

'For us?'

'Yes, Mam and Dad are taking Brian and wondered if we want to go with them.'

'Okay yeah, that sounds good.'

He seemed quite excited so I told Mam we'd love to go with them, and she arranged it all. We were staying in a guest house and had booked two rooms. One had two single beds with a make-up cot for Brian, and the other just had the two single beds. It was decided that Dad, Brian and Peter would share one room, with Mam and I in the other.

I was looking forward to the holiday like the rest of my family, but as the weeks passed Peter seemed to be cooling off a bit. He never spoke about it and started to become a little distant. More and more often he had somewhere to go without me, and even started going away to sea at weekends, with Hans. He said it was to earn some money but I could feel there was more to it than that.

One busy afternoon I was at work on the bread mountain, but feeling quite ill. Eileen said, 'You look terrible, you must have that damn flu bug that's going around so get yourself off home.'

I said, 'I can't afford to take time off, Eileen, we're saving for a holiday.'

'It's alright, you'll get paid for being off sick. Just make sure you get a note from your doctor.'

'You sure?'

'Yes, and anyway I don't want to be catching whatever you've got – half the staff could go down if we're not careful.'

'Ok,' I nodded and started getting my things together.

As I was waiting for the bus home, Peter got off a different bus almost right in front of me. He looked really surprised and it was quite a few seconds before he smiled or spoke.

'Are you alright?' I asked.

'Er, yes are you? You don't look so good.'

'No, I'm feeling quite poorly. Eileen thinks it's the flu and she's sent me home.'

'Oh right. I'm just back from sea,' he said, and flashed me one of his big smiles.

My heart skipped a beat. I'd missed him so much. He waited with me, though we didn't talk very much, and when my bus arrived he got on as well and told me to take a seat as he paid our fares.

'Thank you,' I said.

'No problem. So you're going off sick then?'

'Well, just 'til I feel a bit better. I feel awful at the moment.'

'Well take things easy, get some rest, and I'll come round to see you at home.'

'Will you?'

'Yes, of course I will.'

'When?'

'When's best?'

'Tonight?'

'Okay, I'll come round tonight,' he smiled.

I waited all night but he never turned up, and I knew something had changed forever. My world was shattered and my heart broken in two.

Chapter Seventeen

Hanging on to dreams

I was in a daze for a week after Peter let me down, but Mam kept telling me not to worry.

'He knows you're not well,' she said. 'And probably thinks it's best to stay away for a few days.'

But I knew she was only being kind and trying to soften the blow. I did want to believe she was right, and that once I was better Peter would be back in my life, but deep in my heart the terrible sense of loss was very real. I had to face the possibility that Peter and me weren't meant to be after all.

As soon as I felt well enough I went straight back to work, hoping it would take my mind off worries about the future. At lunch time the first day Evelyn marched over and said, 'Come on you, let's get outside for some fresh air and blow those cobwebs away.'

I smiled half-heartedly. 'We can give it a try,' I said.

We strolled along the main street, chatting and looking in shop windows but secretly, I was hoping we might bump into Peter. I knew he was working just down in the harbour which wasn't far away. There was no sign of him though and it seemed to me that he was staying well out of my way, and keeping a low profile generally.

On the way back to work I remembered that I'd promised to take his young sister Lynne, to see *Mickey Mouse* at the pictures. So when I got home that afternoon I arranged to take Brian and our neighbour's daughter Karen, as well. We decided to go the following evening after I finished work, which meant I'd have to go and see Kathy that very night, to check it was okay for Lynne to come with us. My intricate plan was really just an excuse to see Peter.

Falling in love was absolutely great, but falling out of love was awful and I couldn't understand why he hadn't at least said goodbye and told me it was over. The fact that he hadn't done so cruelly kept my lingering hopes alive, like one of his poor flapping fish, dying slowly on the dockside.

After tea I got changed and tried to look as gorgeous as possible, and walked round to Kathy's house. She seemed pleased to see me, but I think she knew by the way I was dressed that I was really looking for Peter.

'Hello Ann, love,' she said. 'Are you feeling any better after your illness? You look a lot better.'

'Yes thanks, Kath. I'm fine now and back at work.'

There was an awkward, silent pause and my eyes swept around the house as I listened for any signs of my lost love.

'Pete's away out on a driving lesson,' she said matter-of-factly. 'He seems to be doing well and the instructor says he's nearly ready for his test.'

'Oh, I didn't even know he'd started learning!'

'Yeah, he's been at it a couple of months now.'

A couple of months, I thought. How fast they'd flown past. We'd been apart for at least two months. It sounded like an eternity.

'Oh, well I hope he passes soon, tell him,' I responded, maintaining my poise and dignity. 'I actually came round to ask if it was okay for me to take Lynne to the pictures tomorrow,' I continued without taking a breath. 'To see Mickey Mouse like I promised her.'

'Oh yes, that would be lovely. She's never stopped asking about you for weeks.'

Tears welled in my eyes at all that was being lost. I wiped them away with my sleeve and croaked, 'I'll call around for her tomorrow about six?'

'Come and sit down for a minute, pet,' Kathy said, taking my arm and sitting me in the lounge.

I sat there feeling wretched, knowing my make-up was all over the place, yet still hoping Peter might come in soon. As daylight faded and the street lamps flickered on, I thought at least nobody will see the state I'm in when I walk home in the dark. I hated being out on my own at night, and was remembering how nice it was when Peter always walked me home, when suddenly the door opened and in he came.

'Hi,' he said to everyone in general, and went into the kitchen.

I sat a little bit longer but felt awkward. 'Well, I must be off home,' I announced shakily. 'So thanks Kathy and tell Lynne I'll see her tomorrow?'

I glanced over to the kitchen where Peter leant in the doorway sipping a drink, and said, 'Bye, Pete.'

Before he answered, Kathy interrupted, 'Peter, aren't you going to walk Ann home? It's getting late and it's dark outside.'

'Mm, okay,' he answered absently, putting his glass on the kitchen worktop.

I was surprised and thought maybe there was still a little bit of hope left for us. But I felt awkward and uncomfortable as we walked the same route we had so often in the past. Back then we'd stop to kiss under every lamppost. What had I done to change all that? We were so much in love then – weren't we?

When we got to my front door, he kept his hands in his pockets as he at last kissed me - on the cheek! Now I was totally and utterly deflated, and my heart split wide open.

Mam as always, was concerned. She knew I was very unhappy as I never spoke to her and ran straight to my room, where I threw myself on the bed and sobbed my broken heart out. She came in and sat beside me, and said, 'Ann, my love, you're still young and you'll have lots of boyfriends before you find the right one. You need to go out and enjoy yourself.'

It seemed like awful advice to me - finding someone else to fall in love with so he could tear me apart all over again! I carried on with life though and decided not to let anybody know how much I was breaking up inside. Mam was right I decided after a while - I was still young and there are plenty more fish in the sea as everyone kept telling me, though I'm not sure they were the right words to use in my case. I decided to pick myself up off the floor and get on with my life – put my troubles to one side and carry on regardless!

I didn't enjoy Mickey Mouse too much, with my brother and the two girls, but they laughed all the way through and all the way home. As we neared Kathy's house, yet again I stupidly hoped Peter would be around – I just couldn't help myself, but I never saw him. I did see him later from time to time around town, but that didn't help matters and only made me feel worse, wishing and hoping for something I could no longer have.

I started going out in the evenings again with my friends, and the first place we went to was the Tow Bar. Marshall wasn't driving the bus, which was probably fortunate as I was feeling a bit reckless. But as we drove through Egremont I saw a newly-qualified driver who I also knew well. Striding along the road was none other than Peter, with a tall and gorgeous blonde on his arm.

I can't remember much about that night but as we climbed back onto the bus to go home, I came face to face with Marshall, who was driving the return trip. He winked at me as I smiled and sat down, where I sat staring into the darkness outside the window - and inside my mind.

Chapter Eighteen

Blackpool

We were all ready for our summer holiday and waiting excitedly for the bus to Blackpool, which seemed as far away as the other side of the world to us then. I'd started smoking a few months back when I was with Peter. He smoked as did his mother and Hans, so it seemed like the thing to do if I wanted to fit in. Mam found out and was so disappointed. She smoked at one time but stopped years ago when she was pregnant. She thought I'd never smoke because I always hated the smell of it as a child. I seemed to follow others did just to be the same as them – to fit in and be accepted.

Just about everybody smoked in the fifties, and I mean everybody, and everywhere. There was nowhere people didn't smoke. Mam once said, 'I remember going to see the doctor and he was puffing away merrily and blowing smoke all over the place.'

'Really? I asked.

'Yes, it was very fashionable and people thought you were a bit weird if you didn't smoke!'

Dad also stopped smoking years before but said, 'Your mother's right but you're not a child anymore and if you want to smoke, it's up to you, just maybe not around us and the kids?'

I nodded and said, 'You're both right and thank you for not being angry.'

I was grateful and never smoked when they were around, especially on the bus to Blackpool. I could get quite sickly on buses anyway without pushing my luck.

'Don't forget how much you suffered with travel sickness when you were young,' Mam warned me unnecessarily.

I smiled and nodded again. 'I know Mam, I'll be careful and definitely won't smoke on the bus.'

I enjoyed the start of the journey, it was nice to just relax and watch the countryside float past through the bus window. After a while though the miles started to drag by, it seemed to take an eternity actually getting there and inevitably, I kept thinking how different it would have been had Peter been with me.

We arrived eventually though, on time, the weather was good and so was the forecast for the week, and I knew my parents would make sure we all had a good holiday. The guesthouse was nice and so was the landlady when Dad explained that there were only four of us, not the original five. Every time something like that happened though, a knife plunged into my heart and reminded me of what I'd lost so recently.

We kept to the same sleeping arrangements so at least I wasn't saddled with my little brother. Brian was okay but sometimes a chore and well, just not Peter. But we did have a pretty good time overall as it happened. Mam made sure I was never left brooding on my own, we laughed and joked and larked about, and she was really good fun to be with. She kind of knew how to get me out of myself and keep me focused on more positive things.

We went through the hall of mirrors at the fairground, and stopped in the middle where the real crazy ones make you looked weird and distorted. Mam was posing and pulling faces and had me in fits of laugher. I told her to behave as I really needed the toilet and didn't know where it was. The hall was full of people and Dad was embarrassed; telling us both to behave ourselves, the spoilsport! We didn't though and soon I was absolutely desperate.

'I'll have to get back to the guest house,' I said. 'Before I have a little accident!'

'Oh no,' Dad said. 'We've only just got here.'

He was easily flustered but Mam definitely wasn't. Everything was just another little piece of life's jigsaw to her and she took it all in her stride without any fuss, which could prove to be embarrassing at times. I loved her open simplicity though and knew she always meant well.

The week passed quickly but along the way I bought myself a big hat with 'kiss me quick' written on it. Coming out of our room one morning there was a young guy coming out of the opposite room. He winked at me but probably thought I was just a kid wearing that hat. Why did I buy it? Maybe I was already searching desperately for Peter's replacement in my life?

Mam and Dad were delighted every time we went into the fun house or on the trams or anywhere that charged admission, because they were only ever charged for two adults and two children. I was mortified - I was nearly eighteen! Mam said, 'Don't say anything Ann, and anyway it's nice to look younger than your years, especially when you're starting to get a bit of age on you, like I am.'

'But I don't want to look like a child, Mam, even though you probably think I behave like one sometimes.'

On Thursday we were out all day and I was tired, and told Mam and Dad I was going back to the guest house to lie down. It was true, I was feeling a bit weary, but I also wanted to watch *Top of the Pops*. Donny Osmond had been number one in the charts for weeks, and I wanted to see if he was still top with a song I really liked. I don't know why I wanted to inflict such bitter-sweet pain upon myself, and I don't just mean the actual singing! It was about the words of the song and what they meant to me, and to my life, and to my lost love. It consoled me to know that others had suffered what I was still suffering, and survived. It soothed my pain and heartbreak just a little, to know that people can get past it and carry on, and that what Peter and I had, was just puppy love.

Our holiday was over too soon, and early Saturday morning we were all packed and waiting for the taxi to take us to the bus station for our journey back home.

'Are you all ready to go, everybody?' Mam asked, scanning our luggage.

'Yes, Mam,' came the weary reply.

'Everybody have a nice holiday?'

'Yes, Mam.'

'You enjoy it, Ann?'

'I've had a lovely holiday, Mam. We had a really good laugh and Dad is so funny when he wants to be.'

'Mm, and even sometimes when he doesn't want to be.'

Dad grunted but Brian and I laughed. Mam was still looking at me.

'Please don't worry about me, Mam. I'm okay, honest.'

'Well I do worry about you, love, but I'm glad you're feeling a little better, at least.'

I wasn't looking forward to going back home. There was always the chance I would bump into Peter again, probably with his tall blonde in tow, and I knew for certain that would bring back all the feelings of hurt and rejection. I can't recall who quoted at me from an old poem, that it was 'better to have loved and lost than never to have loved at all', but I do remember thinking they must be stupid. They obviously hadn't been through the pain that still hovered over every single part of my life. I've always been interested in poetry myself as it happens, and knew the line was written by Alfred Lord Tennyson in 1849. I think a later verse in the poem was more suited to my situation:

>*'Untouched, the garden bough shall sway,*
>*The tender blossom flutter down,*
>*Unloved, that beech will gather brown,*
>*This maple burn itself away.'*

There was another old poem that I looked up after remembering it from school. It was written by Thomas Hood who lived from 1799 to 1845, and this is the verse that brought fresh tears to my eyes:

>*'Our hands have met, but not our hearts;*
>*Our hands will never meet again.*
>*Friends, if we have ever been,*
>*Friends we cannot now remain:*
>*I only know I loved you once,*
>*I only know I loved in vain;*
>*Our hands have met but not our hearts;*
>*Our hands will never meet again'*

The journey home was quiet most of the way, everybody apparently deep in thought, and passed quickly enough. Mam and I talked about the day we went to the hall of mirrors, and other things that we all did in Blackpool. As we neared home I began wondering how Evelyn was, and if anything interesting had happened while I was away. I'd told her I would go to her house on the Sunday, for some lunch and a catch-up.

When we arrived at the bus-station our connection wasn't due for another half hour, so Mam and I went to the chippie while Dad and Brian waited with our cases. We kept the fish & chips wrapped until we got home, and all the way there the smell tortured us, so that when we finally arrived we were all ravenous. I couldn't wait to get inside the house and devour them!

After tea I went up to my room and played records while unpacking. The very first song I played was *Puppy Love* by Donny Osmond. Tears streamed down my face the whole way through, and I played it a further three times! Why on earth do we punish ourselves so? Is it just to keep our treasured memories alive?

I looked at the clock in my bedroom and it was nearly 9pm, so popped downstairs and told everybody I was having an early night. 'See you all in the morning.'

'Goodnight, love,' Mam said.

'Night-night,' said Dad and Brian, as I went back up to bed.

Travelling is always tiresome and even though my heart was still shattered, I soon fell fast asleep.

Chapter Nineteen

Another change

When I woke in the morning it was another sunny day. I got up, had breakfast and asked my brother Charlie, who'd recently acquired a second-hand car, if he'd take me to Evelyn's. He did and Evelyn was pleased to see me.

'Anything spectacular happen while I was away?' I asked.

'Well, yeah there is something,' she answered flatly.

'Okay?'

'My dad's coming home for good and he's bought a house down in Manchester.'

It took me a few seconds to take in what she'd just said. 'Does, does that mean what I think it means?'

'Afraid so. He's got us a brand new house and we're all moving down there to live.'

I was stunned. 'When?'

'Two weeks' time.'

'Two weeks!' I was horrified.

'I know, just so soon isn't it?'

'You'll have to give up your job!'

'I know.'

'Well,' I said, controlling of my emotions. I'd had a lot of practice lately. 'Well I'll miss you so much, Evelyn. I can't believe you're leaving, and so soon.'

'There's nothing I can do about it, Ann, and I'll miss you too.'

'Promise me we'll write to each other?'

I'd lost Peter already and now my best friend was leaving. How cruel is this life we're all stuck with. It really is full of ups and downs and heartaches.

'Of course we'll write,' Evelyn answered, but even as she spoke I could feel another part of me dying and ebbing away.

'My dad phoned the night before you went to Blackpool,' she continued. 'But I didn't want to tell you then 'cos I knew you'd be upset, and it would've spoiled your holiday.'

'It definitely would have.'

'Then I had to hand my notice in at work the next morning, and I'm going to miss everybody there too, Ann,' she said with a tear in her eye.

'You'll be alright,' I whispered, putting a gentle hand on her arm. 'Life tests us like this, to toughen us up for the long road ahead.'

She looked at me and I don't think I'd made her feel any better. We just sat quietly and held hands for a while. Gosh how I was going to miss her. Life was turning upside down and would never be the same.

The night before she left we arranged a night out with all her friends and some people from work. We enjoyed it but everyone was sad as we parted and said our goodbyes.

'I promise I'll write,' Evelyn said tearfully. 'And you can come visit us anytime you like, and I'll come back over here for the holidays.'

'That sounds great,' I agreed with a smile, remembering how we promised very similar things when I said farewell to Chris - there was no way we weren't going to keep in touch with each other, but in the end - we didn't. Life takes us along different paths, we meet new people and the old parts of our lives fade into the past.

I felt very alone again - no Peter and now no Evelyn. Everything was falling apart but one of Evelyn's friends who came to her leaving party, Susan Graham, kept in touch with me and we started going out together at weekends. Sue also worked at Woolworths and one afternoon she suggested going to the Tow Bar at the weekend. She hadn't asked her parents but her elder sister, Jean, who also worked with us, said it would be fine. Jean had a word at home and it was all systems go for the following Sunday.

Susan and Jean lived at Cleator Moor, a few miles east of Whitehaven, towards Ennerdale in the beautiful Lake District National Park. It was arranged for me to stay with them on the Sunday night, and Charlie agreed to take me over there in the afternoon. Susan's parents were really nice and I chatted away with them for a while before her mother called upstairs, 'Your friend Ann's here, Susan.'

Maybe they'd been checking me out first? Sue rushed to the top of the stairs, 'Come on up,' she said excitedly. We were both looking forward to our big night out.

'My brother's going to run us through to the Tow, Ann, is that okay?' she asked.

'Yeah, that's great.'

'And we can get the bus back home?'

'Fine.'

I was wearing a Crombie dress and a yellow blazer trimmed with navy blue, and looked like someone from TV's *Hi-De-Hi* show! I had on black platform shoes, which gave me a bit of height and Susan said, 'You look great,' and I felt quite good about myself.

When we got there, Sue said, 'My boyfriend, Dave and his friend are coming tonight. Dave doesn't drink so he'll be in his car and we can get a lift home with him.'

'Oh, what about the bus?'

'Oh I just said that 'cos Mum and Dad were probably listening.'

'Oh, right.'

'Dave says you might like his friend, Gordon.'

'Gordon?'

'Uh-hum, he's really nice.'

It was a promotion night for *Double Diamond* beer, so it was quite cheap and we agreed to give it a go. It was really nice and we both had a few, and thank goodness it wasn't a Merry-Down night! Suddenly, Susan said, 'Oh my God, here's Dave and Gordon.'

She seemed a bit embarrassed when they saw us and came straight over, or maybe it was just her shyness, but they both appeared to be really nice blokes. Susan waved a hand and said, 'Ann, this is Dave and this is his friend Gordon.'

I smiled and Gordon said, 'Would you like another drink, ladies?'

I was quite impressed with his politeness and answered, 'Yes please. Double Diamond for me.'

'And me,' said Sue.

He was back in a few minutes and said, 'So, Ann, how are you enjoying the night so far?' as he sat down and poured my drink for me.

Dave sat on the other side of us next to Sue.

'I'm fine,' I answered. 'How are you?'

'Well I'm definitely feeling better after meeting you.'

I blushed straight away like I used to years ago, but smiled and sipped my DD. 'Thank you,' I said, looking up at him through my finely-plucked eyebrows.

It usually felt a little awkward, talking to men for the first time, but straight away I felt kind of comfortable and at ease, and found talking to Gordon quite easy. We chatted for a while, had a few dances together and a few more drinks. It was a lovely evening, quite warm and Dave said, 'Let's all go for a walk on the beach?'

The beach was really close to the pub so we finished our drinks and set off. Susan and I were giggling as it was really dark by then and platform shoes aren't to be recommended for walking on soft sand.

'Definitely not the right footwear,' Sue said.

'I think I'll take mine off,' I said. 'Before I fall over and break my neck.'

They laughed but I wasn't joking. The alcohol wasn't helping either and the fresh air made my head spin. I was stumbling all over the place when suddenly Gordon said, 'Hold my hand.'

I did so and felt quite relaxed and happy, and steadier, as we trudged along hand in hand. The moon was shining, reflecting off the sea which lapped lazily against the shore, and I hadn't felt so at peace with the world for a long time. Suddenly, Gordon swung me around to face him, and kissed me on the lips. I didn't try too hard to stop him and he carried on for what seemed like half an hour! I remember watching a ship on the distant horizon, over his shoulder.

Susan shouted, 'Hey you two, I think the tide's coming in, we better get off the beach.'

It was getting late so we walked back to the car, where Dave said, 'I'll take Gordon home first Sue, is that okay?'

'Yeah that's fine,' she replied, and off we went.

Gordon lived on a farm, which was really big and when we got there he invited us in.

'Another drink, girls?' he asked.

'Could I just have a cup of tea please?' I said.

'Yeah but you'll have to make it yourself, I'm useless at making tea.'

'That's alright, where's the kitchen?'

'Come with me,' he said, leading Susan and me through a wide corridor.

The farmhouse was huge and so was the kitchen, where he pointed to a cupboard and said, 'That's the pantry. You should find everything you need in there. If there's anything you want to eat, just help yourselves.'

When Susan opened the pantry door it was like another room, and we burst out laughing. We had never seen anything like it! I said, 'Shh, he'll think we're laughing at him.'

'Do you like him?' she asked.

'He's okay.'

'Well Dave says he really likes you.'

I shrugged and said, 'Come on, I've found the tea bags and milk.'

We made a cup each and when we finished them Sue said, 'Well boys, we must be going home. Have to be up early for work tomorrow.'

We all walked out to the car and Gordon said, 'Goodnight Ann, would you like to see me again?'

I stopped with one foot in the car and looked at him. 'Would you like to see me?'

'Yes, I would, very much.'

'Okay then,' I said, and got in the car.

As we were driving Dave said, 'Gordon really likes you Ann, what do you think of him?'

'He's okay, I suppose.'

'He really is a nice bloke you know,' Dave persisted.

'Yeah, he's okay.'

I was really feeling tired now and glad to get back to Susan's house, where we were soon in bed and fast asleep.

Chapter Twenty

Is he the one?

Next day Susan and I waited for her other sister, Sheila, and her husband Brian to pick us up for work. Sheila was really beautiful with long blonde hair and was smiling at us when we got in the car. 'Did you have a good time last night then?' She asked.

Susan said, 'Yeah it was a good night and afterwards we went to Gordon Litt's farm. He fancies the pants off Ann!'

'Well you'll be alright there Ann,' said Sheila. 'His family has loads of money!'

Her husband was laughing and I could feel my face blushing again, but soon we pulled in at work. Shelia and Susan were still laughing and joking about last night and as we got out of the car, I realised I was starting to feel better about things, and maybe just a little happier with my world at that moment.

It felt good to be back amongst all the familiarity of Woollies. During morning break we were sitting on the stone steps outside the canteen, catching up with tea and biscuits when Jill, the fruit-counter girl popped her head around the door.

'Ann,' she shouted. 'There's a boy downstairs asking for you.'

Susan shrieked and said, 'I bet it's Gordon, he can't bear to be parted from you!'

Shit! I thought, choking on my *McVitie's Digestive*. I couldn't even remember what he looked like!

'Surely not,' I coughed. 'How would he get here?'

'Probably had the coachman drive him,' she laughed.

I got up slowly, brushed biscuit crumbs from my uniform, and walked back downstairs with Jill. Sure enough, when I went through the doors at the bottom, a slightly familiar young man was standing waiting at the bottom of the steps.

It was good job he'd asked for me because if he'd come straight up, I'm not sure I'd have recognised him. How embarrassing would that be? Must have been the Double Diamond!

'Hi,' he said.

'Hello,' I replied, a little hoarsely, licking a biscuit crumb from my bottom lip.

'I was hoping you might like to go to the pictures with me tonight? *Steptoe and Son* is on.'

'Mm okay,' I answered after a moment's thought. 'That would be lovely, thank you.'

He smiled. 'I'll pick you up at your house at six thirty, if that's alright?'

'Yes that's fine, I'll see you then.'

'Okay,' he smiled again. 'See you tonight.'

He stood there watching as I went back up the steps, turned to wave, and ducked back into the canteen.

'Well?' said Susan excitedly.

'Yes it was him.'

'I know, I peeped out the window!'

'We're going to the pictures tonight.'

'Are you?'

'Yes, to see Steptoe & Son.

'Well that's good isn't it? You don't exactly sound over the moon about it.'

'To be honest, I'm not sure I like him that much but I quite fancy Steptoe & Son.'

Susan was aghast. 'Really?'

'What, Gordon or Steptoe?'

'Gordon – you don't fancy him?'

'Not really.'

'So why did you agree to go out with him?'

'I, I don't know. I'm not sure. Maybe I just didn't want to disappoint him?'

Pretty soon the news was all around the store as the latest topic of conversation.

'Oh, the poor lad,' said Eileen. 'And after he came all that way to see you.'

I smiled and said, 'I like him but he just doesn't float my boat like…'

Everybody went quiet as they all knew I meant Peter. I just refused to let his name pass my lips.

'Dave and me could come as well, Ann,' Susan offered.

'Okay, that might be better.'

'Yes, you could have a foursome,' agreed Eileen.

'Mm,' I conceded flatly.

Gordon was really nice and I did feel bad about not being more enthusiastic, but I just didn't fancy him and there was nothing I could do about that. It'd been fun the night before but a long-term relationship? I just couldn't see that happening.

We did the foursome thing though and he was really polite again, and bought me chocolates and popcorn, which I even took a few nibbles of. During the film he put his arm around my shoulders, but I just wanted to watch the movie so kept my chin down with the popcorn in front of my face. Afterwards he drove me home, so he did have a car at least, and pulled up outside my house. Dave and Sue were snogging in the back. He gave me a goodnight kiss and said, 'I'll call and see you again in the shop if that's alright?'

I nodded and smiled but that essential spark just wasn't there, and I knew he wasn't the one for me. I decided at that moment that I would not, could not, settle for second best. I did feel really bad about disappointing him, but all's fair in love and war, so my dad told me once. I opened the front door and hung my bag over the stairs banister.

'Hello love,' Mam said I as I went in the kitchen to make some tea. 'Did you have a nice time at the pictures?'

'It was okay, Mam but I don't really like Gordon that much, I don't think. He's a really nice lad but he's not the one for me.'

'Never mind love, there'll be others.'

Chapter Twenty One

A new romance?

When I got to work next day, Susan was waiting for me in the canteen. 'Morning Sue,' I greeted her. 'You okay?'

'Yes I'm fine Ann, but poor Gordon was so upset last night. He said it was like flogging a dead horse with you at the pictures.'

That statement upset me. What kind of girl did he think I was? Maybe I gave him the wrong idea the night before when I was full of alcohol?

'Well, I don't really like him, Susan. I know he's a nice bloke but I can't feel something that's not there and is never going to be. I'm sorry.'

'He's going to be so hurt.'

'I don't want to hurt anyone, Susan. I know only too well what that's like. But I can't start living a lie just to suit somebody else.'

She nodded. 'No, of course not. Just such a shame you two didn't get on though.'

'We did kind of get on Sue, and I'm happy to carry on seeing him as a friend, I just know for a fact that I'll never fall in love with him.'

I walked away then and carried on with my work, thinking I was just not going to put myself out worrying about it, or him, or anybody else if I could help it.

That afternoon Marshall came breezing into the shop and to my surprise, I realised that I still looked forward to seeing him. He was a familiar face and had that kind of happy-go-lucky, bad-boy thing about him which is always a little exciting. Sometimes he crept up behind me when I was concentrating on the bread mountain, and I would still blush. I knew I didn't fancy him or anything like that, but maybe I liked him flirting with me for some reason I hadn't yet fathomed?

Gordon didn't give up the chase easily though, however upset Sue reckoned he was. I kind of admired him for that and would always chat to him when he came into the shop, which seemed to be every other day. He often brought me a little present and no way could I be nasty to the lad, and eventually I began to look forward to his company. I think truthfully, I needed the attention but maybe shouldn't have encouraged him, if that's what I was doing. I just could never be brutal enough to tell him I wasn't interested.

I remember going home early one afternoon and the house was empty, not even Brian was around. The schools were still closed for the summer holidays, so Mam and Brian couldn't be far away as the back door was open. I thought they might have gone to see Mabel, who lived over the road and up the street a bit, so went along there. Brian was playing in the front garden and I said, 'Hi Brian, is Mammy here?'

Of course she was, I already knew that. Brian was there so where else would she be? I knocked on the door and called out, 'Hi Mabel is my mother here?'

'Yeah she's here Ann, come on in,' came the answer.

Mabel was close friends with Mam so I knew she'd know about Peter and me breaking up. I was pretty sure she'd be sympathetic and ask how I was keeping, so wasn't surprised when she did exactly that. 'Hello, Ann love, how are you managing with it all?'

'Oh, you know, carrying on with life but thank you for asking.'

'Well always remember there are plenty more fish in the sea, Ann, so you just cast a wide net, love.'

'Will do Mabel, thanks again.'

Mam was smiling and said, 'Guess who I've been talking to today, Ann?'

'No idea, who?' I replied.

'Evelyn's mother's been on the phone asking if she can come and live with us!'

'Oh my…honestly?'

'Uh-hum, I knew you'd be pleased. Evelyn's not happy living in Manchester and she wants to come home.'

Poor Evelyn, I thought. 'So can she, won't Dad mind?'

'No, he's as happy as I am for you both.'

'Wow, that'll be great. So when's she coming?'

'A week on Sunday and I've asked Charlie if he'll go down to collect her.'

'Oh that's wonderful news, I'll go with him!'

I was so pleased to know Evelyn was coming back, and wanted to get home to work out permanent sleeping arrangements.

'Thank you, Mam,' I said. 'I'm going home now so see you later when you get back?'

'I won't be long, love, I'll have to get the tea ready soon.'

I came out of Mabel's with a skip in my step, nearly fell over my little brother in the garden, and noticed a young man walking up Alfie's path.

Alfie and his family were related to us somehow. I think our dads were half-cousins or something like that. The lad had longish hair which was a lovely, burnt red colour. I'd never seen him before but he looked over and smiled at me. I smiled back and he said something I didn't quite catch. I did wonder who he was for a second but carried on home and never thought any more about it.

Susan and I decided to go to the Calder Club at the weekend. It was a private social club run by the massive Sellafield Nuclear Reprocessing Plant, which opened in 1956. Dad transferred there after Winsdcale and we were all members of the club.

They played bingo every Friday and Sunday night, and after that various local groups took turns on stage supported by the club's disco. It was always a good laugh, the drink was cheap as was the entrance fee, so what was there not to like?

The groups were surprisingly good, and played lots of sixties and seventies music which was great to dance to. If a group showed up that wasn't so good, there was always the disco to take over.

I said to Sue that afternoon, 'If you want to stay at mine tonight, that's fine.'

'Yeah, okay that would be great,' she replied.

She arrived just after tea on Sunday afternoon, and we lounged about upstairs in my bedroom playing records. I left Puppy Love in its well-thumbed cover. Mam went to bingo at the club early Sunday evenings, so later when we were waiting in the queue to get into the disco, I watched for her coming out. She was chatting to someone but saw me and called out, 'Hi love, hope you have a nice night, see you later.'

'Okay, did you win anything?' I shouted back.

'No, do I ever?' she laughed.

I don't think she was really bothered about winning, she just liked going to meet her pals and having a good chinwag with them all.

The big act tonight was a local duet: Bill and Pop. They were two local lads who were quite popular around the area, and sang all the songs I loved at the time. They performed for forty minutes then had a break, and during the break the disco started up which got everyone out on the dance floor.

As we twirled around our handbags I saw Alfie and the guy who was walking up his path the other day. They were dancing away to the disco music with some girls. The guy was very smartly turned out and for some reason - I noticed he had very shiny shoes on. Dad used to say, 'The shine on your shoe, says a lot about you!'

The disco was playing one of my favourite David Cassidy numbers. David was one of my favourite singers and I had pictures of him all over my bedroom walls. Maybe Alfie and his pal saw Sue and me looking because when the next number started, they both strolled over and started to dance with us. Alfie leaned across to me and asked, 'You ok, Ann?'

I wasn't completely sure what he said with the music blaring so loud, so I just nodded and smiled. It felt a bit awkward and after the song finished Susan said, 'Should we sit the next one out?'

'Ok,' I answered, but as we left the floor I was amazed when Alfie's friend actually bowed, and thanked me for the dance.

'Don't mention it,' I replied as Susan and I smiled at each other.

We resisted the urge to giggle when we got back to our seats, because the two lads still kept glancing over at us. It was nearly the end of the night and as we listened for what the last song was going to be, Alfie sidled across again with a strange smile on his face.

'Ann,' he said. 'Can my friend Mark, walk you home?'

I wanted to say, Can't he ask me himself? but looked across to where he was standing and thought, Oh well, he's the only one to ask me tonight, so why not?

'Alright Alfie,' I said. 'I'll see him when the last dance has finished.'

Soon the DJ was playing another of my favourites: *The Last Waltz* by Englebert Humperdink - how sad was I! Then the lights came on and everyone headed for the exits. I pretended to look around for Susan, who was behind me, and there was no sign of Mark.

'Come on Sue, let's go,' I said, quickening my pace. 'That lad must have changed his mind about taking me home.'

It was still quite warm outside but we didn't take our time, and as we hurried along I could hear familiar voices just ahead.

'That sounds like Alfie,' Susan said.

Mm, and his friend, I thought to myself.

As we approached, Mark stepped to the side of the path and said loudly, 'Stand back. Let the ladies pass.'

We couldn't help giggling this time as we hurried by. Next thing I knew, Mark was in between Susan and I and linking arms with her! I was amazed and my mouth fell open. I was about to say something when he leaned across to whisper in my ear, 'Aren't we suppose to hold hands?'

The cheek of it I thought. He couldn't be bothered to wait for me and now he wants to hold my hand! He continued to be quite entertaining though and the chit-chat between us was really quite funny. I found myself thinking: He is very funny and also – quite nice. So I came down off my high-horse and allowed myself to enjoy the rest of the walk home. It only took us a few more minutes to reach the house and I said, 'This is where I live.'

I intended to go straight inside to appear aloof and alluring, but he stood there looking like a lost lamb and Susan said, 'I'm going in to the loo, Ann, see you in a minute.'

I muttered 'Oh er, okay. I won't be long.'

Mark started chittering again, a tad too loudly, and suddenly my dad shouted from the front door, 'Ann, it's late!'

I was a little relieved and said, 'Sorry Mark, have to go in now.'

Maybe Dad called me in because he didn't know who I was with, or scarily, maybe he did! Back in my bedroom, chatting and giggling with Sue, I soon put Mark out of my mind. Who cares that he didn't ask for a date? Not me, I was sick of boys who couldn't make up their minds.

Next morning Mam and Dad were straight on my case, wanting to know who he was and where he lived. At least I knew they still cared who I was knocking about with.

'What's his name, love?' Mam asked.

'They call him Mark Murdock, he's the same age as me and lives at Woodhouse.'

'Oh yes, Woodhouse?'

'Mm, but they used to live on Calder Avenue. His dad was a good boxer according to Alfie.'

Whitehaven then was a small, insular town where everyone knew everyone else. Dad was suddenly interested and said, 'I know the Murdocks. They're a decent family as far as I know.'

Mam asked, 'So are you seeing him again?'

'No, I don't think so. He didn't ask me and maybe I would have said no, anyway.'

I could be quite flippant sometimes, but it was usually to hide something else that was going on in my head. Susan was still in bed saying she needed more rest, so I went up and roused her again. Walking to catch the bus for work she linked my arm and said, 'I thought Mark was quite nice, Ann, didn't you like him? I know how fussy you can be.'

She was referring to my meeting with Gordon, of course.

'Yeah, I kinda did, but fancy my dad coming to the door and shouting for me to come in! We'd only been there a couple of minutes as well. Maybe it was fate?'

'Nah, they just worry about us don't they, our parents. Suppose it's better than them not caring at all.'

'Yeah, I suppose so. I don't think Mark liked me very much anyway. He couldn't even be bothered to wait out the Last Waltz!'

We both laughed.

'But he did call us "ladies" a couple of times,' Sue said as we laughed again, and waved to Heather and Jean already waiting at the bus stop.

Since I'd split from Peter I had it in my head that I wasn't pretty enough or such a nice person. It really knocked my self-esteem and maybe I didn't have much real confidence left? I certainly felt very different now from when we were together.

Mondays were always busy in the store and especially at the bread counter, and time passed quickly. The morning disappeared without trace, Marshall had come and gone and I hadn't even noticed him or the time. As I glanced at the clock it was almost lunch time, and all of a sudden Mark was standing at the other end of the counter. He was obviously trying to catch my eye and my bruised heart surprisingly missed a beat. Again I blushed and realised that Mr Murdock must have had more effect on me than I wanted to admit.

Eileen had been speaking to Mark and shouted over, 'Ann, there's someone here to see you.'

I walked over to where they were standing and said nervously, 'I can't stop for long, sorry. We're very busy just now.'

He nodded and quietly asked me, 'I was wondering if you'd like to go to the pictures tomorrow night?'

Not the pictures again, I thought, I'll have to get a season ticket! But I knew *Love Story* was showing at the time so said, 'Alright then. Thank you Mark, that would be nice.'

'Thank *you*,' he said politely. 'I'll call for you tomorrow at six thirty?'

'Six thirty's fine,' I confirmed.

By now my face was like a red ball of fire and that made me even more embarrassed. I wished I could be more like Eileen, who I never saw blushing whatever happened or whoever crossed her path!

'Who's that, then?' she asked with a grin before Mark was even out of sight.

'Oh, just someone I met yesterday.'

'Well tell me all about it then.'

So I told her all about it.

Luckily, Susan was waiting for me for to go for lunch so I said, 'See you later Eileen,' and we went up the stone steps to the canteen.

Chapter Twenty Two

Evelyn is coming back

I was looking forward to seeing Love Story. I liked Ryan O'Neil and a few of the girls who'd seen the film said it was a real tear-jerker. After tea I started to get ready. It was still warm outside so I wore a short skirt and light blouse, and a little summer jacket. When I went into the kitchen Mam said, 'You look really nice, love.'

She never failed to make feel special, just because she was my mother and loved me so much. It was still a little while until Mark was due, so I went outside to sit in the last of the sunshine. Karen, the little girl next door was playing in the garden. She saw me and came running over to sit beside me on the front door step. She was a little stunner with curly hair like Shirley Temple, and we were special friends.

'Where are you off to, Ann?' she asked.

'I'm waiting for a boy who's taking me to the pictures.'

'Aw, that's nice,' she replied.

She was only three. I smiled and kept looking at my watch because the time was dragging. Karen just sat there quietly, gazing down the street. It was 6.35 and I thought - he's late for our first date - our first and last date quite probably.

'Would you like to go for some sweeties, Karen?' I asked.

'Yes please,' she replied instantly.'

'Go tell Mammy then.'

She looked at me.

'Go tell your Mammy that you're going to the shop for some sweeties, with Ann.'

She ran off but quickly came back and said, 'Mammy said it's okay.'

There was a pub at the bottom of the road with an off-licence which sold sweets and crisps and bits & bobs. Karen held my hand all the way there and back and chatted to me non-stop. There was a large grassed area which hadn't been cut for weeks, with a path through it leading from the other side of Mirehouse. The grass was so long I only saw Mark coming at the last minute. I was a bit aloof again and said, 'You're late.'

'Sorry,' he replied. 'I was late in from work.'

'Mm. Well you'll have to wait while I take Karen back home.'

'Okay.'

She skipped along the path sucking her red lollipop. 'Bye Karen,' I called as I watched her go into the house.

'Bye Ann, thank you for my lolly.'

Mark smiled and we started to stroll into town. It was a lovely evening and although the buses were quite regular, I preferred to walk. We chatted along the way, asking each other questions and just getting to know one another. We seemed to get on well and I found I was enjoying Mark's company, and this time without any assistance from alcohol.

I was mesmerised by the movie and never spoke all the way through it. I couldn't speak because I was so choked up, and could hear other girls crying in the audience, it was such a sad story. It still makes me cry today and I've watch it at least five times since on television repeats. Mark didn't complain though, maybe he was a little upset himself, and as we were leaving he asked, 'Would you like to get the bus home, Ann?'

'I'm happy to walk if that's okay with you?' I answered.

'Fine by me,' he said, and as we set off to walk he took my hand.

We walked all the way home hand-in-hand, and talked non-stop about the film and how his mates would laugh at him for going to see Love Story. There were lots of couples in the pictures though and I thought, what's wrong with taking your girlfriend to see a romantic movie? I supposed it must be some macho thing but I know now, that real men don't feel the need to hide or deny their feelings.

We arrived at my house and stood outside awkwardly for a minute or two, before Mark pulled me close and we kissed. I was nervous though and said, 'I must go in now Mark, I don't want my dad coming out and chasing you off again.'

He didn't say anything and I wondered if he'd ask me out on another date. I wasn't certain by any means that I wanted to go out with him again, but I'd feel insulted if he didn't at least ask!

All of a sudden he pulled away and said, 'Goodnight then.'

I smiled to myself but just said in return, 'Goodnight.'

Well that romance didn't last long, I thought, pushing the door open and finding Mam in the kitchen.

'What was the picture like, then?' she asked brightly.

'Oh Mam, it was so sad and Ryan O'Neil is fabulous. He made the film feel so real.'

'And are you and Mark going out again, then?'

'No,' I sighed. 'He didn't ask me out again, but I'm pleased because I would've said no, anyway.'

It was a bit of sour grapes on my part but I shrugged my shoulders and thought, well, I did quite like him so it's his loss. At work next day Susan asked about the film.

'You must get Dave to take you, Susan,' I said with real enthusiasm. 'It's a brilliant film but take plenty of tissues. I guarantee you'll need them.'

Dave was a farmer's son like his best friend, Gordon, and at that time of year they were always busy harvesting, or whatever it is they do in their tractors. There was only Dave, his father and a brother-in-law working on the farm so Susan didn't get to see him that often.

'I doubt he'll be able to make it, Ann. He's up at the crack of dawn every morning at the moment, and still working when it gets dark again.'

'Well you should try to go see it with somebody. I loved it even though it made me cry.'

'I heard it makes everybody cry, even some of the blokes!'

'Wouldn't be surprised,' I said, knowing Mark wouldn't be one of them.

'So when are you meeting Mark again, by the way?' she suddenly asked.

'I'm not seeing him again because he didn't ask me to,' I answered flatly.

She was silent.

'Guys,' I said with disdain. 'You just can't weigh them up can you? Maybe he just wanted somebody to see the film with?'

We were about ready to head down to the shop floor and I decided to change the subject: 'Evelyn will be back next week,' I said cheerfully. 'My brother and I are driving down to pick her up in Manchester.'

'Oh right, I'd forgotten about that.'

'Yeah, she'll be back at work Monday. Can't wait to see her.'

Evelyn hadn't been away very long but I had so much to tell her. I decided to forget about boys and just get on with trying to enjoy life with my girl friends.

Early Sunday morning me and Charlie were out on the open road to Manchester. He had a little blue Austin which he loved, and it got us there without any problems. Well, it did rattle a bit when we were doing more than sixty, but never gave up the ghost on us.

Evelyn was ready and waiting when we arrived, and after a quick cuppa and sandwich we were off back home to West Cumbria. We managed to get there just before dark and my parents had managed to find a double-bed for us. I was tired after the return trip, but couldn't wait for bedtime so I could make a start on all the news I had to tell Evelyn. She laughed at the story about Gordon, and although I didn't think it was so funny for him, I knew she meant well. I also told her about Mark and asked what she thought about the situation. She said, 'Who knows how men think. I'd just chill out and see how it all goes if I was you.'

Not bad advice I thought, but not easy to follow because wherever I went I seemed to bump into Mark. We always seemed to be in the same pubs at weekends and although I never went out with Mark, I always ended up coming back home with him. Evelyn and me still went to the Tow Bar but not as often, as we now liked the Calder Club and that was right on our doorstep. Mark was always at the Calder so most

Sundays, he walked me home. I was quite sure he didn't want to commit to anything long-term though, and I was quite happy with that freedom too, especially now Evelyn was back home.

Charlie was going out with a girl called Margaret, and they seemed very much in love with each other. My other brother, Albert, was still young, free and single, and Mam said she didn't think he'd ever get married. I think he really liked Evelyn but only as a friend, he said.

Chapter Twenty Three

Mam and Dad's anniversary

My parents' Silver Wedding party had been arranged for months. My sister and her husband and my little niece, Pauline were all coming to stay, even though nobody quite knew where they all would sleep. Mam said I should invite Mark as well so the next time he took me home, I did. I thought he'd have something more important to do, or even laugh, so was surprised when he accepted.

It was on a Saturday night in the Calder Club and went really well. Mam and Dad's relatives were all there and everybody really enjoyed it. I think Mark felt a little out of it because he didn't know many people, and am sure he regretted accepting the invitation. Strangely though, he started to pay me a bit more attention after that night and would always make a follow-up date. He even took me to meet his parents one afternoon!

His father seemed like a nice man and joked that I was far too good for his 'no-good' son. He said to him, 'You've landed a right bonny lass there Mark, so think on and make sure you treat her right.'

His mother just sat on the sofa with her coat and hat on, and hardly ever lifted her head out of the book she was reading. It must have been a very interesting story. Billy, Mark's dad said to her at one point, 'Mary, put the kettle on and make the lass a cuppa tea.'

'No, it's alright,' I interrupted quickly, not wanting any fuss on my account. 'I'll do it. Anybody else want one?'

I went to the kitchen and Mark followed me to say, 'Take no notice of my dad, he always says things like that about me, but he doesn't really mean any of it.'

Poor Mark, I thought when I realised how the things his dad said must affect him. How awful to say things like that about anybody, never mind your own son. My dad would never denigrate any of us like that, especially not in front of strangers, in fact he'd do just the opposite. I felt a bit uncomfortable then and after sipping my tea I said, 'I'll have to go soon, Mark.'

He shouted through to the living-room, 'Mam, can I borrow the car to take Ann home?'

'Yes, alright,' she answered in between chapters. 'But fetch it straight back.'

When he parked outside my house he said, 'Ann, can I see you again?'

I answered, 'You see me all the time, Mark.'

'No, I don't just mean bumping into each other at the end of the night. I mean can we meet up and go out together?'

Wow, I thought, what brought that on? 'You sure?'

'Positive.'

'Okay, if you can make it on time?' I said, referring to our first date.

'When?'

'Well er, what about tomorrow?'

'Oh no,' he replied. 'I've got football training tomorrow and Thursday.' He played for a local club and was reputedly very good. 'How about Saturday? I don't think we have a match this week.'

So that's how it got serious. The days were shortening as darkness fell earlier, the schools had resumed after the holidays, and summer was in hasty retreat. Mark and I became kind of an item and Peter was dumped in the past, at least that's what I told my heart and anyone who asked. I did like Mark a lot but at times, it seemed as if he didn't really like me so much.

It was September and not far off my birthday, and one day Mam asked if I'd like to do anything special. It was my 18th and a lot of people seemed to be celebrating that more than their 21st, maybe because we were legally able to drink in the pubs and clubs?

'You can have your money this birthday, Ann, or wait until you're twenty-first?' she said about the cash that her and Dad had been saving up for years, for each of their children.

'I think I'd like it now, Mam,' I decided. 'Who knows what might happen in the next three years?'

'I thought you probably would. Makes sense I suppose. Tell you what: I'll make a little 18th birthday tea for you and a few friends. What do you think?'

'That would be great. I'll invite Evelyn, Susan Graham and Susan Cass if that's alright?'

We had a really nice day together and I got £25, which was a lot of money to me then. But that was it, there'd be nothing when I turned twenty-one. I could drink alcohol legally now, but as it happened, I probably drank less and was never ever a big drinker. Honestly!

Mark bought me a bouquet of lovely red roses and a box of chocolates, which helped to make my birthday memorable, but we'd already drifted into a really up and down, volatile relationship and were always falling out over something or other. Somehow we stayed together but Mark could be very moody and jealous, and I could hardly do anything at all without him thinking I was doing something wrong.

We'd arranged to meet one night and I stood waiting for him at the bottom of the road next to the off-licence. He was late and I looked nervously at my watch several times, but eventually he arrived in his work van and we drove down the B5345 to St Bees, where the big posh, public school is.

We went to a nice little pub with a view out to sea and Mark said grumpily, without even looking at me, 'I'm having chicken-in-a-basket, what do you want?'

I wanted to say, I'll have soup in a basket, just for a laugh, but could see he wasn't in a humorous mood.

'I'll have the same, please.'

We sat in silence, gazing out of the window until the chicken came, with chips on the side, and it was very nice. We ate in silence and Mark hardly said a word to me all the time we were there. After we finished he said, 'Come on, let's go.'

I wondered why we'd even bothered going there at all as we climbed back in the van and screeched out of the car park. He drove back to Mirehouse like a total lunatic along the little road just east of Sandwith, and I was absolutely terrified. I really thought he was going to crash and kill us both. Why on earth was he doing this? What had I had done to upset him so much? I'd done nothing to cause this crazy behaviour, but was beginning to think that me breathing was enough to upset him.

116

I was relieved when he lurched to a stop outside my house and we were both still in one piece. I tried to talk to him gently and asked what the problem was, but he never responded apart from giving a couple of revs on the accelerator, as if he couldn't wait to get going again. It really was a waste of time so I said in a louder tone, 'Mark what on earth is wrong with you? What have I done?'

He still refused to speak, so I unfastened my seat belt and grabbed the door handle whilst telling him exactly what to do with his childish moods, in a very unladylike manner. He suddenly got hold of my arm and said, 'Ann, look I'm sorry, but what would you do if your friends told you were hen-pecked?'

Hen-pecked!? I was mortified. My boyfriend, hen-pecked – by me? In fact I was more than mortified – I was bloody furious. I turned towards him sharply, 'Are you serious?'

He looked at me and nodded.

'Right Mark, if that's what your friends think and you choose to believe them - so be it.'

He gawped at me and looked surprised.

'Now get off my arm,' I said, trying to wrench my sleeve out of his grasp.

He kept hold but had calmed right down. 'I'm sorry, Ann, please don't go,' he pleaded, and then kissed me passionately!

At first I resisted, but then gave in and he was a completely different person to the maniac who'd driven me home. We sat silently for a short while, obviously thinking our separate thoughts before I said, 'I have to go in now, Mark. It's getting late.'

He looked hurt and asked, 'Can I see you tomorrow?'

'Maybe,' I answered. 'Have a think about whether you really want to.'

'I want to,' he replied, kissing me again before I left him twiddling his gear-lever.

I thought about what had happened well into the early hours. Why was Mark so strong in some ways but showed such weakness in others? I wondered. Ours was a very topsy-turvy relationship, but he had something about him that always made me forgive his erratic behaviour. Maybe I wasn't strong enough to resist and I don't know if I'd always been so insecure, or if he was making me that way, or if he just did whatever came into his head at any moment without considering the consequences? Or maybe he knew there were no consequences because I always forgave him? Like Evelyn said, who knows what men think?

Mark continued to have his silly little outbreaks every now and again, and every time I let it go, and things would be fine again until the next occasion. He was always apologetic afterwards and I think he knew Evelyn was in the background, and that if he pushed his luck too far I might just call it a day with him and start going out with her again. He promised to improve though and things were fine for a few weeks after the hen-pecking thing.

We went out one night and I was staying at his parents' house afterwards. Their house was expensively-furnished, well-kept and very clean, but also cold. They obviously had plenty of money but apparently didn't like spending it on heating the place. Mary and Bill were already in bed when we got home, Mark said goodnight and went to his room straight away, and I closed my bedroom door quietly so as not to disturb anyone. I slid into bed and pulled the sheets up to my chin, but was still cold. I kept reminiscing about the hot-water-bottle I had as a kid, or the electric-blankets some of the neighbours had, and thought I'd never get warm. I was awake for what seemed like hours but eventually nodded off.

Something woke me with a start and at first I couldn't register what it was. And then I did. Someone had their hand over my mouth. I tried to scream but the hand pressed harder, and as my eyes got accustomed to the darkness, I stared up at Mark.

'Shh, it's ok,' he whispered. 'It's only me.'

I mumbled, 'What are you doing?'

He smiled and moved his hand over my breast.

I said urgently, 'Your parents can hear us!'

'No, it's okay. It's okay,' he said, climbing on top of me.

Suddenly the light switched on and his mother stood silhouetted in the doorway, staring straight at us. He rolled off me and shielded his eyes from the overhead light. I clutched the sheets to my throat and after a few seconds she turned and went back to her room. Mark waited until it went quiet again, then disappeared. I thought about sneaking out of the house and running home in the dark, but decided to wait until the light of morning. I stayed fully awake.

Next morning I was still wary, and angry, and couldn't look either of his parents in the face. Once again though Mark apologised profusely and begged my forgiveness, and once again I relented. Why? I have no idea except that I think I was desperately in need of something in my life that wasn't there. Whatever it was and whatever happened that night, or nearly happened, the incident was forgotten and we carried on with our crazy relationship.

Mary Murdock often went to bingo at the Calder Club, but Bill preferred the pub. He'd been in a bad accident years before and was partly paralysed down his left side. He still got himself out

119

to the pub every night though so Mark and I had a lot of time on our own. He had a young brother still living at home, Terry, but he was always out and about with his mates. So with the house empty for hours at a time, we often had the opportunity to be really intimate and Mark made the most of it.

Chapter Twenty Four

Charlie and Margaret's Wedding Day

Evelyn was quite settled in at our house. She still called my parents Mam and Dad and we all still loved her, and it seemed unfair that I saw Mark every night. I can't say that I was falling in loving with him, but I did like having him around for company, and needed some male reassurance after the devastation caused by Peter. Mark and I had a bumpy ride along the way most of the time, but I always hoped his behaviour would settle down, then I'd fall in love with him, and in time it would all work out nicely for us.

At work we were preparing for Christmas which was only weeks away. The store was beautifully decorated and festive songs played every day, and I sang along with them all. My brother Charlie asked me one evening if Mark and I would like a night out with him and his girlfriend, Margaret. I said I'd ask Mark but couldn't see it being a problem, and did so when he came to call the following day. Mark was quite happy about it so we arranged a date.

On the agreed evening Charlie collected Margaret and we all went into town for a drink. We had a really good time and they were great company. Just before closing time, Charlie leaned over to Mark and me and announced, 'Thought I better tell you, Margaret's pregnant.'

'Oh that wonderful news,' I said. 'Congratulations to you both.'

Mark had a beaming smile on his face but Margaret didn't look very happy at all, and seemed to be on the verge of crying at any moment. Charlie was much more composed and patted Margaret on the knee. He was named after Dad, which was very fitting as they were so much alike in so many ways, and always coped well in a crisis. Was the pregnancy a crisis? I wondered, watching the interaction between them.

Mark and I kept quiet as Charlie said, 'It's alright Margaret, we'll be fine.'

She didn't seem convinced though as she turned to me and said, 'I'll flush this baby down the toilet when it's born.'

What a terrible thing to say about a poor little unborn baby, but I think she was still in shock from finding out herself. Charlie put his arm around her and whispered, 'Don't say things like that darling. You know I love you and I'll always take care of you and the baby.'

Mark and I glanced at each other but still said nothing, but I thought that was so lovely of Charlie and felt sure he'd make a good husband and father, just like our own dad. He said to us, 'Can I ask you both not to say anything to anybody yet? We haven't even told our parents.'

'Of course we won't Charlie, if you don't want us to,' I reassured him.

Suddenly Margaret brightened and asked, 'Ann, will you be my bridesmaid? I don't have a sister, just three brothers.'

'Oh, so have you decided to get married?'

'Yes I think so,' she answered. 'Well, Charlie's asked me to.'

'Well yes, I'd be delighted to be your bridesmaid. I've never done that before.'

It had been planned that I'd be bridesmaid for my sister a few years back, but she got pregnant too and they married in the Registry Office, so didn't really need me.

Then Charlie looked at Mark and asked, 'I was hoping you might be my best man, Mark?'

'Yes, 'course I will Charlie,' Mark replied after a surprised pause.

'Well at least we've got that bit settled,' Charlie smiled at Margaret, who nodded and almost broke into a smile herself.

I did as promised and never said anything to anybody, but unfortunately Mark told his mother and she passed the news on to my mother, who was quite upset by it. But Margaret seemed a lot happier with it all out in the open, and both families could now concentrate on planning the wedding, which helped my parents come to terms with the situation. It wasn't that they were opposed to the marriage, it was just that they were staunch traditionalists and preferred it come before the pregnancy. Anyway, the big day was duly booked for 12th December, well before the forecast birth date.

Margaret didn't want to impose too much expense on her parents, so I borrowed a dress from Susan Cass who'd been a bridesmaid before. It was a really lovely, petrol blue colour with 'leg-of-mutton' sleeves. When I tried it on I was pleasantly surprised by how well it fitted, how slim it made me look, and with my new shoes on I looked quite tall and elegant. Needless to say – I liked it a lot! Fortunately, I was the only bridesmaid so didn't have to colour-match with anybody else's dress. Mark already had a nice suit and looked quite dashing in it, but he was always smart and well turned-out.

I was at his house one evening and it was nearly time for me to go home. I hadn't felt very well all evening and kept getting a really bad pain in my stomach. Mark asked with a puzzled frown, 'Are you okay?'

'I'll be alright,' I answered with a grimace. 'But I'd like to go home now, please?'

He was in the bad-books with Mary so didn't bother asking if we could use her car, and we set off to walk. Their house was partway up a big hill so at least going home was all downhill, but with every step the pain grew worse. I thought I was going to be sick and was starting to worry that something serious was wrong with me – perhaps something inherited from my mother.

Mark'd had some kind of argument with his mother earlier that night, and that's why he didn't ask to use the car. He could be sulky but his mum was easily riled, so things could be pretty volatile between them.

'Wish I'd just taken the damn car now,' he hissed, obviously concerned about me. 'Just take your time, Ann, it's not far now.'

As soon as I stumbled into the house Mam knew something was badly wrong. 'Whatever's the matter, love?' she asked, reaching out to steady me.

'I don't know but I feel terrible,' I gasped, bursting into tears.

By now the pain was almost unbearable and Dad said, 'Jessie, send for the doctor right away.'

She called the out-of-hours emergency number and was told the doctor would be with us soon. I crawled up to my room and was climbing into bed when I heard a car pull up outside.

There was a loud knock on the front door and Mam came thudding upstairs with the on-call doctor. She examined my stomach and asked, 'Have you got a boyfriend?'

'A…a boyfriend?'

'Yes, a boyfriend.'

I was puzzled but nodded.

'Are your periods regular?'

'Er, yes,' I grunted, but wasn't prepared for the next question, particularly with my mother standing right there listening.

'Are you having sexual intercourse with your boyfriend?'

I hesitated because we'd been brought up to never tell lies. Mam would be furious if I said yes, but if I said no she'd be disappointed with me for lying - a no-win situation.

'Ann?' the doctor persisted.

'Well, yes, occasionally,' I confessed, avoiding looking at Mam.

The doctor did look at her though when she said, 'It looks like it might be the early stages of pregnancy.'

Mam ran out of my room and down the stairs. 'Charlie,' she cried.

'What? Oh no, what is it Jessie?'

'Our, our Ann's pregnant.'

'Pregnant? Our little Ann? Never. Are you sure?'

Mam nodded, wiping tears from her cheeks with a handkerchief she kept tucked up her sleeve.

Dad put his head in his hands and said, 'Oh no Jessie, not Ann as well, where did we go wrong?'

I felt absolutely awful and ashamed, and even worse when I heard Mam say, 'What on earth will the neighbours think?'

125

But Dad was recovering fast and replied, 'What's it got to do with the neighbours? I don't ask them to look after my family!'

Mark heard all the commotion and came up to my room, passing the doctor on her way down. Neither of my parents would ever allow a boy into my bedroom normally, but they likely thought the damage was already done so where's the harm.

'Is it alright to come in?' he asked.

I nodded.

'Are you okay?'

His face was white and I'm sure his hands were shaking.

'Are *you* okay?' I asked him.

He nodded, 'I think so, but what's the problem?'

'The doctor thinks I'm pregnant.'

'P…pregnant?'

'Yes, bloody-well pregnant so listen, you better go home now and give my parents time to calm down.'

'Alright,' he quickly agreed, leaning across the bed to kiss me. 'I'll see you tomorrow?'

'Uh-hum, goodnight Mark.'

Before leaving, the doctor told Mam to make sure we took a urine sample to the surgery the following day, as soon as possible.

Before I got the results though, my period started, so I wasn't pregnant after all. Mam was relieved and advised me to go on the pill, but I'd heard so many scare-stories about side-effects that I decided against it. Dad wasn't sure one way or the other.

Everything calmed down and got back to normal very quickly. We were all ready for Charlie and Margaret's wedding and on the appointed Saturday morning, Mam had booked me into the hairdressers with her. I decided to have loose ringlets and they looked really nice. Charlie told me what bus to take and the directions to Margaret's house and luckily, I arrived in good time. She was in such a state when the door opened and I stepped inside.

'Look at my hair,' she frowned.

I thought it could certainly look better for her big day.

'Can you do anything with it for me, Ann?'

'I can try?' I answered but didn't really have a clue what to do. 'But I'm not a hairdresser, you know?'

'I know but I don't want to spend more money on hairdressers and there's no time anyway, now.'

I did the best I could, and when I finished she definitely looked better than when I arrived. I could not believe it when she took out her wedding dress - it was exactly the same as mine but in pale lilac, but looked like it had been washed a hundred times at least. Mine looked brand new compared to hers and although it was borrowed, I felt a sharp pang of guilt. When we got dressed I avoided standing next to her in front of the mirror, in case she lost confidence. Poor Margaret I thought, wondering if she regretted refusing the big expensive wedding her parents had offered to pay for. It was a noble gesture by her, but it could be a once-in-a-lifetime experience.

She showed no sign of regret as the wedding cars arrived though, and we gathered up our bouquets. I had a little nervous flutter as I left first and very alone, wishing I hadn't agreed to be the only bridesmaid.

I was standing by myself at the back of church when Mam and Dad arrived. Mam came over and whispered, 'You look lovely.'

I told her quietly about Margaret's hair and dress and she said, 'Don't worry love, everything will be alright.'

I could see Mark standing with Charlie and they both looked very smart. Margaret and her father finally arrived and the wedding march started to play. Mam smiled at me as I passed her in the aisle. The ceremony was really nice, and didn't drag on too long before Charlie and Margaret were declared man and wife. He kissed his new bride and a group of us signed the register. After a few minutes the registrar said we were done and we all moved outside. Although it was December, the sun was shining so we shuffled around congratulating the newlyweds, throwing confetti and posing for photographs.

We were booked in to the Dolphin pub in Whitehaven for the reception, or bun-scuffle as Mark called it, and the whole day turned out really well. Margaret and Charlie didn't go away on honeymoon, but both seemed more than happy just being with each other. I wasn't really involved in the previous discussions, but Mam and Dad made our dining-room into a bedroom and living space for them, and suddenly we had an extra person living at our house!

Chapter Twenty Five

23rd December

Mark and I both had a lovely day at the wedding. Charlie gave Mark a little gift-box with a new 50-pence piece in it, and told him to keep it for good luck. There was a little card inside with the wedding date and time, printed on, and an inscription saying: Best Man: Mark Murdock. It really was very nice but I don't know what happened to it. Never saw it again. I got a little gold necklace for being bridesmaid.

Mark must have been inspired by the whole thing because he asked me to marry him that same night, after we'd had a good few drinks. I accepted his proposal without much consideration and we agreed on the 3rd August 1973. We didn't have much money so he ordered me an engagement ring from Mam's clothing catalogue, and paid for it weekly. It was gold with a sapphire - my birthstone, in the middle and little diamonds around the edge. We decided to get engaged on 23rd December, which was my grandma's birthday, but even then I wondered why I'd agreed to it all, because we still had a very rocky relationship and I was pretty sure I didn't love him. It felt like I was being swept along by an army of other people, and I was just so used to doing what I thought was expected of me.

One night just after he proposed, he had one of his tetchy turns, stopped speaking to me and I had no idea why. We'd been at his parents' house all night and everything had been fine as far as I was aware, so I retraced my steps as I always did, to see if there was anything I'd unknowingly done to upset him again. Suddenly I remembered that his mother had been in the shop that afternoon, buying her bread and Gordon was also in there chatting away to me as he always did. Despite knowing about Mark, Gordon had never given up on me and still came in the shop quite regularly to say hello.

So I then knew right away what the sulky silence was all about, and although Gordon was only talking to me, I could appreciate that it might be easy for an onlooker to interpret what they saw differently. Mark borrowed his mother's car to take me home, and all the way there he never said a word. He pulled up outside my house and I turned to him for a goodnight kiss, but he totally ignored me. I shrugged and got out of the car and said, 'Will I see you tomorrow then, Mark?'

'No, I can't make it tomorrow,' he replied.

'What about the day after?'

'No.'

I went through every day of the week and got the same answer, so feeling a bit stupid and humiliated by this time I said, 'Oh well sod off then and if you think I'm getting engaged to you, you are very much mistaken!'

Tears were running down my face as I ran into the house and Mam asked, 'Are you alright?'

When I never answered and ran straight up to my room, she knew there was something wrong and followed me up. She sat beside me on the bed, where I was lying face down sobbing, put a gentle hand on my shoulder and asked, 'What on earth is wrong now, love?'

'I hate him,' I replied, and when I finally stopped crying I explained about Gordon being in the store that afternoon, and how Mary came in and that she must have told Mark he was there.

'Oh dear.'

'But we're just friends, Mam. We were only chatting so why should Mark think it's a problem and why is he always so nasty to me? Aren't I allowed to have any friends of my own?'

'It'll all be alright again by tomorrow love, just you wait and see.'

'I don't care if I never see him again, so he can forget about tomorrow.'

I know how you feel Ann,' she said. 'But it will turn out alright and I'm sure you'll feel a lot better about everything in the morning.'

Next day Mark still hadn't been in touch and when Evelyn came home from work, she asked if I'd go out with her that night. She was going to the Three Tons which was a pub in town. It was a bit of a hippy place and not one of my favourites, as they played heavy rock and everyone looked like they were well off their heads. But I had nothing else planned and owed Evelyn a few nights out, so agreed to go.

Dad was busy putting up Christmas decorations again and the house was upside down as usual, but I knew that when we came home he'd be finished and the house would feel special as it did every Christmas. Just the thought and spirit of Christmas made me feel a lot happier. Evelyn and I sat in the Three Tons talking to one of my brother's friends, Gary, who said, 'You're far too young to be settling down yet, Ann.

You're only a bairn and should be out enjoying life with your mates.'

Evelyn nodded but didn't say anything.

'I'm not that young, Gary,' I said as he took a long swallow of his pint. 'And I like the idea of settling down.' I'm just not sure it should be with Mark, I thought.

'Too young to be getting hitched,' he added. 'But if that's what you want...'

I knew he was right but didn't want to pursue the matter any further, not when me and Evelyn were supposed to be out enjoying ourselves. We did actually have a good time at the pub, which surprised me a little, but it was so nice not having to be careful about what I was saying all the time, and being careful not to smile at anybody, and not having Mark watching me like a demented bloody hawk.

The house was in darkness when we got home and when I switched the living-room light on, all the Christmas tree lights came on with it. It cheered me up even more. Dad always did a good job and the house looked warm and cosy, and bathed in sparkly brightness. Many years later I wrote a poem about how happy our house always was, especially at Christmas, and it won an international award!

We loved the lights but tried to keep quiet, as Margaret and Charlie were asleep in the ex dining-room. We drank our tea quickly and went up to bed, as Mam stage-whispered, 'Goodnight girls.'

She just couldn't settle until we were all home safe and sound. Before nodding off I said, 'Thank you Evelyn for taking me out tonight. I did have a nice time and it did me good as well.'

'Don't mention it,' she mumbled.

We were both tired and fell asleep quickly, and I woke in the morning to the sound of Mam clattering in the kitchen. She was always up and about first when we were kids, and couldn't kick the habit. The kettle was already boiling when I went down and Mam turned and said, 'Mark called round last night, but I told him you were out with Evelyn.'

'Mm,' I replied with raised eyebrows. 'That won't have gone down too well, I bet?'

'He was quiet. I'm sure it's just a lovers tiff,' she smiled. 'It'll all be alright in the end.'

I didn't just want it to be alright though, I wanted to be loved and not rejected or humiliated like Mark so often made me feel. Evelyn followed me downstairs and we sat and ate our toast with hot tea in front of the roaring fire, and I felt warm and cosy, and safe. As we left for work we both shouted, 'Bye Mam.'

She came to the door to wave and said, 'Bye, see you both later.'

Chapter Twenty Six

Christmas engagement

Woolworths was always extra busy as Christmas approached, especially in the mornings, and when I remembered to look at the clock this particular morning it was nearly lunch-time. As I turned back to the rapidly diminishing bread mountain, Mark was standing at the counter right in front of me with a smile on his face, and my stupid heart missed a beat. Why does it do that? I asked myself. He treats me like shit and my heart jumps with delight! Maybe I did love him after all? Or did I see him as a challenge which I shouldn't back down from? I returned his smile anyway and he asked, 'Can we meet for lunch, and talk?'

I looked at him for a long moment. 'Talk about what?'

'About us.'

'Us?'

'Yes, us. We're a couple and I want to marry you.'

He knew exactly what to say and as always, I gave in. 'Alright,' I said flatly, and carried on with my work.

He left and I told Evelyn he'd been.

'And what happened?' she asked.

'I'm meeting him for lunch.'

'Really?'

'Uh-hum.'

'Okay,' she said. 'Whatever you think is best.'

Evelyn was a true friend and only wanted for me what I wanted for myself. I still didn't know for sure if that was Mark, but he certainly seemed to have some kind of hold on me. I went outside and he was standing there smiling. He took a little box out of his pocket and handed it to me. It was my engagement ring and once again he said, 'I'm sorry Ann, for how I was with you the other night. Are you still going to marry me?'

I paused but then heard myself saying, as if from a long way off, 'Yes, alright. Are our plans are still going ahead? We have an appointment to see Father Taylor next week.'

What was wrong with me? Why was I so terrified of being left on my own? Because I'd already been dumped once, that's why, and it had completely destroyed my self-confidence. I was desperate to find someone to fill the gaping hole in my life, and despite his faults, Mark had come closest to doing that.

As we walked along the street he said, 'Yes, of course they're going ahead, try your ring on.'

I did, and was disappointed that it was slightly too big.

'What a shame,' I said.

'Never mind,' he smiled. 'We can soon get it altered.'

Despite my doubts and misgivings, I was committed to being married before I got much older, and said, 'We could take it to *H. Samuels* and see if they can do it?'

'Okay, let's do that.'

'But can we wait 'til tomorrow so I can show the girls at work first?'

'As long as you don't tell them we got it out of the catalogue?'

'They won't care about that Mark. They're not millionaires either.'

'I know, but why not say we've been to H. Samuels already and just got engaged?'

I hated having to lie but did feel slightly embarrassed myself, that my engagement ring came from a clothing catalogue. But most of all I didn't want to have another fall-out with Mark, I did not need the stress so just went along with his story. The girls thought the ring was gorgeous and all gathered round to have a look. I told them it was a little too big and I was getting it altered the next day. It was only 14th December so there was still plenty time for it to be done in time for the 23rd.

Mark was off work the following day and met me outside again when I finished. We went to show my parents the ring first. Mam was so happy for us and I told her the official engagement date was 23rd December.

'That's Grandma's birthday,' she said with surprise.

'I know,' I replied. 'That's why I chose it.'

The engagement went ahead without any problems, though we didn't do anything special as we had a night out planned for the following day, so for now, everything in the garden looked reasonably rosy again, as long as I didn't look too hard.

Mark and I had tickets for the Christmas Eve disco at the club. When we got there the room was already full but we managed to find seats. Although Whitehaven is a small town I didn't know anyone at our table, but it was nice getting to know new people and we had a great night. We were sitting with three other couples but they were a lot older than us, and halfway through the night they got out packs of homemade sandwiches and asked if we'd like one. We took one each to be polite, and they were very nice.

It was my first Christmas Eve with Mark and we both enjoyed the evening, and afterwards he walked me home. I wanted to be with my parents for Christmas morning and dinner, at least for this year which might be the last before I was married. Mark came in to say hello to everyone as they never went out on Christmas Eve, and when the door opened we could smell the turkey, ham and pork cooking. I don't think I knew anything about veganism or the horrific slaughter of animals back then, but at least there were freshly made mince pies cooling on the side.

Dad was sitting in the living room watching TV but stood up when he heard us. 'Hello Mark,' he said jovially. 'Merry Christmas lad, would you like a drink?'

'Yes please,' Mark answered as he sat on the sofa.

'Is beer alright?'

'Er, have you any lager?'

I was still in the kitchen talking to Mam as Dad called through, 'Ann. would you like a drink?'

'No, I'm okay, thanks Dad, I've just put the kettle on. We're having tea.'

We went through to join the men with some mince pies and nibbles on a tray. I'm not too keen on mince pies to be honest, so made sure there were some chocolate biscuits on the tray. Mark didn't want anything to eat and was happy to sit with his lager. Everybody was chatting away and obviously getting on well together, and it felt comfortable and kind of, right, I suppose. For once I felt sure that I was making the right decision - about getting married not the mince pies.

'Did you both have a nice night? Mam asked us.

'Yes, it was really good,' I said.

'It was great, we even got a free sandwich!' Mark laughed before finishing his lager and getting up to leave.

'Are you away already?' Dad asked.

'Yes, I must go now but thank you for the drink, Mr & Mrs Chambers.'

'We'll see you soon, then.'

'Merry Christmas to you both and goodnight,' Mark said as I walked him to the door, where he gently kissed me.

'I'll call round tomorrow afternoon,' he said, and then whispered, 'I love you.'

'I…love you too.'

Mam was smiling when I went back inside and she asked, 'Everything okay love, and you both had a good night out?'

'Yes we did, it was really nice and so was our company.'

Christmas felt somehow different that year, but I knew the same family feeling would still be there at home. I can't remember what presents I received, maybe as you get older presents aren't as important as when you're younger, and other things take their place? Evelyn, Albert, Charlie and Margaret all arrived home together and we sat talking for another hour. Eventually I said, 'I'm going to bed, goodnight everyone. See you all in the morning.'

Charlie and Margaret had already gone to their room and Mam was tidying around in the kitchen. 'Goodnight love,' she called through.

'I'm going up as well,' Evelyn said, dragging herself off the sofa.

On Christmas morning Brian was up early. He was still only eight so very excited, and we all sat and watched as he opened his presents. After everything was torn open and the whole floor covered in wrapping paper, Mam made tea and toast but by then we'd all eaten too much chocolate.

Dad always helped in the kitchen and pans of all sizes were boiling and simmering. The telephone rang and it was my sister, Dorothy wishing us all a Merry Christmas. Margaret and Charlie were busy moving belongings around in their living space, so we could re-use it as a dining room for Christmas Dinner. It just never felt right calling it Christmas Lunch, as though it had been demoted to some lesser kind of snack instead of the celebration of family life it had always been for us.

The meal was great and we chatted and told stories as always about previous Christmas Days. I got up to wash the dishes and Evelyn came to help. It was a gesture I always made to thank my parents, who had worked all morning and part of the night before, preparing it for us.

I was all ready to go when Mark pulled up outside, and I waved to let him know I'd seen him. I was staying over at his parents' house that night so said, 'Goodbye everybody, see you all tomorrow.'

As I clambered into the car I still felt so full, and wondered how on earth I could face a big tea at Mark's house. When we arrived the house was unusually warm and cosy and Mary already had the table set. There was enough food to feed Mark's football team and I wondered how many people were coming. But it was just the usual family members, plus Mark's sister Maureen and her husband David, who were also staying overnight. The conversation was easy-going and humorous, and I felt just like part of the family, and also managed to eat far more than I should have. I felt happier and more settled than I had for a long time, and was definitely beginning to look towards the future more positively.

Chapter Twenty Seven

Happy New Year

Back at work the shop was already busy as people re-stocked their supplies after the holidays. The Christmas decorations were pulled down and stored away for next year, and immediately we were preparing for Easter. Chocolate eggs were piled high on the shelves, life carried on remorselessly and my wedding plans began to take shape.

I'd been christened in the Church of England but Mark was a Roman Catholic, and it was important to both him and his family that we had their traditionally long, marriage ceremony. We planned to have children and knowing they would be raised as Catholics, I decided to change my religion so as to be fully involved with everything that they were.

I had to go see Father Taylor, who was our local priest at St Benedict's church. I loved the church and had often been there with my friend Lynda, who was also Catholic. It always had a serenely warm feeling about it and the subdued music was really relaxing. Father Taylor had a look of Rock Hudson about him with a cheeky smile, and was a truly nice person. He was always kind and considerate and we got on well. He began instructing me in the ways and rituals of the Church for my induction, and I'd been going to see him regularly for a few weeks. Mark hated having to trail along with me but knew he was expected to.

One night it was really warm in Father Taylor's house, sitting in front of a roaring log fire, and when we came out I felt a little sickly. I was wondering what the cause could be when I suddenly realised I hadn't had my period that month.

'Mark, I'm late,' I said. 'What if I'm pregnant?'

'Well that's okay Ann, we're getting married anyway so we'll just bring it forward if need be. But remember last time you thought you were, and weren't?'

'Yes but that was different, that was the doctor assuming I might be pregnant because of my stomach pain, and I wasn't late then.'

Like most women I knew my own body and my period was never late, and I just felt certain that this time, I was really pregnant. When we got back to my house Mark came in and we sat and talked for a while. I told him what I was thinking and he said, 'Do you want me to be here with you when you tell your parents?'

'No, it's okay Mark, I'll wait a few more days just to make sure, then pick the right time to tell them myself. It'll probably be easier for them if you're not there at the time.'

It was getting late and Mark got up and said goodnight to everyone before leaving. I saw him to the door and as I went back inside, Mam followed me into the kitchen and asked, 'Is everything alright love?'

She knows something's not right already, I thought, so might as well get it off my chest right now. I knew I'd feel better afterwards if I did.

'I think I might be pregnant, Mam.'

I reasoned that it wouldn't be as bad as the first time when the doctor just announced the possibility out of the blue. Both my parents obviously knew Mark and I were having sex now, so the shock wouldn't be as great, would it?

'I told you to go on the pill, Ann.'

'I know. I'm sorry Mam. I didn't want to take it because some of the girls at work said it made them feel sickly and gave them bad headaches, and they felt really awful.'

'Well never mind, it's too late now. You'll be okay. I'll call the doctor tomorrow.'

I went to see my GP two days later with the usual sample, and Mam came with me. This time I saw Dr Galloway, who'd been our family doctor for years. He asked what the problem was and I told him what I suspected.

'Lie down on the bed, Ann and I'll examine you,' he said straight away. 'It may be a little early but have you done a urine sample yet?'

'Yes,' I replied. 'I brought it with me today.'

After examining me he said, 'Yes, I think you're in the early stages of pregnancy but the sample will give us a better picture.'

We both thanked the doctor as we left, even though I wasn't overjoyed at the news he'd given us, and sure enough, when I went back for my results they confirmed that I was indeed, pregnant.

Mark's face went as white as a newly-washed sheet when I told him it was definite, and that my parents were going round to see his about the situation. He told his mother what was happening and when we arrived, there was already a very tense atmosphere in the house. Both sets of parents started talking straight away, so Mark and I left them to it and went through to his room. Voices were raised at times downstairs, although we couldn't hear what they were saying, and Mark told me that his parents had been shouting at him just before we arrived.

'Why were they shouting?' I asked.

'Oh, you know, they think we've messed things up, and my dad says we should get married in the registry office.'

'What? Why?'

'Well, because you're pregnant.'

I was shocked and deeply hurt. 'Well if that's the case and that's what you and your family think of me, there's no way I'm marrying you.'

Who the hell do they think they are, to tell me where I should get married? I thought indignantly as the hurt turned to anger.

'And how do you feel about it?' I asked Mark.

'I feel a little bit frightened, I think, but I'll be okay.'

I could hear cups clinking in the kitchen and Mary shouted up, 'Ann and Mark, would you like a warm drink?'

'Yes please, Mrs Murdock,' I replied politely.

We both went down to the living room where everyone was smiling, surprisingly, and as always Mam asked if we were alright.

'Yes, we're fine Mam, thank you.'

We drank our tea quietly. It appeared that all talking had been done, and Mary put some chocolate biscuits on a plate. We nibbled but soon Dad said we should go.

Mark's father said, 'Take Ann and her mam and dad back home as soon as they're ready, Mark.'

'We're ready now, thank you Billy,' Dad replied.

We left and nothing was said about the meeting all the way home. Mam and Dad got out of the car and I said, 'I won't be a minute.'

'How do you think it all went, then?' Mark asked.

'No idea but no doubt we'll hear all about it soon enough.'

'Yeah, at least they were smiling at each other at the end, so there might not be as much shouting going on when I get back.'

'Best of luck with that one, Mark.'

He gave me a goodnight kiss, said, 'See you tomorrow,' and was gone.

Chapter Twenty Eight

14th April 1973

After Mark left for home I went into the living room where Mam and Dad were talking.

'I was really annoyed tonight, Chuck,' Mam was saying. 'When Billy said Mark should take her down the back streets.'

I was dumbfounded and stood gaping at them with my mouth open.

'Oh, Ann,' she said turning towards me. 'I didn't realise you were there.'

'What did Billy say?'

'Well er, I don't know if Mark mentioned it but his father suggested you should get married in the registry office.'

Mark had mentioned it but I still could not believe my mother was actually saying it, and I started to cry. 'How dare he say Mark should take me down the back streets,' I blubbered. 'Does he think I'm some sort of riff-raff?'

Dad said, 'Don't you worry, love. I told him straight - no one is taking my daughter down any back street.'

'Well I am not getting married if it has to be in the registry office. Dot's wedding was there and it was nothing like the kind of wedding I want.'

'Don't worry love,' Mam said. 'It's this Catholic thing but there is no reason why you can't get married in church. In fact I'll make arrangements to go and see Father Taylor myself tomorrow, if you still want to go through with it?'

She had a chat with the priest and made an appointment for Mark and me to see him, so the next day I told Mark, 'We have an appointment to see Father Taylor, tonight at six thirty.'

'Okay Ann, I'll see you about six.'

We walked slowly up to the priest's house, which is right next door to the church. I knew I'd feel embarrassed having to tell him I was pregnant, but it had to be done. Mark knocked on the door and the housemaid, who I knew really well, answered. She smiled at me and said. 'Hello Ann, are you okay?'

'Yes I'm fine thank you. And you?'

She nodded and took us through to a reception room, and said Father Taylor would be with us soon. We sat for five or ten minutes when suddenly the door opened and he came bustling in to stand opposite us.

'Hello er…Ann and Mark,' he said.

'Hello Father.' we both replied.

Then we all just looked at each other so I started talking:

'As you know, Father, we've booked our wedding at the church for 3rd of August.'

He nodded.

'Well, we'd like to know if we could bring the date forward please because…well because I'm pregnant?'

Why had I been made to feel like I'd done something shameful? I hated feeling like this. It was the 1970s not the 1870s. Did anyone really believe that every bride who walks down a church aisle is a virgin? I'm sure they've just been luckier or more sensible than me, and used contraception which the Catholic Church doesn't condone either!

I could hardly look the priest in the eye and was dreading what he might say, as he got up and walked slowly across the room. I thought he was just going to leave us sitting there but he stopped by his desk and fumbled in the drawers. An image of him pulling out a handgun and shooting me dead flashed across my mind, and I glanced at Mark, who looked like a rabbit caught in a poacher's lamplight. Then the Father turned back to us with a little book in hand, and asked, 'What date were you hoping for, Ann?'

'Oh,' I said, a little taken aback. 'Around the middle of April sometime, please Father, if that's convenient?'

He flipped a few pages and said, 'You could get married on the 14th of April?'

'That sounds ideal,' I answered, looking at Mark for confirmation, but he still wasn't in communication mode.

'But as it's Easter weekend,' continued the priest. 'There can be no flowers in church.'

'Oh?'

'Although, you could have flowers on the day, as long as they're all completely removed from the church by Easter Sunday.'

'That's fine, we can do that, and we've decided to have the shorter ceremony so they won't even be in there very long.'

So it was all agreed and re-booked for the fourteenth. When we went home and told my parents, they said they'd re-arrange the cars and everything else for that date.

The following weekend Mam and I went to the bridal shop in town to look for a dress. She said I should pick an ivory one because of my condition, but the dress I liked was white satin with a lacy bodice and hood. I tried it on and loved it, and hoped Mam had forgotten about ivory when she said I looked beautiful. I looked in the mirror and for once in my life, I believed her.

'Do you have this one in ivory?' she asked the young girl who was attending to us.

'I'm really sorry but we don't have it in ivory at the moment. We could order one for you though. Do you have a date in mind?'

It was the end of February and we only had seven weeks to get everything arranged.

'It's my daughter's wedding day on the 14th of April,' Mam told the girl.

'Oh, I'm really sorry but that's too short notice for us. Would you like to see what we have in ivory?'

'Yes please,' Mam replied.

The girl was very patient and efficient; no doubt she was well-used to picky & choosy brides-to-be, and showed us some beautiful, ivory-coloured gowns. But there just wasn't another that looked as nice on me as the white one I'd already tried. I took my time looking closely at them all, but eventually said, 'Mam, please can I have the white one? It looked really lovely on me and I don't think I'll ever find another that I feel so happy with.'

She smiled and told the girl, who was also smiling, that we would have the first one I'd tried on - the white one.

'I'll sort it with your dad,' Mam said, as we picked out some pale lemon bridesmaids' dresses.

We made an appointment for my bridesmaids to come in for fittings, Mam paid a deposit and said we'd be back the next day. We arranged with Gladys, our next-door neighbour, to take her little daughter Karen to the shop, and Mam rang

149

Dorothy for my niece's measurements, as they lived in Carlisle. I also arranged for Susan and Evelyn to meet me there the next afternoon. It was all sorted the following day and my bridesmaids looked adorable. Dorothy said she would come through the following weekend to make sure Pauline's dress fitted okay. I chose hats with wide brims for Susan and Evelyn, and the two younger bridesmaids had lacy bonnets. Everything was done and we were assured that all would be ready for the big day.

I was pleased that the arrangements were going so well. Mam and I even went to the florists to order all the flowers and they had just what we wanted. I couldn't believe everything was going so much to plan, so easily. Mam and Mary Murdock decided who was coming from Mark's family, Mam and Dad made a long list of our family, and all the invitations were posted out. In total there were 123 guests, though the majority were from my family. I remember it being said by someone, that there should always be more family than friends present at a wedding. I thought was an outdated rule but it worked out that way, and all there was left to do was wait for the day to arrive.

Chapter Twenty Nine

Wedding, or no wedding?

Mark and I were busy with our wedding plans and didn't have much time to think about anything else, but one night after I'd been to his house he had one of his sulky tantrums, and dropped me off at home without making any future arrangements. Maybe things were going too fast for him, I wondered? His feet hadn't really touched the ground since we discovered I was pregnant, but neither had mine and I was annoyed at his dismissive attitude. I thought his behaviour towards me had better improve or I'd be having second thoughts about marrying him at all. Or was it third thoughts?

At work everyone asked about the wedding and wanted to know every detail, and it was always exciting to talk about my dress and the bridesmaids and the flowers…but I wondered what would actually be left after all those things had gone? This particular day I felt really negative, wondering what was wrong with Mark and when his next big sulk would be, and was quite distracted. Just after lunch I was standing behind the counter daydreaming, when he came marching into the store.

'Ann,' he said quite brusquely. 'Can you call round to my work this afternoon, before you go home?'

'What? Why?'

'It's important, please come if you can make it?'

'Well, alright then, I'll see you later,' I replied flatly while pretending to do something important.

It'll just be another one of his apologies coming up again, I thought, for his childish behaviour. I really did wish he would grow up and stop sulking over nothing, but went round to his job as promised, thinking positively. When I arrived I could see he was really busy but when he saw me, he came over right away.

'I'm sorry about last night Ann, it's just that everything is going so fast.'

'Yeah, I know it is,' I replied calmly, but was thinking: It's not just about you - it's me who's pregnant - how frightened of the future do you think I feel!?

He was just about to reply when his boss, obviously annoyed about something, shouted over, 'Are you going to be long, Mark?'

I didn't want him to get into any trouble because of me so said, 'It's okay, you go back to work and I'll see you later.'

'Okay, I'll pick you up from home.'

He came to the house later in his mother's car, so I knew he'd been home after work first. As we drove along the backroads he slowed right down and looked at me, then said, 'Ann, I lost my job today.'

'Oh no, really?' I asked in surprise, putting a hand to my mouth.

'Yeah, I got so angry with the boss for shouting at me when I was talking to you. We ended up arguing and I told him to shove his job where the sun doesn't shine!'

'Oh no, we're getting married in a few weeks and I'm having your baby. Why did you do that?'

He didn't answer and we pulled up on his drive in silence. As soon as we entered the house his mother said to me, 'Did he tell you what he's gone and done?'

I nodded, looking at Billy's empty armchair. He'd obviously scarpered down to the pub.

'He's had that job since he left school,' she went on. 'The boss has been on the phone tonight, and told him he can go back tomorrow and no more will be said about it, but we can't talk any sense into him.'

I looked at Mark but he turned away.

'I am not going back there,' he said, and stormed off to his room.

I followed him and said softly, 'Just go back tomorrow, Mark. You've always liked your job and this will soon blow over, and then everything will be alright again.'

He wouldn't answer so I went back downstairs. Mary was standing in front of the living room mirror and turned to show me a small cut above her eye.

'Oh dear,' I commiserated. 'What happened there?'

'It was him,' she answered.

'Who?' I asked, suspecting that maybe Billy had done it before escaping to the pub.

'Mark.'

'Mark?'

'Yes, he got angry and threw a comb at me because I was telling him how stupid he was being.'

I didn't know what to say but just then Mark came in. 'Ann,' he said, without looking at his mother. 'I'll walk you back home now.'

We walked all the way and he hardly spoke a word. When we got to my house he gave me a quick kiss and said, 'I'm going.'

It seemed a strange thing to say and I asked, 'Going where Mark, back home?'

'No, I don't know where I'm going but I'm going. I'm sick of everything and the wedding's off.'

He left and I stood for a few moments, watching him disappear into the distance, before closing the door behind him. I wandered into the kitchen and sat at the table. I was confused, worried about my future and the baby's welfare, and had no idea what to do at that point. I felt so alone and, so young and vulnerable.

Mam sensed something wasn't right and came through. 'Ann, is everything alright?'

'No Mam, not really,' I answered as if in a dream.

'Well, what's wrong? Where's Mark?'

'He's gone.'

'Gone? What do you mean? Where's he gone? I don't understand.'

'I don't know where he's gone and I don't think he knows either, but it's not back home.'

'Ann love, you're not making any sense.'

'He said goodbye, Mam. He's gone for good and the wedding's off.'

Her mouth dropped open and she went straight through to tell Dad. Next thing I knew Dad came hopping through pulling his shoes on, grabbed his coat and flipped his cap on.

'Where are you going?' I asked.

'I'm going to find him.'

He was gone for hours but did eventually find Mark. I never asked where but he brought him back to the house. We all talked for a long time and I can't remember one word of what was said - I was still in dreamland. Later he took him back home and the two of them talked some more in the car, and when Dad finally got back, he told me not to worry because everything was going to be fine.

Chapter Thirty

Wedding Day

Mark never went back to his old job. Whatever happened between him and his boss, he'd taken it very much to heart, but soon found alternative employment at a local weaving factory. Two weeks before our wedding, he got a sleeve caught up in one of the looms, and it broke his arm. He was in plaster for the big day but at least it matched my white dress. Something seemed to have gone missing from the whole wedding thing anyway. Neither of us bothered with a hen or stag night but at least I had all my bridesmaids staying with me the night before, well, except for little Karen from next door, who was only four, bless her.

I think my friends knew I was feeling a little strange about things, because they definitely tried to cheer me up that night, and were very successful. I was with friends again and Susan, Evelyn and I laughed all night about nothing in particular. I think I finally fell asleep about three o'clock in the morning.

We all got up at eight-thirty and went downstairs for breakfast. Mam advised us to eat plenty as I wasn't getting married until one-thirty, and it would be about three in the afternoon before the photographer finished taking pictures. The reception wasn't booked until four, and there would be drinks and toasts and speeches before we got anywhere near any food.

Gladys from next door did my hair, her daughter Karen's and my niece Pauline's. Mam and Dot went to the hairdressers and were away all morning. My aunts from Manchester and Blackburn arrived and the house was crowded. All the presents were put on display in the dining-room, after Margaret and Charlie cleared their things away again. Such was life.

Karen and Pauline got on well and were really well behaved. Evelyn and I dressed them and they both looked adorable. After she and Susan were dressed and ready they both helped me. Mam peeped around the door and told us we all looked beautiful.

The taxis arrived and lots of neighbours lined up outside waiting to watch us leave. It was a lovely, warm day with the sun shining brightly and a light breeze blowing in from the sea. Dad had been to the pub the night before and made sure he came home with a pocketful of change, which he threw to the local kids waiting outside. They cheered and laughed as they scrambled around collecting coinage off the road.

Mam and the bridesmaids then left, leaving just Dad and me at the house. As I came downstairs, I was two steps from the bottom when I stopped. I stood there with my bouquet in one hand, and the front of my dress in the other so I didn't trip over it, and I just froze. I stared at the wall right in front of me, but didn't see it. In my mind I was watching the rest of my life stretching out, and couldn't move forward.

Dad was waiting for me at the door and asked, 'Are you alright, Ann?'

I heard him but didn't answer, and kept staring straight ahead.

'You don't have to do this if you don't want to, you know,' Dad said. 'I'll always look after you and the baby.'

I'd always been more of a mummy's girl but at that moment, I loved my dad easily as much, and knew he loved me. I felt a strong urge to say, 'I don't want to marry him, Dad,' and all the confusion in my head would be over. But I can only think that at that point in time, I really didn't know exactly what I wanted, or even who I wanted, and felt afraid and nervous because Mark was so moody and unpredictable. Then I remembered all my friends and family waiting for me at the church, and imagined what they'd say if I didn't turn up, leaving poor Mark standing there all alone at the altar. It would be so embarrassing for everyone, particularly my dear parents, and that would haunt me for the rest of my life.

'I, I'm okay Dad, just give me a moment. I'm just a little nervous.'

'Well that's understandable, love. Just take your time, there's no rush.'

I knew he and Mam would have taken care of me and my baby for as long as I needed them to, but I got my feet off that second step, tottered outside and carried on with the life I'd made for myself.

Half an hour later Mark and I were married and posing for photographs outside St Benedict's. We sat at the big table in the reception, smiling and chatting to everybody and drinking toasts. It all made me realise how young we both were and at one point, by chance my eyes met Mark's, and he looked as lost as I felt.

His brother stood up and read the cards and made a lovely speech, and had us all laughing. Then my dad said a few words before Mark got nervously to his feet. He thanked everybody for coming before turning to me and saying out loud, 'Just look at my beautiful bride.'

My heart skipped and my eternal optimism said maybe everything would be alright. The whole of the reception went well and afterwards we all went back to my parents' house, where neighbours popped in and out all afternoon wishing us well and admiring our presents.

Mark and I went upstairs to get changed and for some reason, I put on a navy and white polka-dot dress with white, high heeled shoes. I hated that outfit with a passion afterwards and have never worn navy clothes or white shoes ever again. I was already starting to look pregnant so already felt fat and unattractive, and that feeling had been exacerbated at the reception: My new brother-in-law took Mark to the bar to talk in private, and every time I happened to glance over at them, he was looking back at me and laughing. I might have been over-reacting I suppose, but felt absolutely awful. This is supposed to be one of the happiest days of my life, I thought, and because the pregnancy made me feel a bit queasy, I couldn't even enjoy a drink to drown my sorrows!

For our honeymoon we went to Mark's sister's house in Carlisle for a week. Carlisle is a beautiful, vibrant city with a fascinating, borderland history but I enjoyed the week even less than my wedding day, which was not at all. Maureen and her husband, David made us really welcome but I was so pleased when it was all over. Now all I had to worry about was the rest of my life, which was immediately daunting as we were going to live with Mark's parents!

My wedding day, 14th April 1973

Chapter Thirty One

Tragedy and trauma

One night shortly into my new life as a wife, I received a phone call from my mother: 'Ann, Margaret's in hospital and the baby's been born early.'

'Oh, really?'

'Yes, Margaret and Charlie have a baby boy and have called him Paul.'

'Is he okay?' I asked, knowing the baby wasn't due for many weeks.

'No love, I'm afraid he's very poorly. His lungs haven't developed properly and he's struggling to breathe.'

'Oh, oh my God.'

'But the doctors say that if they can get him through the next forty eight hours, he might have a chance.'

Mam went to the hospital next day but little Paul was still very ill. I was at work but she rang me to say how beautiful he was. Not long after, my brother came into the store and stood at the counter as if waiting to be served. I knew by his face that

161

he hadn't brought good news. I reached out and touched his arm and he said, 'Ann, the baby died.'

'I am so, so sorry, Charlie.'

I could see tears welling in his eyes. 'How's Margaret?' I asked, knowing it was a silly question but unable to think what else to say.

'Well, not very good. She keeps crying and I don't know what to do. I feel absolutely useless.'

'Tell her I'm thinking of you both, and of baby Paul, and if there's anything at all that I can do, please just let me know.'

The baby lived for two days and his funeral was arranged for very shortly after his death. I was at work on the day but Mam advised me not to go in, and to avoid the funeral as it would be too distressing for me, expecting my own child soon. She said Paul's little coffin was only as big as a shoe box, and the service was terribly painful. I was worried for months afterwards, fearing there would be something wrong with my baby, and at the same time felt awful that I was still pregnant when my brother had lost his longed-for child.

Wednesday was still my day off work but every week I got up early with Mark. I made Mary & Billy tea and toast and took it up them on a tray, then hoovered through the house and tidied up. Only then did I get myself ready and go to spend the day at my parents' house. I missed them, and Evelyn and little Brian, so much. Although Mary & Billy made me feel welcome, I would have much preferred us to live with my parents, but Charlie and Margaret were still there and didn't need any extra problems at the moment.

Mark's dad was an ex-boxer who had a serious accident years before Mark was born, and by all accounts had been lucky to survive it. He was snagged and dragged along the road by a van whilst riding a pushbike, sustained serious injuries and was only given six weeks to live. Evidently, because he was so fit and tough from his boxing training, he lived for many years afterwards. He was though, paralysed down his left side and Mary cared for him throughout their married life. She obviously loved him but understandably, did get stressed out from time to time. Having me suddenly land up to live with them, and soon to have a noisy new baby, was undoubtedly more stress for her to cope with. I helped her with chores all the time, but she always made me feel that I didn't do enough. We'd only been living with them for a few weeks, but it seemed for like a month of very long Sundays.

I always got back from my parents' before Mark arrived home from work, and had everything ready for him, apart from one occasion. On this particular day I'd been really tired and fallen asleep on Mam's sofa. When I went in to Mary and Billy's, they were both in the living room and called me in.

'Hello Ann,' Billy said. 'You okay?'

'I'm fine thanks, Billy, how are you?'

'Not bad. Your mam and dad okay?'

'Mam and Dad are both well, thank you, but I haven't been feeling very well today so I think I'll go and lie down. Is that alright?' I asked, looking to Mary for permission.

'Yes, I suppose so,' she replied, with a blank expression.

I went upstairs but could hear them talking quietly as I went into the bedroom. I usually made tea for Mark coming in so wondered if my not doing so this one day, was regarded as a fault on my part. Despite living within a family I felt very lonely and wished Mark and I had our own house. I never usually went to bed so early but felt awkward, out of place and uncomfortable. I hadn't been sleeping well either and was genuinely exhausted.

I'd been lying on the bed for a while, dozing but not sleeping, when I heard raised voices from downstairs. Then there was a thump, thump, thump of feet on the stairs and Mark appeared in the bedroom doorway.

'Are you alright?' he asked abruptly.

'Yes I, I'm okay. I wasn't feeling too well before so I had a lie down. Is that a problem?'

'My mother's complaining that you don't do anything to help her around the house, and you know how stressed she gets, looking after my dad.'

I felt hurt because I knew that I helped enough, certainly considering I was pregnant, and also suspected that the real reason for Mary's complaints, was that my mere presence interfered with her cosy little routine. Mark's face was white with strain and I knew that we would never ever, be free from stress and family problems until we were on our own. I waited until his breathing steadied and said, 'I think we should find somewhere else to live.'

Mark let out a long, pent up gasp and asked, 'Do you think your parents would let us stay with them?'

A ray of light shone into my world, and I felt sorry for Mark as I knew he'd been arguing with his mother and father, who had made him feel that he was stuck between the devil and the deep blue sea. 'Come on,' I said with a smile, kissing him on the cheek. 'We'll go and see what they say.'

Mark went back downstairs and into the living room. 'Can I use the car, please?' he asked politely.

'Yes lad, you can.' Billy replied.

Mary didn't speak. I put a few essentials in a bag. We didn't have a lot of stuff there, as some of my clothes and all our wedding presents were still at my parents'. We walked out and I certainly didn't look back. As we drove away I asked what his mother had actually said. He repeated exactly the same thing and I assured him that I always helped out as much as I could. 'Does she want me to do everything for her?' I asked.

He shook his head and spread his hands in exasperation, and I hoped that was the end of that particular chapter, so never mentioned it again. I actually felt quite sorry for Mary, as I'm sure life was hard for her because Billy certainly wasn't the easiest man to live with. But I also wondered how much stress and demand she's piled on Mark over the years, and what effect it all had on him. Perhaps his tempers and tantrums were signs of the turmoil he carried around in his head as a result?

My parents' house seemed so much more relaxed, but also more alive, in contrast to Mary's which was always quiet and gloomy, in my opinion. I loved being back home and because of that, was pleased that Mary had provided the opportunity for us to return.

'Hello love, and hello Mark. Are you both okay?' Mam asked when we walked in carrying our bags and looking hopeful.

'Not sure yet,' I said, glancing at my new husband. 'Can we stay here? It's just too much for Mary having us living at her house.'

Mam didn't answer but looked over at Dad. He shifted round in his chair and said, 'Why aye lass, we'll sort something out room-wise.'

In another quirk of fate, Charlie and Margaret had just received word that they'd been offered a council house, so would be moving out in about a week. We were back with my family and a lot more happiness.

Chapter Thirty Two

Health scare

I was much happier being back at home with everyone I loved, and so much closer to the hospital, the doctor's and my job, although I was off sick at the moment as the work was quite strenuous. I had to move big, heavy bread trays around every morning, and all through my pregnancy I suffered with nagging backache so the extra strain wasn't helping at all. Back then there was no general right to maternity leave, so it was normal to work through the first six months and then finish altogether, with no right to return.

Every morning I still got up to see Mark off to work, and then I'd talk with Mam for a while. Life was so much better for me and Mark seemed calmer and happier. Charlie and Margaret moved into their new house, and Mam and Dad had the dining-room for their bedroom. Soon Margaret was pregnant again, with the baby due in January. We were all so pleased and hoped and prayed that everything would be okay this time around.

Our house was always full of people, which was one of the things I missed when living with Mark's parents. My dad was a very patient man, nothing ever seemed to faze him and for as long as I can remember, he always looked out for all of us. Many years later I wrote a poem; the following is part of it and every word relates to him:

> *My dad is a real good man,*
> *Always doing the best he can,*
> *To borrow a pound he's always good,*
> *And all his promises are solid as wood,*
> *His failing health puts him at risk,*
> *But there's always money for the shopping list.*

Mark got a new job: cutting all the grassed, public areas for the local council. He'd hated working at the factory so I was pleased when he left. It was shorter hours at the council and once all the grass for the day was cut, he could come home. Mam and Dad always made Mark very welcome but probably like me when I was at his parents, I don't think he was ever fully at ease. He never complained though; still played football for the same club, trained two evenings during the week and had a match every Saturday during the season. So unlike me whilst living with his parents, he wasn't in the house too much. He usually came home from work or football, ate his tea and not long afterwards was ready for bed. We still kept in touch with his family and visited Mary and Billy every Sunday.

Mam always carried a little weight but had been going to a slimming club for a while. She lost quite a few pounds and looked really well, and was very aware of her health and fitness. She was tinkering in the kitchen one morning and shouted through to me, 'Ann, come and feel this.'
    'Feel what?' I asked, walking in from the living-room.

'I've found a lump in my breast, here look, can you feel it?'

I knew by her expression that she was worried, and was shocked when she showed me where the lump was - I could actually see it. I stayed calm though and said, 'It'll be okay Mam, just get the doctor to check it out.'

I tried to sound convincing but wasn't sure I succeeded. She phoned the surgery later that morning and got an emergency appointment right away. Within the week she was being examined by a consultant surgeon at the hospital. He was quite concerned and Mam was booked in for an operation the following week. I was worried about her but Dad didn't want me to go the hospital after her operation, in case it upset me and the baby I was carrying. I went away. Her operation was exploratory and the lump tissue was cut out and sent off for analysis. Luckily it was a non-cancerous cyst, and we all breathed a massive sigh of relief. Mam had told Dad to look after me as she knew I'd be distraught if anything was wrong, and she didn't want anything to harm her unborn grandchild.

The surgeon said Mam could come home if there was someone available to take care of her, so everyone rallied around for her release the following day. Lots of relatives came to the house to welcome her home but for some reason, I felt very tense and on edge. I'd expected to feel relieved knowing she was alright, but felt the need for something to keep me occupied while waiting.

When she finally arrived I was in the kitchen making fried egg sandwiches for everyone. Mark was out at work but Dad, Albert, Charlie and Margaret were there. I could hear the buzz in the living-room and wanted to go through to welcome Mam home, but couldn't leave the sizzling eggs. The fat in the pan was boiling by then and when I tried to lift one out, I dropped it because I wasn't concentrating. It fell back in the pan and splashed hot fat onto my arm. It hurt like hell and I lost control of my emotions and myself, and started to cry. I felt so frustrated, and then angry and reacted by throwing the damned eggs all over the kitchen! Albert came in to see what all the noise was about, then shouted through to the others, 'Ann's plastering the kitchen walls with fried eggs!'

Dad came through and said, 'Go and sit down love, I'll knock something up.'

I know it was only the stress being released, after being so worried about my mother and now so pleased she was alright, but I can imagine it being quite alarming for others at the time. We laughed about that day for years, but I realised I had quite a temper hiding away under my ever-calm exterior.

One night not long afterwards, Mark and I went to bed early and later I heard lots of voices downstairs. Mark had already nodded off but I was heavily pregnant now and finding it hard to sleep, so I got out of bed, found my dressing gown and went downstairs to see what all the fuss was about. When I went into the living-room, Evelyn's parents were there with Evelyn and her new boyfriend, Frank. Her parents were over in Whitehaven to meet him and visit Evelyn's grandma.

'Hello,' I said to everyone in general and Evelyn said, 'My dad thinks your parents are wonderful and must have the patience of saints.'

I smiled and I said, 'Yes, they must have.'

'He wants to take me back to Manchester because he thinks it's not right for them to have all these extra people living here, especially with your new baby coming soon, and Mam having her recent health scare and goodness knows what else to worry about.'

Evelyn always called my parents Mam and Dad and I wondered how that would go down with her own father.

'We don't mind, do we Jessie?' my dad said. 'And Evelyn has never been any trouble.'

I knew Evelyn and Frank were very much in love though, and would soon want to be together all the time, but the house definitely couldn't take another couple who'd probably want babies of their own. Frank was in the navy and worked from different ports, so it probably wouldn't matter much to him if Evelyn moved to Manchester, although his own family lived in Whitehaven.

Next day Mam had obviously been thinking about it and said, 'I'll miss Evelyn when she goes.'

'I will too,' I said. 'I know we don't do a lot together any more, but it's nice to have someone close to talk to like a sister, and she was a good help to you around the house wasn't she?'

Mam just nodded and didn't say anything, and I could tell that like me, she was thinking that something which had been good in our lives, was about to end. Evelyn left shortly afterwards, and went to live with her parents in Manchester.

Chapter Thirty Three

New arrival

I was busy getting everything ready for our baby's arrival, and was now so big I wondered how the child could move inside me. I felt so full there didn't seem to be any room left! I hated being so big but would sit for hours watching my baby move around, stretching my stomach into funny shapes. Sometimes it would poke its knee or foot into my ribs and that was often uncomfortable. We were all at home one night watching England playing in the World Cup qualifiers against Holland. They played well for 90 minutes and did everything right except score a goal. It was exciting though, and the poor kid must have wondered what was going on when my heart missed a beat every time England nearly scored.

The birth was due on 20th October which was only a few days away. Evelyn and Frank arranged their wedding for 3rd November and wanted me to be bridesmaid. It was disappointing knowing that I wouldn't be able to go because I'd have the baby to care for, even if it came early, so had to turn down the invitation. On 20th October nothing unusual happened and no baby arrived.

'Never mind love, the baby will come when it's ready to,' Mam told me.

Nine months seemed forever and now I was over my due date. I was booked into hospital for Monday the 22nd and Mary kindly offered to drive me there. I saw her car pull up outside and shouted, 'Bye Mam, see you later.'

'Okay love, I'll keep my fingers crossed.'

Mary stayed in the waiting-area when they called my name and I went through into a cubicle, where I was told to get undressed. I lay there naked waiting for the doctor, shivering slightly, and could hear him speaking to other expectant mothers. Finally he got around to me.

'Hello Mrs Murdock, are you feeling well?' he asked cheerfully.

'Yes thank you Doctor, just a bit tired of waiting for baby to make a move.'

He examined me, ummed and ahhed a bit and said, 'I think we'll have you in hospital tomorrow. Maybe this baby just needs a little prod to wake him up.'

'Alright, thank you,' I said, and got myself dressed after he left the room.

Mary was reading a magazine and smiled when I re-emerged and said, 'Hello, I'm here.'

'Is everything alright?'

'Yes, but I have to come back tomorrow morning, and if the baby doesn't come on his own, they're going to start me off.'

'Oh, they're going to induce you?'

'Uhum.'

'Well that'll speed things up.'

I felt quite excited but also nervous, as I was only nineteen and didn't yet know much about babies or giving birth.

'I'll come and pick you up in the morning Ann, and take you back to the hospital,' Mary offered as she dropped me off at home.

'Thank you very much,' I told her and hurried into the house to let Mam know what was happening:

'I have to go back to hospital in the morning. They're going to induce me if baby doesn't make a start himself.'

I kept thinking of the baby as a boy but had no idea of its sex. I don't know whether internal scans were available generally back in 1973, but I certainly wasn't offered one so just had to wait for the actual birth. Mark was hoping for a boy but I really wanted a girl - a little girl who would love me as much as I loved my mother.

When Mark came home from work he was excited at the news and said, 'That's great Ann. I won't be able to come to hospital with you but I'll be up as soon as I finish work.'

'That's okay, you shouldn't miss work. Mam thinks I might even have the baby tonight, anyway.'

I didn't sleep very well that night, half expecting to go into labour but no, baby decided to stay right where he was. I got up with Mark for work and made his breakfast, and as he left he kissed me and said, 'I'll see you later Ann, maybe our baby won't be long now?'

'Hopefully,' I answered, smiling as I closed the door behind him.

I heard Mam getting up as I went into the kitchen to put the kettle on.

'Are you okay?' she asked, coming sleepily into the kitchen.

'Just a little nervous but I'm fine.'

'You'll be alright love, and you'll soon have your little baby with you.'

All through the pregnancy I'd been worried in case there was some kind of emergency, and I had to be whisked off in an ambulance with blue lights flashing all over the place. That scared me because it meant something was wrong, so I was relieved when Mary drove around the corner and into the street. I had my case packed with all the things for the baby, and was ready to go to the hospital for my induction. Mary came to the door and Mam kissed me goodbye.

'I'll come and see you this afternoon,' she said as we got in Mary's car.

'Ok Mam, love you lots.'

The hospital was only about five minutes from where we lived, and we soon arrived outside the maternity unit. Mary came in with me and made sure I was settled, before saying, 'Ann, I'll have to go and make sure Billy's okay. He wasn't too well last night.'

'Yes that's fine Mary, I wasn't expecting you to stay.'

'I'll phone later to make sure you're alright, and tell Mark to let us know when the baby arrives?'

'Okay, no problem and thank you for the lift again.'

I was simply going-with-the-flow and doing more or less what I was told. I was still young and quite naïve and underneath my apparent calmness, a little terrified! I was in the ante-natal part of the maternity unit, which was downstairs, and would be moved up when the baby was born. My bed was one of four in the ward and as soon as I was settled down, a girl came over to talk to me:

'Hello,' she said. 'My name's Pam. Is this your first?'

'Oh, hello Pam. I'm Ann and yes it is my first. I'm overdue now. The baby was due on Saturday and they've said they'll induce me tomorrow, if he doesn't come on his own.'

'Mm, they'll give you an enema tonight before lights out. That usually gives baby a kick start but if not, they'll break your waters tomorrow!'

It all sounded quite gruesome but Pam was very laid back. She seemed so much older than me and very knowledgeable, but it was her second baby and she was just in for monitoring as her blood pressure was high. Mam arrived as promised and I was pleased to see her, even though it was only hours since I'd left home. We sat and talked and Mam said hello to a lot of the nurses who passed by. She'd previously worked at the hospital for years as a cleaner, and knew a lot of the staff. The visiting-hour passed quickly and a nurse came along, ringing a hand-bell calling out, 'Home time, ladies.'

Shortly afterwards the nurses brought us some food and although I was quite a fussy eater, there was plenty on the tray that I liked. When we'd all finished a nurse came by and told me she was going to give me an enema. It was quite busy on the ward and she didn't come back until just before evening visiting-time. As soon as she gave me the enema I felt awful. My stomach was gurgling all the time and when Mark arrived for visiting, I spend most of the time in the toilet.

'Sorry Mark,' I kept saying to him, as I had to go again and again. It wasn't one of my favourite experiences and I didn't stop running to the loo until just before the end of visiting, so we hardly had any time to talk. I walked down to the end of the corridor with him and said, 'Goodnight Mark,' before giving him a kiss.

'Goodnight Ann. I'll see you tomorrow and hopefully we'll have our baby by then.'

As I walked back to my bed, passing the day-room, Pam waved and I joined her to watch television for a while. My stomach was still bubbling though so I didn't stay long before flopping back into bed. The nurses came around with medication and drinks before lights-out, and I had a cup of *Horlicks*. Pam came in from the day room and we chatted for a while. She was really nice. During the night I woke up in a lot of pain and must have been groaning as I heard her say, 'Ann, are you ok?'

I rolled over and she was right by my bed. 'No Pam, I'm in a lot of pain.'

She said, 'Just hang on and I'll get the nurse for you. It'll be the baby on its way.'

The night-nurse came straight in and examined me before announcing, 'Well Ann, this is it. You're in the first stage of labour.'

Another nurse came in and they wheeled my bed into a side ward. They popped in and out of my room several times, keeping an eye on me before asking, 'Would you like some pain relief?'

'Yes please,' I replied.

They gave me some drugs but they didn't help much.

'Would you like some gas and air?' they asked. 'It does help.'

I put the mouthpiece between my lips, and felt like I did years back, when the dentist put me to sleep before operating. I hated that feeling and refused it. So I lay alone in pain, crying quietly into my pillow without making a sound that anyone could hear. The nurse who'd been taking care of me all night came by and said, 'Goodbye Ann, I'm off home now. Hope baby comes soon and it all goes well.'

'Bye,' I managed to reply. 'And thank you.'

Her replacement on the morning shift came in shortly afterwards and said, 'Good morning, how are you today?'

Silly question I thought - I was in agony, but she fussed around and left again. She never came back for a while and I pressed the call button, I was in so much pain. She returned and gave me a quick looking over, then called for help. Suddenly I realise that this really was it - my baby finally wanted to come out into the world! Pain, fear and excitement all rolled into one came over me in those first few moments. They wheeled my bed round to what was called the labour-room, where I felt my waters break and knew the baby was on his way. Thankfully I didn't have long to wait and at 9.15am on 24th October, my son Craig was born, weighing 9 pounds 1½ ounces. It's easy to say now but childbirth wasn't really too bad, though I was seriously glad it was over and I had a beautiful, healthy boy at the end of it.

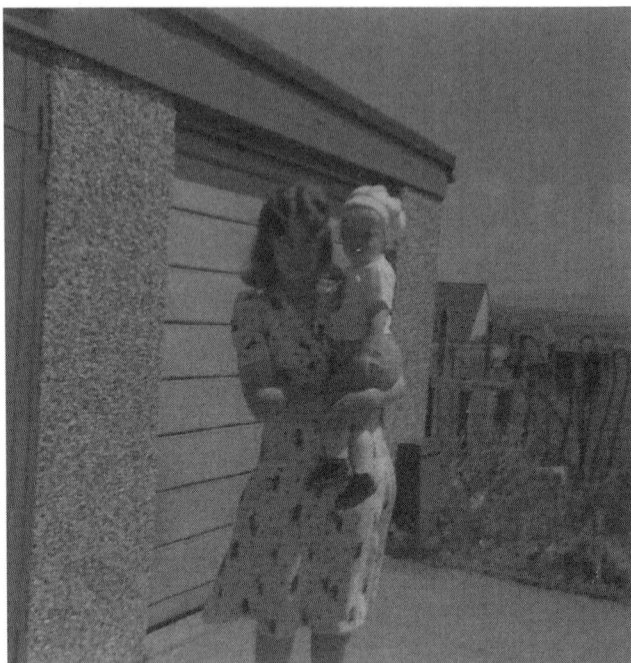

Craig and me in 1975

Mary and Billy with Craig, 1975

179

Chapter Thirty Four

Motherhood

Little Craig was adorable and though I'd only seen him for a few minutes, I already loved him to bits. I needed stitches but that didn't bother me considering the wonderful thing that had just happened, and then the nursed help me into a clean night gown. I was tired, sore but very happy as I was taken up to the post-natal area and put in a room of my own. It was right down the corridor at the far end of the maternity ward, and I lay there in bed wondering where my baby was. I must have fallen asleep but suddenly heard someone in the room. It was a very young nurse who had brought me something to eat. 'Is everything okay, Ann?' she asked with a smile.

'Yes, I'm fine thank you.'

I was really hungry and the chicken & chips looked very nice, but my mouth was so dry, probably from the pain relief I'd had earlier that morning, that I couldn't eat. She took it away and brought some ice cream which I managed quite nicely. When she came back for the dishes she asked if I was feeling alright. I answered, 'Yes I'm fine but when can I see my baby?'

'Have you not seen him yet?' she asked in surprise.

'Only for a second when he was first born,' I replied anxiously.

'Oh, that seems odd. I'll go find out what's going on.'

I waited for what seemed like hours, listening for footsteps in the corridor and watching the swing doors for any movement, but nothing happened. I was starting to get really worried and decided to find out what was going on myself. I was halfway out of bed, feeling stiff but determined, when the doors swung open. The nurse was holding a little bundle of linen and I couldn't tell whether she was smiling or frowning. She looked away and my heart lurched, but then she turned his beautiful little face towards me and placed him in a little cot beside my bed. I looked down at him and he looked straight back at me. Even though he was quite a big baby he seemed so tiny lying there, completely helpless with his little hands opening and closing. I touched his pink fingers and pulled back the blankets to see his toes. He was a perfect baby and I felt so proud that such a beautiful little boy was mine.

I heard people in the corridor and realised it was visiting time. My mother, Mary and Mark came in together and they were all smiling. I knew Mark would be delighted with a son. Mary looked in the cot and said, 'He looks just like Mark did when he was a baby.'

I had to agree that Craig looked more like his dad than me. Mam just smiled at me and said, 'He's beautiful Ann, and well done, he's a good healthy weight.'

I now knew why his knee or foot was always sticking in my ribs before he was born - he was 21 inches long! I was only 5 feet 2 tall with a small torso and long legs for my height, so am not surprised he hadn't much room in there.

I received lots of cards from the girls at Woolworths, and Craig got so many little romper suits and clothes that I wouldn't need to buy any for quite a while. It was fortunate having a room of my own at the hospital, as the general rule for visitors was only two at a time, but no one seemed to care how many there were with me. I liked visiting times but they were always over so quickly. Dad didn't make the first one but Mam gave me a kiss and said he'd be up tomorrow to see me.

Craig was the first grandson for my parents as my sister had two girls: Pauline and Caroline. Mark stayed back for five minutes after the others left and said, 'Well done Ann, he's a lovely little boy.'

'Thank you,' I smiled.

He smiled back and turned to leave. 'I'll see you tonight.'

'I'll walk to the door with you, Mark.'

I could see Mam and Mary waiting for Mark at the end of the ward, and waved goodbye to them all. They waved back and I walked back to my room. There were a lot of new mothers chatting in the dayroom and some were smoking, which was allowed in 1973. I looked in to see if Craig was asleep and as he was, went to sit in the dayroom with the others. But I felt like a fish out of water as all the other mums seemed so much older than me, and they all apparently knew each other. Most were waiting to go home but enjoying the rest from their daily chores, and had become friends after being in hospital for a few days together. The general rule was a ten-day stay, though nowadays it's not usually even ten hours!

I was soon chatting away with them though, as we all had a major topic of conversation – new babies! Some of the older mothers weren't as excited as us younger ones, understandably;

they'd probably done it all before and knew the routines. Babies were crying off and on all the time and because my room was so far away down the corridor, I had to keep leaving to check Craig was alright. I loved just watching him lying there sleeping, and eventually decided just to stay in my room with him.

The nurses came in and out to check on us and soon it was tea time, which I enjoyed as I was starving. I went to the bathroom after tea to wash and make myself look respectable. The nurses checked everyone was ready to receive visitors, and I sat on the edge of the bed to wait for Mark. I could hear him talking to someone out in the corridor, and when he came in he was with Albert.

'Hi Albert,' I said, hugging them both in turn. 'I thought visiting was only for daddies in the evenings?'

'Well they must think I'm a daddy then,' he replied after saying hello to Craig.

I was pleased to see my big brother. He can be so funny and had Mark and me in stitches at his jokes.

'I've just seen an old lady running down the road in her nightie,' he suddenly said.

'You're joking again, right?'

'Honestly Ann, I did. She'll have come from the A Ward.'

'The A Ward?'

Albert looked out of the window. 'That's the A ward, down there.'

'You sure?'

'Uhum.'

'So what's the A stand for?'

'Ah'm away home if I get the chance!'

We all laughed and Mark asked, 'Are you okay Ann? You don't look as tired as you did this morning.'

'Yes I'm fine but I'll be even better when I can come home, there are so many rules and regulations here I can hardly remember them all.'

'Really?'

'Yes, the most awkward one is that we can only feed our babies at designated times, which are every four hours, but Craig seems to be hungry all the time and he lets me know about it.'

'That's what baby boys do,' Albert said. 'Make a fuss to let you know when they're hungry.'

'Some grown-up boys too,' I added, looking at Mark.

We all laughed again and it was the quickest hour ever. I hated having to say goodbye to Mark and Albert so soon. It felt like I'd been in hospital for weeks but it was only two days. I felt like making a run for it myself, with Craig of course.

The following day Mam and Dad arrived and soon afterwards Margaret and Charlie came. Margaret stood in the doorway with a ghastly look on her face, then burst out crying, threw Craig's present at me and ran off. I was flabbergasted and wondered what I'd done wrong. Charlie followed her and came back after a few minutes. 'I'm sorry Ann,' he apologised. 'But this is the same room Margaret was in when she had little Paul.'

'Oh no,' I said. 'That must have been awful for her.'

'It was a bit of a shock and the memories really upset her, but the good news is she's six months pregnant again, so I suppose her emotions are all over the place as well.'

Chapter Thirty Five

Release

Craig was ten days old and I was really fed up with being in hospital, but at least we were going home today. I had to wait for the doctor to say it was okay for us to be discharged, but knew we had no health problems so waited patiently. Finally I was told we could go so I called Mary, who came to pick us up. I'd previously made Craig a pram-suit and dressed him up in it to take him home, and he looked adorable. I didn't have a mobile phone, don't think they'd really been invented then, or a camera with me so all those very early memories were never captured, but all the nurses admired his hand-knitted clothes. I was so proud of him.

Mary arrived and I said goodbye to the other mums as one of the nurses carried Craig to the car. It was her responsibility, she told me, to make sure the babies were safe until they left the hospital. I didn't argue and was grateful for the care I'd received, but was fit and well-rested now, and ready for release.

Mam was excited when I got home as she adored all babies, and especially this one. She had Craig's pram already parked up in the corner of the living room, well away from any draughts. Mary said, 'I can't stay Ann, I better get back and see to Billy. You know what it's like.'

'Well thank you so much for bringing me home Mary, and I hope to see you soon.'

Mam fussed over the baby and me although I was really possessive about him. I hated people just picking him up randomly and would let them know about it. If Craig cried and I wasn't there, Dad would say, 'Jessie, just leave him. You know she'll tell you off again for interfering.'

Poor Mam, I must have been really awful to her and she did not deserve it. But Craig was a good baby and I didn't want him being woken up all the time for no reason. He cried when he was hungry and then would go back to sleep after being fed. Every time anyone came to visit us he was almost always asleep, and that really pleased me because it showed he was happy and well cared for. Craig was my whole world now, and I loved him so much that I didn't want to share him with anyone, not even Mark!

Mark was at work all week and still training or playing football, so didn't have much time to spend with the baby anyway. Anyone else only got to nurse Craig if I said they could – usually in the little time-slot when he'd been fed but before he went off to sleep again, but I really hated sharing him.

Mark and I hadn't had many tiffs recently, probably because we were living with my parents, but came very close the Sunday after I got home from hospital. Mark's mother and sister, Maureen, came to see Craig but he was fast asleep all the time they were there, so they never got a chance to hold or cuddle him. When they left, Mark went out and said goodbye to them but when he came back in, I knew there was something wrong. He never said anything until we went to bed that night: 'Ann, my mam wasn't very happy because Maureen didn't get to hold the baby.'

I shrugged and said, 'Well he was asleep, why should we wake him just for a cuddle? They could have stayed longer until he woke up again.'

It was little things like that we sometimes argued about. We were both young and I suppose it was a lot of responsibility looking after a baby. It caused tension and maybe I was obsessively possessive, but now I had something in my life that was completely my responsibility, and nobody could take it away or tell me how to behave. I was a mother and wasn't going to let anyone criticise me for that. My son was the little part of my world which I alone controlled.

One day we'd been arguing because I found out that Mark had lied to me about something. Maybe I shouldn't have but I told Mam about it, and just as Mark walked back into the room she replied, 'Well, they say you can catch a thief but not a liar.'

Mark heard her, guessed what she meant and stormed off. He calmed down though and never mentioned it. We still visited his parents every Sunday and walked up the long hill with Craig in the pram, which always sent him off to sleep. Maureen was there one day and as soon as we entered the house, Mark took Craig out of the pram and sat him on Maureen's knee. I was furious. I know it was nothing but it made me so annoyed. I was being selfish and Maureen was Craig's aunt, but aren't mothers supposed to be selfish when it comes to their children; isn't that how we protect them best? Or was I suffering from some mental aberration, which is what I'm sure Mark and others thought.

Most days I had all the time in the world to be happy with my baby, and quickly noticed any little changes. When he was about six weeks old he got really restless and wouldn't take his bottle, and cried all morning. I tried all the usual remedies I or my mother knew about, like gripe-water which usually did the trick, but not this day. Mam watched and fussed and finally said, 'Ann, why don't you put Craig in his pram and take him for a walk? He might just have wind and a little fresh air might settle him down.'

It was a lovely sunny day even though it was December, and exceptionally mild for the time of the year. I walked up to the shop at Mirehouse but Craig screamed the whole way there and back, and when I finally got home I was frantic with worry. Dad was home from work and sitting in the newly reinstated dining-room having his tea. He heard Craig screaming and came rushing through.

'Jessie,' he shouted to Mam who was upstairs. 'Phone the doctor - this baby's in pain.'

Dad never beat about the bush and when the doctor arrived and looked Craig over, he said the baby had an ear infection and prescribed him some antibiotics. Poor Craig, that's why he was crying so much. It hurt me that I hadn't known to do something sooner, but it was a lesson I learned well.

Chapter Thirty Six

A new place to live

It was nearly Christmas again - which was the time of year my family loved most. Obviously Craig was too young to know what it was all about, so we decided not to buy him too many presents. It was nice to buy some things for him though, even all the new clothes which he'd grow out of before he had chance to wear them! We had Christmas dinner with my parents, then went to Mary's house for tea. I met his brother Colin and wife Brenda with their two children, Andrea and Gary. They lived in Holland as Colin was stationed there with the RAF. Maureen and David were at the house too, and younger brother Billy with his wife Sylvia. They were all fussing over Craig, which I hated but had to put up with, for one day at least. I couldn't wait to get him back home.

Mark and I decided to go out on New Year's Eve and my parents agreed to look after Craig. It was the first time I'd left him with anyone since leaving the maternity ward, but I knew he'd be well cared for. I did enjoy myself but was glad when it was over. Mam said Craig was no bother and I knew she'd loved having him. I bet she cuddled him all night with me out of the way.

On 2nd January Mark and I received a letter from the local council, offering us a house and saying we could collect the keys on Monday 7th January. We were so excited and luckily it wasn't very far from my parents' house. Mam was tinkering in the kitchen so I ran through and told her, 'We've got a house Mam! It's a three-bed semi-detached on Steeple Close, and we can collect the keys on Monday!'

'Oh that's great news Ann! It's a lovely area; Ginny's daughter – Carol, lives up there.'

'Will you look after Craig, please Mam? So Mark and I can go have a look at it?'

'Of course I will. Off you go, you both must be so excited.'

It was only a ten minute walk but all uphill. Two hills to be exact and both quite steep, hence the name: Steeple Close. I thought a better name would've been Steeple Chase, like the horse races Mark was so fascinated by. Right at the top, tucked into the corner of the close was number 7 - the house which was to be our new home. A friend's parents, Mr and Mrs Ash, lived on the close and directly opposite number 7, which had two flights of steps up to the front door, and a well-kept garden shaped like a two-tier cake.

We walked up the steps with our hearts pounding, partly from the steep ascent but mostly from excitement. I thought about Craig in his pram and said, 'It'll be a toil of pleasure, getting the pram up and down here.'

'It's steep but we'll manage,' Mark replied. 'It'll keep us fit.'

The front room had a big bay window and we peered in to see that luckily, the house was in good condition inside as well as out.

'Come on, let's have a look around the back,' Mark called over his shoulder as he made off in that direction.

There was a good-sized kitchen with separate dining room, and was exactly the same layout as my parents' house except for the bay window. The back garden was quite small; up three steps from the path as the ground was still rising, but bordered onto an open field just the other side of a low perimeter wall. I was already certain that I liked the house, and couldn't wait to get the keys. A lady from the next door came out and said, 'Hello, are you the new tenants?'

'Yes we are,' I answered with a big smile. 'And we're hoping to move in on Monday when we get the keys.'

She smiled back. 'You're lucky getting this house. There were a lot of other people after it.'

'I know - we're very lucky. I'm Ann by the way, and this is my husband, Mark, and we have a little baby boy called Craig, who's only three months old.'

'Well I'm pleased to meet you both, and my name's Mary.'

We chatted for a few minutes before Mark and I said goodbye, and walked back down to Mam's to tell her about the house. It was much easier walking downhill but I made a mental note to take care with the pram on the steep descent, or little Craig could end up in Whitehaven harbour! Mam was sitting in the living room and Craig was fast asleep in his pram.

'The house is lovely,' I told her. 'And it looks so clean. The only problem is that it has lots of steps leading up to it, and that's after climbing all the way to the top of two hills to get there!'

She laughed. 'Well, it'll keep you fit, trailing up and down there every day.'

I called into the council offices on Monday, collected the keys and paid our first week's rent, which was £7 including

191

water rates. When I got back Mam said, 'Always pay your rent on time Ann, and always make sure you have potatoes, bread and eggs in the cupboard. That way you'll always have a roof over your head and food to eat under it.'

I had lunch with Mam that afternoon. Dad was at work and Craig was asleep in his pram, and the house was unusually quiet and peaceful. Mam said, 'Ann, your dad says you and Mark can have the bed you're using, and we'll give you some bedding and curtains to get you going in the new house.'

'Oh that's great, thank you, and Mark says Mary knows someone who has a three-piece-suite. It's in good condition and we can use it 'til we can afford one of our own.'

'That's good of them to help you out. You'll soon have all the things you need. It always takes time to set up home for the first time.'

Mark finished work early that day and Mary drove us up to the house. I was so excited again, and we were delighted when we went inside. The house looked like it had been recently painted and was so clean. The bathroom colours weren't to my taste as they were mint green with a black border, but it was sparkling clean and quite big. The back bedroom was a very strong blue colour. I love blue but this was just a bit too blue even for me! Everything else was just about perfect.

We couldn't get our carpets fitted until the following week and were going to wait, but then decided to move in without the carpets. By the end of the week we had our sofa and chairs, bed and everything else that we owned or had been given, up in the new house. On Saturday 12th January, we moved in.

Chapter Thirty Seven

Another new job

It was a whole different world having our own house, although I did miss the hustle and bustle at my parents' place. I got up every morning to light the fire and make Mark some tea and toast. I'd make up his sandwiches the night before to save time and Craig would be awake most mornings to see his daddy off to work. When Mark left I would tidy the house and if it was a dry day, hang out any washing that I'd done the night before, then have my own breakfast and get Craig ready to go to see my mam and dad.

We walked down the long hill, often meeting Margaret with her baby, Julie, and then we all spent the day with Mam. I always took a clean romper-suit for Craig in case he needed it, although Mam laughed at me, but I hated walking back home with him in dirty clothes – I might have to stop and chat to somebody I knew!

Margaret and I spent a lot of time together when Craig and Julie were babies, as there was only three months age difference between them. We would compare experiences and if there was anything worrying either of us, we always asked Mam for her opinion. The days passed pleasantly and I loved being a mother. Craig was by far the biggest part of my world and I talked to him constantly, telling him all my thoughts and worries and even though he didn't understand one word, it made me feel better.

The neighbours popped in and out of Mam's when Margaret and I were there, all keen to see her two new grandchildren, and we would all sit around chatting, laughing and joking. I hated to leave when it was time to go but always made sure I was back home with Mark's tea ready for him, when he got back from work. Margaret and I walked home together and said goodbye when we reached the end of my street. Our house always seemed empty and very quiet after being out and even though I loved it, I did miss being with my mam and other people.

One day when I arrived home, the postman had left a letter marked *Private and Confidential,* which was addressed to Mark. When he came in I was busy in the kitchen talking to Craig, who was always beside me in his pram. I heard the door open and shouted, 'Hi Mark, I'm in the kitchen.'

He came through, kissed Craig and said, 'Have you had a nice day?'

'Yeah, I'm okay. We've just been to Mam's. There's a letter for you in the living room. I think it might be about the job you applied for.'

'Oh, great,' he said and went through to get it. 'Ann,' he called back. 'I've got an interview for a job at Sellafield!'

We were both so excited because although he did sort of like his current job, as he was effectively his own boss and was on his own most of the time - the money wasn't great.

'It'll be so much better if I get this job,' Mark said. 'We'll have much more money to spend.'

'When's your interview?' I asked.

'Thursday, next week.'

'That's quick. You'll have to ask for the day off.'

We had our tea and I gave Craig his bottle, bathed him and put him to bed. He was such a good baby and though still not sleeping right through the night, always went back to sleep as soon as he was fed so we didn't have many sleepless nights.

Mark arranged for the interview day off and asked Mary to drive him there. She told him he could use her car as she didn't want to leave Billy on his own for so long. I stayed home doing the housework, and soon saw him climbing the steep slope to the house on his return. His head was down, looking at the steps and I thought no, he hasn't got the job.

'Ann, I got it!' he announced with a big smile, striding through the door.

'Oh, that's great!'

'I start in two weeks so will have to put my notice in to the council tomorrow.'

It seemed so quick and simple but in the early seventies there was plenty of work available, and most people knew that if they didn't like a particular job - they could soon get another.

'Put Craig's coat and hat on and we'll go tell everybody,' Mark said, and I hadn't seen him so positive since we got the house.

Mam could see we were both happy, and smiled when she opened the door. 'Good news?' she asked.

'Yes Mam, Mark got the Sellafield job and starts two weeks on Monday.'

'Oh, that's great news, Mark. You might be working somewhere near Chuck.'

195

'It's a massive place though, Mrs Chambers. It's like a separate town all on its own.'

'We can't stay long, Mam,' I interrupted. 'We have to take the car back and tell Mary and Billy.'

'Ok love, and well done Mark.'

We were both a lot more optimistic knowing there'd be extra money coming in each week. I know they say money isn't everything but it certainly does help, and I think we both hoped it would also correct what was not quite right in our relationship, because something wasn't.

Mark handed his notice in and the fortnight dragged past. On his first day at Sellafield I got up as usual and made tea and toast. He had to walk to the local shops to catch the work's bus, and Craig and I waved him goodbye.

'Daddy's starting a new job today,' I told Craig, who looked at me and smiled. 'Let's get ready and go see Nana and Grandad.'

I was always up and away early to visit my parents, once all the chores were done and the house was clean and tidy, with some washing flapping on the line. My electric bills were always low as I was there most of the day, so never used any at home. Mary was also really helpful and said one afternoon, 'I'm getting a new sofa Ann, would you like this one?'

Mary's house was lovely and she liked buying new things, so we always inherited what she didn't want, which helped as we were still struggling to set up home. Everything was going tolerably well financially, except that Mark did like to gamble on horse-racing, and sometimes if we didn't have any spare cash it caused arguments. I accounted for every penny I spent and always knew exactly what I had left. It had to be like that for me to manage the housekeeping effectively, and my maths were still very sharp. I had to buy things for the baby and the house, as well as the weekly food and rent and whatever else was needed, so needed to keep track of our money to avoid falling into debt. If we missed paying the rent we risked losing the house. I regularly counted up the cash in my purse, and often found that there was some missing. At first I thought I'd counted wrongly but soon concluded that I hadn't. After it happened quite a few times and I'd dropped several hints, I asked Mark outright, 'Have you taken some money from my purse?'

'No, I haven't,' he replied, but after it happened several times more, I knew he was lying.

Usually I hadn't been anywhere to spend the missing money, or to have lost it because I always kept my purse very safe. One Friday I sat for hours adding up everything I'd spent through the week. This caused an argument when Mark saw what I was doing, and eventually my loss of respect for him after it continued. I was angry and thought, why can't he just admit he's taken some money, or ask me for it instead? At least that would save my sanity. Apart from hiding my purse there wasn't a lot else I could do to prevent what he was doing. I tried but he always found it anyway.

If he won on the horses he'd always give me some of the winnings, so I was never quite sure what the point of his dishonesty actually was, but I had to question how he had any money to gamble in the first place if he had to steal from his family to continue it? He always shrugged me off with some excuse so I'd let the matter go to avoid the inevitable friction.

With his first wage from the new job I pleaded with Mark to buy some paper and paint to decorate the dining-room, before the extra was handed over to the bookie. I noticed that after he started at Sellafield, his moodiness got worse and we argued a lot more. One day I asked, 'Don't you like the new job, Mark?'

197

'Well, I have to go to work so whether I like it or not doesn't really matter does it?'

Mark was always gloomy before work and tense on the days of his football matches. He spent all of one Saturday morning cleaning his boots prior to a big match that afternoon, and was visibly anxious. I tried to avoid his volatile mood, and kept myself busy with papering and painting all morning. We hardly spoke until he was all ready to go out, when I made a mistake by saying, 'Have a good day and don't worry, I'll manage the decorating on my own.'

He interpreted that as a jibe and glowered at me. I hadn't really meant it that way because I was glad to see the back of him and his sulky mood, but the situation made me tense and after he slammed the dining-room door, I threw down the paint-brush and turned my back on him. He walked across the room, picked up the brush and threw it back at me. It hit me on my spine and I fell to the floor, as much through shock as anything else. He then stormed out, slamming the front door behind him. I picked myself up, retrieved the confused brush, and carried on painting.

I worried all afternoon in case he had a bad game, knowing that would worsen his mood which he'd then bring home with him. Thankfully, when he got back all was apparently forgotten as he'd played well and was awarded 'Man of the Match'.

He was always apologetic after an argument or display of bad temper, but would never discuss why it kept happening. It was probably partly my fault too; maybe I shouldn't complain or have an opinion about anything concerning him, who knows, I certainly didn't. I finished the decorating though, and the dining-room looked lovely. We continued to have little hiccups from time to time but I thought maybe this is how married life is for everybody. We were young and had to adjust to coping with the pressures of a new life, new home and new baby, and all the associated pressures and responsibilities.

Chapter Thirty Eight

Two false starts

I'd really hoped that Mark's new job and income would help to make things better between us but unfortunately, it didn't. I don't think he liked the job from the start, though he never actually said so, but it included more holidays than council grass-cutting, and had a system involving 'red inkers', which meant that if a worker fell ill but had no paid sick-leave left, he had an additional seven days to fall back on. These seven days were an annual concession but Mark began to use them like extra holidays. When he was off sick he got a little bit extra pay as his tax deduction fell, he said, so the incentive to use the inkers was always there, even though the employer would obviously take note of his dubious absences. I thought he was taking liberties with a relatively secure and well-paid job, but had learned by then not to argue or even disagree with him.

Our wedding anniversary came along and we received cards from family and friends, but chose not to have an organised celebration. It would mean arranging baby-sitters and although my parents always loved having Craig, I still hated having to be apart from him for any length of time, or sharing his care with anyone. Mark and I didn't go out socialising much anyway, and were both were quite happy staying at home with our baby. Mark still trained twice a week for football and played matches most Saturdays and Sundays, so he saw his friends a lot. I spent as much time as I could with my parents, and in the quiet evenings at home I continued the knitting I'd learned and loved as a child. It sounds quite sad now when I think about it, but as long as Mark and I weren't arguing, I thought we were doing well. We never planned for his holidays, as he was happy just not having to go to work, and never did anything different except that I wouldn't go to my parent's when he was home.

Craig started teething quite early and by the time he was one year old, had a full set. He was really clever and I'd sit for hours on the mat, playing with him and his toys. I read to him and confided in him when I was unhappy, which was most of the time. On his first birthday he received lots of clothes and toys but we didn't organise a party. It seemed a bit silly as he was far too young to understand or enjoy it, but I baked a cake and we sang Happy Birthday to him, which made him smile. He was soon walking and investigating every little nook & cranny around the house and garden, and keeping him safe involved a lot more work. We fitted locks to the drawers and he was still too small to open doors, which I was at least thankful for.

Soon after his birthday we got ready for the first Christmas in our new home. I couldn't wait to put up the tree and decorations, hoping they would lift my spirits. We collected streamers and trinkets bit by bit each week and both sets of parents helped out, and at the beginning of December I was ready. I'd noticed that Woolworths and most other shops had all decorated so I decided to do ours. Craig watched with his mouth open as I got started, and I played Christmas music on my record player to add to the festive mood. Many of my favourite tunes were on Max Bygraves' Christmas album, and Craig said many years later that he could still remember them from those early times in his life.

Christmas was still a special time for me as it reminded me of my own happy childhood with my parents and siblings, and because I wasn't truly happy at this point in my life, listening to the songs made me feel sad at what I'd lost. Nobody ever knew how I really felt then; not even Mam as far as I'm aware. I'd made my bed, I knew she'd say, so now I must lie in it. I always kept my head up and mouth shut, and wore a smile for the world.

Craig had a little teddy bear toy that had been a present for his birthday, and was playing with it near the Christmas tree one afternoon. It was the last working Friday before the holidays, which in Cumbria and other areas is known colloquially as Black-Eye Friday, because so many blokes and some women, come home with one after finishing work early and going to the pub to celebrate. I was in the kitchen and it was quite dark as I only had the decorative lights on, giving the house a lovely, soft glow.

Craig was playing in the living room and I had a safety-gate around the open fire. I was busy making tea for Mark, who was running late but I thought he'd probably gone for a drink with his workmates. That was fine though I did ask him in the morning whether he was going, so I knew when to make his meal, and he told me he was coming straight home. I suddenly realised that Craig was very quiet and when I went through to the living room, the fire was roaring and the room was all lit up. I panicked for a second before realising that Craig was standing to one side, watching the blaze. He'd thrown the teddy into the flames, where it caught fire and fell down into the grate. I managed to poke him out onto the hearth though poor teddy was already cooked, but I think this fright must have put me on edge.

Mark never arrived home until 8.30pm. I know that's not such a terrible crime but it seemed so to me at the time, obviously after the scare with Craig and probably partly because of my underlying unhappiness. Craig was in bed by then, which irritated me further as Mark had promised to see him before bedtime. Tensions boiled over and the first Christmas in our new home, started with a bad-tempered argument between us.

Chapter Thirty Nine

Christmas Day 1974

Mark and I were awake at 7.30 on Christmas morning, but Craig was still asleep so we put our arguments aside, crept downstairs and made a pot of tea. We got the fire blazing and the living room was soon warm and cosy. The house didn't have central-heating and had to be warmed room by room, before we opened our few presents and waited for our son to wake up. It wasn't long before he did and I ran upstairs to get him. His little face lit up when he came into the living room, with the Christmas lights on and his presents piled under the tree. We sat on the floor and helped him open them, and then spent an hour or so playing along with him and all his new toys and getting him to try on the new clothes he'd been given. There was a knock on the door at 9.30 and I knew it would be my parents and brothers, Albert and Brian. They bustled in out of the cold and Mark made us all a nice, hot cuppa.

I know it can't be the same for everybody unfortunately, but for me Christmas is all about being with family, and when it happens I find it quite magical. What I've always liked so much about that time of year, is that everyone seems happy regardless of the problems they might be going through, and for one day or even for a moment, it's absolutely lovely and nothing else can compare with it in my experience.

They stayed for an hour then moved on to see Charlie and Margaret and their new baby. I cleared away all the wrapping paper, peeled and chopped some vegetables and prepared our dinner. We had Christmas crackers with it and laughed at the silly jokes that were hidden inside each one. Craig fell asleep straight after lunch; all the excitement tiring him out, and Mark and I washed the dishes together. We then set the table up in the corner of the living room and filled it with party-food wrapped in foil, to keep it fresh until Mary and Billy arrived.

Craig woke up and kept asking when his Nana Mary was coming, but they never arrived. We didn't have a phone to contact anybody so it was 4.30 in the afternoon before we were finally certain that they weren't coming. It was so disappointing and I knew Mark was really sad that they hadn't been to see their grandson on Christmas Day. We made the best of the situation though, snacking on the party food throughout the evening, and eventually put what was left in the fridge. I often wondered why we had any tea on Christmas Day, as I was always still so full from dinner.

We'd arranged to visit Mary and Billy on Boxing Day, and Mary duly arrived to pick us up. She said Father, which is what she often called Billy, hadn't been very well the day before but she hadn't been able to leave him or let us know. Mark's brothers and sister were at the house and we had a really pleasant day. We laughed and joked and I enjoyed the merriment and good feeling between family members. After we came home and put Craig to bed, Mark and I sat together and watched some of my favourite Christmas movies. So after a bad start on Black-Eye Friday, Christmas turned out quite well and some of my waning optimism returned.

On New Year's Eve we made some food for the evening, and watched *Andy Stewart's Christmas Special* on television. At midnight we wished each other Happy New Year, kissed and went to bed, and that was it for 1974.

With the festivities over it was back to work for everyone, and life carried on exactly as before. Mark and I regularly fell out over something or other, and then made up again, but the majority of our arguments were still about money. I often wondered if all our problems would disappear if we had lots of the stuff, but somehow knew they wouldn't. I realise now that I'd slowly lost my trust and faith in Mark as a provider for his family, and therefore some of my essential respect for him. Things would be going along quite nicely for a while, when totally out of the blue he'd say he wasn't going to work that morning. I became so worried about our financial position, and our ability to pay the rent and feed the baby, that I started asking him every night before I went to sleep, 'Mark, are you alright?'

'Yes, I'm fine,' he'd reply. 'Why?'

'So you're going to work tomorrow?'

'Yes, of course I'm going to work, now go to sleep and give me some peace.'

Many nights I'd lay awake thinking he wasn't going to go the following day, but always made up his sandwiches before going to bed in the hope he would. I set the alarm and each morning when it rang, I'd nudge him gently to make sure he was awake and whisper, 'Are you feeling okay this morning, Mark?'

'Yes, I'm fine,' he'd say.

'Are you going to work?'

'Yes, I am,' he'd reply, so I'd get up, put the kettle on and make him some toast for breakfast.

I'd then sit at the table watching the clock with increasing dread, as I always suspected he was going to change his mind. I'd call upstairs, 'Mark, are you getting up? You'll miss the bus if you don't get a move on.'

This occurrence was so regular that it became a way of life for us, and I hated it so very much. Eventually I'd go back upstairs feeling deflated but also angry at the disrespect with which he treated me, though I suppose I should have learned the lesson by then and put my optimism to bed for good.

'Why can't you just be honest with me?' I shouted at him one morning, the tension in me boiling over. 'I needn't have gotten up so early if you'd no intention of going and…and now your sandwiches are wasted!' I added because I couldn't think of anything else to say.

He never replied, just turned over to face away from me and went back to sleep. Later he asked me to telephone work and ask for a red-inker or a day's holiday, depending on which he had any left of. The exasperating part of it all is that he wasn't lazy; he was a good worker by all accounts, it was just getting him to go that was the problem. Or is that an essential component of laziness? Hard to be a good worker if you're not even there!

With all the shouting Craig was now awake. 'Come on Craig,' I said. 'We'll get ready and go see Nana Jessie.'

My parents' house became a refuge for me. Although I'd always gone there most days, it was to enjoy their company and avoid being on my own when Mark was out at work, but now it became essential to preserve my sanity and give me the strength to cope with the life I was living. I constantly wondered whether I was doing something wrong; something that made my husband the way he was. I actually asked him more than once and though he never answered, I did sense that there was something bothering him deep down in his heart.

Despite what I saw as a major problem, I realised that many people wouldn't and we did still have some good times, and it was those times that helped me through the bad ones. Mark constantly told me that he loved me and would ask, 'Do you love me, Ann?'

'Of course I do, Mark,' I would always reply, wondering why he needed constant reassurance.

I realise that I never ever, as far as I remember, actually said to my husband, 'I love you, Mark.'

Maybe I never did truly love him. Probably I didn't and that fact almost certainly had some effect on him. It's a reality that I have to live with and remember when I think of the problems we had in our years together. But I wanted to – I wanted desperately to love him so that our lives and that of our baby son could be truly happy. I wanted to love, and I needed to be loved by somebody I could love in return.

Over the land is April,
Over my heart a rose;
Over the high, brown mountain
The sound of singing goes.
Say, love, do you hear me,
Hear my sonnets ring?
Over the high, brown mountain,
Love, do you hear me sing?

(Robert Louis Stevenson, 1850 – 1894)

'Hello, Mam,' I called as I opened her back door. Craig ran in and sat in front of the roaring fire.

'Morning Craig,' Mam smiled as she gave him a hug. 'Morning Ann, is everything alright?'

I just shrugged and set about making a cuppa, but then she asked the question I always dreaded, 'Is Mark alright?'

'Who knows?' I answered.

'Has he gone to work today?'

Did my face and demeanour tell her what she already suspected? I don't know as I didn't ask – I was too embarrassed. I looked back to the steaming kettle and whilst turned away from her, lied that my husband was at work, before busying myself with cups and spoons. Mam went quiet then and didn't pursue the matter. Craig was only eighteen months old but looked at me strangely, as if he knew I was lying to my mother about his father. I never told him what to say or what not to say, but he knew whether his dad was at work or lying at home in bed. He never spoke though and it seemed as if he knew how much it hurt me, feeling the need to lie to my mother.

Despite the debatable reasons not to, I must have still had some feelings for Mark, or why else did I never tell her the truth? I told her absolutely everything else. It can only have been to protect his reputation, and mine I suppose, being his wife. But it wasn't me that constantly refused to go to work and provide for the family, it was him and I was ashamed that my husband was lazing in bed when he should be out at work earning an honest living. Mam was only making conversation, and would've been horrified if she'd known how much I hated the questions she asked, and that they upset me so much.

One day Mary came to pick me up at Mam's; she was taking me to a doctor's appointment for a check-up as I'd been feeling a bit depressed. She was talking to Craig and said, 'Where's your daddy Craig, is he at work?'

Craig nodded his head and I think that even at such a young age, he'd picked up signals from me which told him that Daddy wasn't always where he was supposed to be. He was clever enough not to answer, 'No, Daddy's still in bed,' as I think most children his age would.

In effect, Craig had already learned to lie as an unfortunate consequence of his parents' actions. A few days later Mam said, 'Ann, there's a part-time job going in a little baker's shop in town. It's owned by a nice couple called Mr and Mrs Laidlaw.'

I smiled immediately at the possibility.

'Why don't you apply for it? I think it's only two days a week - Thursday and Saturday, but it'll give you some extra cash and I can have Craig on Thursdays when Mark's at work?'

I phoned the shop, arranged an interview and got the job. My first day was a Thursday and I got Mark up for work whether he wanted to go or not, then dressed Craig ready for Mam's. I took an extra set of clothes in case she wanted to take him out, so he'd have a clean set to come home in - I still hated him not looking sparkly white! Mam laughed and said I was just making more washing for myself.

I was a bit nervous, not having worked since being at Woolworths, but also determined to make a success of it and wondering why I hadn't thought of something similar earlier. Most of the employees had worked there for years and were all a lot older than me, apart from one girl who was closer to my age and seemed a really nice person. They all offered me advice and said the boss-lady was very strict. 'Always look like you're busy,' they told me. 'Even if you're not!'

For most of the day however, we were constantly busy as customers flocked in for fresh bread and teacakes. It was also nearly Easter, and the smell of hot-cross-buns brought more people in than usual. Mr Laidlaw was downstairs in the actual bakery from very early in the morning; usually starting work at 4am every day.

Working with bread again reminded me of my happy times at Woolworths. I soon memorised all the prices as I did there, and loved my new little job. We had the chance to buy pies and fresh cream cakes at a cheaper rate, and then got another 20% off! I think I used to spend most of my wage on pies and cakes, and had to be careful not to pile on the pounds. I loved being part of a working team again, but missed Craig although I knew he was fine and being well looked after by my mother.

Mark didn't work on Saturdays but he did play football, so she took care of Craig on Saturday afternoons too. Things seemed to get a little easier as we had a bit more money coming in now I was working, so Mark and I would have a night out occasionally. Mam would always baby-sit and Craig stayed over at her house, which he loved because he was spoiled the whole time.

We still didn't go out much though and even when we did, it usually ended badly. He would tell me numerous times that I was the best-looking girl in the place, but then always spoil the night by accusing me of looking or smiling at some other man. I was simply a friendly person and if someone smiled at me, I would smile back out of politeness. It didn't mean I fancied anyone but this was another feature of Mark's insecurity, so I was content to stay home with our baby most of the time.

While I was working, Mark didn't take many of his days off but I could never figure out why. One Thursday when I went to collect Craig after work, I sensed something was wrong because Mam didn't look very happy at all. Craig came running to me and I gave him a big cuddle and a kiss as I'd missed him so much, and asked, 'Is everything okay, Mam.'

'No, I'm afraid it's not,' she said.

'Why, what's wrong?'

'I took Craig for a walk today, and all of a sudden he shouted, 'There's my daddy, Nana.'

I looked and it was Mark so I said, 'Oh yes, he must have finished work early.'

I shook my head in confusion.

'Ann, it was Mark and he was coming out of the bookie's shop.'

My heart lurched.

'He said hello to Craig and me, and then carried on up home to your house I presume. You know I love having Craig, but why didn't Mark come and collect him if he wasn't at work, and save you the bother?'

'I don't know Mam,' I lied again, knowing he wouldn't be able to go to the betting shop if he had Craig with him.

We'd just started to get on our feet again and I loved being back at work. It made me feel like a real part of the human race and I loved seeing my baby afterwards, and taking him up home to our house on the hill. Why did Mark always have to wreck my little world and our small slices of happiness?

'I'm sorry Mam,' I said, holding back my tears. 'I'll ask him what's going on.'

'Well, it's just that you're out working to make some extra money for the family, and he's throwing it away in the betting shop. It's not right, Ann.'

I just smiled but we both knew she was right. I would never criticise him in front of anybody else though, and definitely not tell my mother about the many times he didn't go to work. It would seriously worry her and I didn't want that. The worry it caused me over the years was quite enough without letting it affect her too much as well.

Chapter Forty

A fictional friend and a love affair

When I got home Mark was all ready for me when I asked, 'How come you weren't at work today?'

He replied, 'Your mother looks after Craig so you can go to work, so if I was at work or not she would still be looking after him.'

'Yes she would and actually was, but she does it to help us get some extra money in, not for you to go spending it in the betting shop.'

'Well, it's nothing to do with your mother anyway.'

'No, but it's a lot to do with me. So why weren't you at work again?'

'I didn't go in today, that's all.'

'Yes you did, or at least I thought you did. I got you up and you left the house to go for the bus.'

'Well I didn't get on it.'

'So where did you go?'

'Nowhere.'

'Nowhere?'

'I just hung around the shops until I knew you'd left for your mother's with Craig, then I came back home, okay?'

So many times he deceived me and made me feel stupid, and that Craig and I weren't even worth getting out of bed for, yet he still told me that he loved us both more than anything. After a few days silence we carried on as normal and no more sightings at the bookies were reported, though the truth is that he probably took more care and made sure he wasn't seen again.

It was nearly Craig's second birthday, and I worried about how much he would remember of Mark and I arguing and sulking with each other, especially after learning to lie to his grandma about his dad. But we both loved Craig so much, I can't fault Mark on that score, and tried our best to make life as good as possible for him. He was obviously a happy little boy, and I made a cake for his birthday to go with all the presents we managed to buy him. There weren't any children of the same age that lived on our road, nor any pre-school nurseries where Craig could mix with other kids, so his birthday party comprised just him, Mark and myself. We all sang Happy Birthday though and he had a lovely time.

One day shortly afterwards I was walking down the road to visit Mam, and Craig was lagging behind. I stopped and said, 'Hurry up Craig, let's get to Nana's before it rains.'

He looked behind him and said, 'Hurry up Dorgie.'

'Who are you talking to?' I asked.

He replied, 'It's my new friend.'

'Okay,' I said. 'Well both of you hurry up before it rains.'

I kept turning around to watch him and all the way down the hill he kept talking to someone, or something.

'Hi Mam,' I called as we let ourselves in the front door.

'Hello Craig. Hello love, is everything alright?'

I didn't answer but knew she would be putting the kettle on so followed her into the kitchen. 'Mam,' I said quietly. 'Craig was just talking to someone all the way down here, but there was no-one there.'

Mam looked around at me in puzzlement.

'When I asked him who he was talking to,' I continued. 'He said it was his friend, Dorgie.'

'Aw bless him, he must be lonely Ann, so he's made up an imaginary friend.'

'Oh, right.'

'Maybe it's time you had another baby?'

Craig never asked us to make meals for his new friend or anything like that, but he was always with us as Craig would often say, 'Mammy, can Dorgie come too?'

We didn't discuss Dorgie and just let Craig be happy with him around, even if only in his own mind. Apart from that, life just carried on as always. I still worked at the baker's and Mark hung onto his Sellafield job, though sometimes I wondered how. We fell out regularly and then made up again just as often. As time went by he refused to go to work even more, Craig and I visited my parents more, and nothing changed for the better.

One Thursday evening Mark was going football training and got changed after tea. I was getting Craig ready for bed as Mark shouted, 'Bye Ann, I won't be late back. Say goodnight to Craig for me.'

After putting Craig to bed I sat watching television and doing some knitting, which I found very relaxing and therapeutic. I was knitting myself a thick pullover for the winter as it was far cheaper than buying one. I always felt a bit down when I was alone and Craig was asleep. I didn't really like peace and quiet, as some people do, but preferred plenty of hustle and bustle like there usually was at my parent's house.

It got to 10pm and Mark was usually home long before that, so I began to wonder if something had happened as he never usually went anywhere after training. At 11pm I convinced myself that he'd decided to go for a drink after training with his pals, and went to bed. I didn't sleep though, but lay awake worrying more and more as it got later and later. Eventually I heard the door open and Mark came straight up into the bedroom, laughing and telling me how much he loved me, 'I do Ann, I really love you.'

'Quiet,' I hushed. 'You'll wake Craig up.'

He kept laughing, loudly, and the more he laughed the more annoyed with him I became.

'I've been for a drink with the lads,' he said. 'And we got talking and I really know just how much I love you.'

'Alright,' I hissed, losing my patience. 'Now be quiet before you wake Craig up.'

He clambered up on the bed, still mumbling drunkenly how much he loved me, and unfortunately it annoyed me so much that I pushed him away and he fell off. He lay on his back on the floor, and carried on laughing. I stayed rigidly still and silent, and finally he climbed back into bed and fell asleep.

I was surprised how angry he'd made me feel; so annoyed by such a relatively innocent thing, and decided for certain that I definitely did not love my husband. It was a sad realisation but I had to be honest with myself at least, that this was not the kind of life I wanted, not for myself or for my son, and in fairness to Mark, he deserved somebody who could truly love him in return. I finally admitted that I'd never been happy as Mark's wife, and was always hoping that something would happen to change things. In fact I'd go so far as to say that I really hated my life, apart from Craig of course. I love my son far more than my life. He had become my whole world and the reason I carried on my existence. He made my suffering, because that's exactly what my marriage was most of the time, feel at least worthwhile.

Chapter Forty One

Big decisions

Craig started waking up every night and coming through to sleep in our bed. Mark went to sleep in Craig's bed so he wasn't disturbed again. So when I woke some mornings to find Craig in bed with me and not Mark, it was no surprise. I knew Mark wouldn't go to work in the mornings if he didn't feel like it, so after a while I didn't even bother asking him. One morning when he stayed home he called through from Craig's room, and of course Craig ran through to see his daddy. I could hear them both giggling and went into the bedroom and said, 'Come on Craig, we're going to Nana's.'

'What's wrong with you?' Mark said, sensing my mood.

'I'm fed up with you missing work all the time, and in fact I'm fed up with you full stop, so I'm going back home to live with my parents.'

I think Mark might have been expecting it because he replied straight away, 'You can go but Craig is staying with me.'

He knew I wouldn't leave Craig but I couldn't be bothered discussing it and just said, 'Come on Craig, let's go.'

Mark put his arms around Craig and said, 'No, he's staying with me.'

Poor Craig was crying Mammy, Mammy and holding his little arms out for me to take him, but Mark wouldn't let go. I burst into tears of frustration, swore at Mark and ran down the stairs. He came down a few minutes later and said, 'I don't want you to leave, Ann. Please stay and we can talk about this?'

I felt so deflated and didn't want any more pain or stress, so eventually agreed when Craig came downstairs and sat on my knee. I cuddled him and he snuggled up to me.

When Mark went out for a drink with the lads after football without warning me, it was nothing really but it caused a crisis, because it came on top of all the other things he did and the way he so often made me feel worthless. Now he made me feel that all our problems were my fault for trying to get away from them, and him. I know many people would think Mark's behaviour wasn't so terrible and that in effect, he wasn't a bad husband or father. But I had great difficulty accepting my life as it was, and that I had nothing more to look forward to. I did continue to seek any positives though and as usual, things got better after a few days. After a few more days our problems resurfaced all over again.

I was at my mother's one day having a cup of tea. She was playing with Craig on the floor and suddenly said, 'Ann, I'm going over to Dot's for a few days. Would you and Craig like to come?'

Dot was my sister, Dorothy, who lived in Carlisle, and I knew Mark wouldn't mind me being with her and my mother.

'Yes please,' I answered with a beaming smile. 'When are you going?'

'Next weekend, so I'll let Dot know you and Craig are coming too. Mark won't want to come will he?'

'No, definitely not,' I replied too quickly.

She smiled. I was so excited. I loved going anywhere with Mam; we always laughed about everything and she made me feel so much better.

Mark seemed quite pleased that I was going away for a few days, and said he hoped we all enjoyed it. He knew I wouldn't get up to anything he didn't like with my mother there, not that I would anyway but he still didn't trust me. I asked for the Saturday off from the bakery, and everything was arranged.

We caught the train early in the morning and Craig was soon mesmerised by the scenery whizzing past outside the window. The rhythm of the train relaxed me and took me back to the happy days of my childhood, and after a few miles I whispered to Mam, 'Can Craig and I come and live with you and Dad?'

'Why, what on earth's wrong, Ann?' she asked in genuine surprise.

'I'm so unhappy, Mam. Mark won't go to work and I just can't cope with the worry and stress of it all anymore.'

'Well don't you worry anymore love, it'll be fine. Your dad and me will look after you both if necessary.'

I felt relieved and elated and we had a lovely time at my sister's house. Her daughters, Pauline and Caroline loved playing with Craig, and we all enjoyed the whole weekend. I felt so relaxed and happy and so much more like the person I'd been when I was younger, and single. We stayed at Carlisle until the Tuesday and then came back home. Dad said I could stay from that very night but would have to sleep with Mam for the time being.

'That's fine,' I said as Mabel from along the road popped her head into the kitchen.

'Hi Jessie, it's just me,' she announced. 'Oh hello Ann, you okay?'

'No, not really Mabel,' I replied, glancing over to where Craig was playing with some of the toys he kept at the house. 'Mam will tell you all about it, I don't want to say too much in front of the lad,' I whispered.

Mam took her out to explain and Mabel immediately said I could stay at her house until we got things sorted out, one way or the other. So I moved in with Mabel and her husband, John, who were both really kind and treated me like one of their own from the start. I enjoyed talking with them, especially in the quiet evening before bed-time, and thanked them more than once for allowing me to stay. I wasn't even sad about not being at my own house, and as long as Craig was safe next door with my parents, I was content.

Mam asked if I wanted to go to bingo with her and Mabel the following night, saying Dad would keep an eye on Craig. Why not? I thought, and got myself spruced up to go. I said goodbye to Craig and told him to be a good boy for Grandad, and that I'd see him the following morning. 'Why not tonight?' he asked.

'Because you'll be in bed when we come home and I'll be sleeping at Mabel's, next door.'

I wasn't a big fan of bingo but knew Mam and Mabel were being kind by asking me to go, and they didn't want me sitting at home brooding about my current predicament. Mam even paid for my bingo cards, too. As we waited for the first card to start Mam nudged my leg and nodded, and I looked up to see Mary walking over to us.

'Hello Ann,' she said brightly. 'Did you have a nice time at Carlisle?'

'Yes,' I answered, nodding nervously.

'And is Craig alright?'

'Yes, we had a lovely time thank you,' I answered politely. 'And Craig is fine.'

Mary looked puzzled to see me there, obviously because Mark had told her I'd gone to Carlisle and wouldn't yet know I was back. Then again I hadn't told him I wasn't coming back, at least not back to the house I'd shared with him.

Chapter Forty Two

Another lost job

A few days passed, Craig and I were at least content if not perfectly happy, and I hadn't heard from Mark. I hadn't had my period either, but I put that down to all the upset and changes to my routine. I was normally as regular clockwork, so a little concerned, and mentioned it to Mam.

'Don't worry too much yet love,' she said. 'It's probably with everything that's going on at the moment. You could just be a bit late.'

She did make me feel better, but I wasn't too sure. With my luck, I thought, could it ever be that simple?

'You could take a urine sample to the doctor,' Mam suggested. 'But don't worry and remember - everything happens for a reason.'

I thought about that but couldn't think of any valid reason for me being pregnant again, apart from giving birth to another beautiful baby of course. I hoped and prayed that I wasn't expecting though, now I'd made a break for freedom, but knew

Mam and Dad would still take care of me so it wouldn't be a total disaster. Those serious considerations took my thoughts to Mark whose weaker points, after a week or so apart, had faded a little. I knew he wasn't a bad person, or stupid or lazy, we just saw life differently and had separate priorities. We were far too young to get married when we did, and too reckless when we had Craig, and the big realisation sprung back into my mind – I didn't love Mark. Did I?

I was sitting in the living room with Mam and Dad, assessing my life and future. Craig was watching the horse-racing on TV and my dad said he was so clever, knowing what all the betting odds meant. Yes, I thought, he'll have learned that from Mark, but I wasn't so sure that knowing how to gamble was such a good idea at nearly three years old, however much intelligence it showed. Suddenly Mam said, 'Ann, Mark just walked passed the window.'

I looked up and at the same time heard a knock at the door.

'I'll go,' Dad said, getting up.

'Hello lad,' I heard him say.

I couldn't hear Mark's response but then Dad said, 'Yes Mark, she is here, come on in.'

Craig jumped up and ran over to meet him, shouting, 'Daddy, Daddy.'

Mark picked his son up and gave him a cuddle. I saw the expression on Mark's face, and knew how much he must have missed the little boy he loved so much. It melted my heart. He said hello to Mam and then politely asked if he could have a word with me. We went into the dining room. Craig followed us but I told him to stay with Nana and Grandad. He sat back on the carpet and said, 'Daddy, the horses are on the telly.'

Mark nodded and smiled as we left the room, then asked, 'Ann, when did you get back from Carlisle?'

225

'A few days ago,' I answered flatly.

'So are you not coming back home?'

'Mark, I'm sorry but I just can't cope with the way you are. You won't go to work so I'm worried all the time, and it makes me so sad and depressed.'

He was silent for a moment before saying, 'I really am sorry, Ann. I will try to be a better person but I've come to show you this.'

He handed me a letter which was official notification from Sellafield, for him to finish work because of ill-health. I was puzzled and said, 'I don't understand, Mark. Why are they finishing you because of ill-health? You're fine, aren't you?'

'Well,' he said, looking at his feet. 'They were going to sack me, because my name was in the Whitehaven News for scoring a goal at football, while I was on the sick.'

'Oh no.'

He nodded. 'My manager said it wouldn't be so bad Mark, but you play for the opposition,' and then he smiled at me.

I just had to laugh at the way he said it, although I was crying inside, but at least he was being honest with me, for once. I looked him straight in the eye and said flatly, 'I think I'm pregnant again and now you have no job, again.'

His smile faded fast and he looked straight at me. I started to cry and he whispered, 'Please don't cry, Ann. We'll be alright. You know I love you and I've missed you and Craig so much.'

'Well it took you long enough to come and find us,' I replied angrily.

'I didn't even know you were back from Carlisle until my mother saw you at the bingo.'

I felt desperately trapped and lost in a world not of my choice. I was only twenty years old, had a baby not even three and probably having another, and a husband who said he loved me but couldn't keep a job to provide for us.

'I'll go back home Ann, and let you think about what you want from life,' Mark said.

This time I looked at my feet, clad in a pair of my mother's pink slippers, and tears welled in my eyes again. Mark looked back from the door and called, 'Bye Craig and goodbye Mr & Mrs Chambers.'

I went back into the living room and burst out crying. Craig ran over to hug me and said, 'Don't cry, Mammy.'

'Ann, what's going on?' my dad asked.

I blew my nose, noisily, and said, 'Mark has lost his job but he wants us to go back home, because he loves and misses us.'

Mam and Dad looked at each other with troubled expressions.

'What...what if I'm pregnant again?' I stammered through my sobs.

'You have to do what's best for you and the boy, Ann, but we'll always be here for you if you need us,' Dad said.

'I know you will,' I sobbed.

We were all quiet for a short while and I finally stopped crying. I hugged Craig tightly and asked him, 'Craig love, do you miss not being with Daddy?'

He looked up at me and nodded.

'So should we go back home?'

He looked up again and this time smiled, and nodded. He was still only a baby but I knew he loved and missed his father, which didn't really leave me much choice.

Chapter Forty Three

Another new baby

I spoke to Mabel and John and thanked them again for their hospitality, and told them Craig and I were going back home.

'You take care, Ann,' Mabel said as she waved goodbye to us. 'Everything happens for a reason.'

'I know, Mam tells me all the time. Bye Mabel.'

When I told him we were coming back, Mark said he would drive over for us and help with our things. As we waited Mam said, 'Ann, Dad says you know where we are if you need us.'

I gave them both a kiss and thanked them for everything. Craig was watching out of the window and when he saw Mark arrive he was so excited. It's always the children that suffer most when relationships go wrong, I thought. I was still very doubtful about the future but could see no other way forward, so hoped and prayed that things would get better.

For a little while Mark and I got along reasonably well and life ran quite smoothly, possibly because he had no job to shirk from. I got my test results from the doctor and yes, I was pregnant with a baby due in April 1977. This time I grew really big and the summer of 1976 was very warm. There was even an official water-shortage declared and nobody was allowed to use paddling pools or hoses in the garden. I was very hot carrying Craig's sibling around inside me all summer.

Mark's brother, Colin, came back from Holland with his wife Brenda, and almost immediately got a council-house a couple of doors from us. They had two children, Gary and Andrea who were both older than Craig, but were happy to play with him and they all spent some happy times together throughout those summer months. Brenda and I became really good friends as well as being sisters-in-law, and I would often go to her house to confide in her when the men were out. She was a really good and understanding friend to me, and we used to laugh about all sorts of things. I felt a lot happier with her around and living so close to us.

Mark was also happy with me and his brother's wife being good friends, and never complained when I spent time with her. I left the baker's shop as carrying the bread-trays around was heavy work, and Mark still didn't have a job. Craig's third birthday arrived and we had a little tea for him, Andrea and Gary. In 1976 the government awarded families Child Benefit for their first child. It wasn't a great amount but I was pleased with a little extra to help out with our finances. Mary was still generous and often gave us things for the children or the house. Most of the furniture was second-hand but never very old. I think buying stuff might have been one of Mary's coping-mechanisms to get through the difficult times caring for her husband. Maybe husband-problems ran in the family? I don't know but I never bought a pair of curtains for years!

When we got our Child Benefit book it had my name printed on the front, and I felt so relieved that we had some extra income that I could control. But when Mark received his

Unemployment Benefit the following week, they'd taken off the amount of Child Benefit I received. Oh well, such is life, I thought, back to square one.

Christmas wasn't far off and Craig was excited this year, as he now understood what it was all about and that he'd get some presents. By the time it came around I was very heavily pregnant, with people asking me all the time, 'Haven't you had that baby yet?'

It amused and sometimes annoyed me, because the baby wasn't due until April, three months down the line! I was so big that the only thing I had which fit me was a green and white dress. It was fortunate that I liked it and it was really comfortable, because I never seemed to have it off my back!

Colin & Brenda invited us round for Boxing Day at their house, and I looked forward to that. Mary & Billy came, also Mark's brothers: Terry and young Bill, and Bill's wife, Sylvia. It was a really good day and we all agreed to take turns doing the same on future Boxing Days, at each other's houses. It was arranged for it to be at our house the following year, and though I loved the thought of regular family get-togethers, I couldn't help wondering whether Mark and I would still be together in a year's time.

1977 arrived and I was looking forward to having the new baby. Brenda was also excited about it and kept trying to talk Colin into having another. He wouldn't even discuss it even though poor Brenda was so broody. I still walked down to visit my parents every day and Mark found himself a job: He was taken on as a labourer by one of his footballer mate's father, who was a builder working on a new housing estate, not too far away. Building was a whole new experience for Mark, and he was always exhausted when he came home after a long day's hard work. He stuck at it though and I felt quite proud of him for that.

It was getting close to 18th April, which was the predicted birth date. Craig and I were walking down to see my parents when suddenly I tripped and fell. I was back on my feet quickly but felt a little dizzy. A young lad came over to help but I told him I was fine, but still felt shaken up when I reached Mam's. Craig ran ahead to tell her I'd fallen, and she asked, 'Are you alright, love?'

'I..I'm not sure,' I answered.

'Well sit down and I'll make us a brew.'

After a rest I felt okay but the sudden fall did continue to worry me a little. The 18th came along but no baby did, and I immediately thought that this pregnancy was going to be just like the last - late after induction. I was tired, mostly because of the extra weight I was carrying, and so big and round it disrupted my sleep.

On 21st April I woke early about 4.30am, feeling very uncomfortable, knew the birth was imminent and asked Mark if he'd phone for an ambulance. He walked to the public telephone at the shops and got back just before the ambulance arrived. Despite the early start our new baby wasn't born until 1.30 in the afternoon. Darren arrived weighing 9 pounds 15 ounces and was in perfect health. He was beautiful and even though he was a big baby, looked so vulnerable lying there in his little cot.

Mark, my mother and Mary came to see me later that day. I was still waiting for the doctor to come and stitch me up, as I'd been cut to help the baby out, so only Mark was allowed in to see me. He was so proud of his second son and asked if he could take him out to show him off, so I asked the nurse and she said he could. I was disappointed that my visitors couldn't come in, because Craig was with them and wanted to see his mammy and baby brother. Mark promised to bring him the next day.

I was looking forward to seeing Craig but he wasn't very impressed with the new baby, and cuddled me all through the visit. I waved cheerfully to everyone when visiting was over, but was wishing I could go home with them. I did manage to get home a little earlier however, as Craig was really missing me and not feeling well, so they let me out after 8 days. Mark, Craig and Mary came to pick me up and I was happy to be going home at last.

Life went along smoothly for a while, though Mark hated the hard graft of the building sites. But he stuck with it all through summer and then applied for a job as Caretaker's Assistant at a local school. He got the job and although his wage wasn't great, he liked the work and got on well with the caretaker - Pat. So for the first time in years, Mark had a job he liked and never took any time off unless he was genuinely ill. It's just about horses-for-courses; simple as that, I thought optimistically. Brenda was finally pregnant again and there were so many other positive changes going on, that I felt better about my own life and future than I had for a very long time.

Chapter Forty Four

My new job

The first few weeks with Darren were really hard and distressing. He had bad colic and though we took turns carrying him around for hours on end, rocking him gently, he still sobbed his heart out and clenched his little legs up to his tummy. I thought he was still hungry because he was a big lad and milk wasn't enough for him even then. I would have fed him some baby-porridge but the health visitor said it was too early, and I didn't want to take any chances with his health. He settled down after a few months though, when he was eating more, and soon Craig's fourth birthday was almost upon us.

Things were still running quite smoothly and at 7 months old, Darren fit well into our daily routine: Mark got up for work, I made his breakfast and saw him on his way, before getting the boys ready to visit Mam. I still liked seeing her every day, and also Margaret with her two girls who also visited. She had a new baby too so the house was full of little ones, and always hectic. Poor Mam, it's a wonder she wasn't sick of us and all our kids. Maybe she was but too polite to say.

I think she liked a buzz about the place as much as we did though, at least I hope she did and that's what I told myself.

'Hi Ann,' she greeted me this particular day as we arrived. Hello Craig and Darren.'

'Hi Mam,' I replied.

'Hi Nana,' said Craig.

Darren just gurgled and smiled.

'I was at bingo last night,' Mam continued.

'Oh yes, have a nice time?'

'Yes, and guess what?'

'Go on.'

'They're looking for a new caller.'

'Oh, right,' I said, suddenly more interested.

'What do you think?'

'Er, yes, I think I might be interested. I could go when Mark gets home from work.'

'But there are the Thursday and Saturday matinees as well?'

'Oh right, forgot about those.'

'I could watch Craig and Darren for you though?'

'Wouldn't you and Dad mind, every week?'

'No, no we'd love to have them, and you know what Dad always says: the more the merrier!'

'Okay,' I smiled, and phoned the bingo hall right away.

I got an interview, was offered the job and started that same weekend. I worked every night from 6.45 'til 9.30 except Sundays, and also had Thursday afternoon off so Mam only needed to watch the boys on Saturday afternoon, when Mark was playing football.

I liked the job right away because I was dealing directly with customers again. I enjoyed chatting as I sold bingo books to them, and even went around during the interval, selling ice-creams like at the pictures. I met some lovely people and the other girls were a good bunch to work with. The manager was fine too and I was treated like a person, not just a number, and of course the extra income was a big plus for us.

Mark and I were still getting along reasonably well at the time. We didn't go out much despite the extra money, which was probably fortunate because Mark remained as jealous and possessive as ever, but while we were on our own at home, there were no real problems. After starting work at the bingo hall we were like passing ships in the night, so maybe the lack of contact helped too. We were both always too tired to argue anyway.

It was nearly Christmas yet again and the girls at the bingo were arranging a night out for us all. They were taking names for a meal out in Workington, and then drinks around the town. One of the girls, Maureen, who had worked at the bingo for years, said to me, 'Ann, are you coming on our night out?'

I stuttered for a second before replying, 'Can I let you know? I'm not sure my husband will be over the moon about it.'

'Oh, you'll be okay with us,' she said. 'I'll put your name down.'

It felt churlish to protest, and I really did want to have a night out with my new colleagues, so paid for my meal and bus ride. I knew I had a right to socialise with my workmates, or indeed any friends, but still never mentioned it to Mark. I decided to wait until a couple of days before to tell him, as I knew I'd be interrogated when I did, so might as well cut the torture to a minimum. In fairness to Mark, he never actually stopped me going anywhere that I wanted to, but he would nearly always go into one of his silent, sulky moods and I just could not take any more of that nonsense.

I was so looking forward to going out with my new friends but couldn't mention it in my own house. I confided in Brenda and she said, 'What's wrong with him? It's just a night out with the girls from work, for God's sake. Colin's totally the opposite.'

I just shook my head.

'Colin never bothers himself when I go out,' she laughed. 'I think he's pleased to get rid of me for the night!'

'You don't know how lucky you are.'

When I did tell Mark I added what his sister-in-law had said, and I think that might have made him think about his behaviour. The big night came and I thoroughly enjoyed it, but made sure I was back home on time. We did exchange angry words nevertheless, because Mark still could not bring himself to trust me despite the fact that I had never, ever, given him cause not to. His insecurities ruled our lives. I took it all philosophically though, as I did more often now, and life carried on again in our version of normality.

Christmas came and went reasonably happily, and as arranged the previous year, we had another good family get-together on Boxing Day, at our house. Brenda was waiting patiently for February when her new baby was due, and with only a few weeks to go, I was secretly hoping she'd have a boy who'd be a future playmate for Darren. With only 10 months between them, on 7th February, Brenda gave birth to a healthy, bouncing boy who she and Colin named Lee.

Chapter Forty Five

Andrea & Martin's wedding

$\mathbf{M}$ark and I were still getting along reasonably well, though two small children and both of us working at different hours of the day, meant we didn't see much of each other which certainly helped. As long as Mark felt he'd played well at football at the weekend, everything was fine. If he was sulky or bad-tempered when he came home, I knew he'd had a bad game so tried to keep out of his way.

We were invited to my old friend, Andrea's wedding reception. Andrea and I had played together whilst growing up and our mothers were also good friends. I was looking forward to it and bought myself a new pair of trousers with a blouse, and although I hadn't lost all my pregnancy weight since Darren's birth, I was quite slim.

We asked Mary to baby-sit at our house, as my parents were also invited to the reception. We didn't ask Mary very often but Terry volunteered to stay in and look after his dad. It was all arranged and I got the night off from bingo without a problem. The reception was in the big hall at the local hospital nurses' quarters, which was often hired out for weddings. It went really well and of all the nights out that Mark and I had together, this was definitely one of the best I remember. We were up dancing, laughing and talking and it felt that we were really close to each other. I thought maybe we'd turned a corner in our marriage and things would carry on in the same vein. Mark could be really nice at times, when he wanted to be, and everyone that knew him really liked him. He was a good father too and loved the boys.

We had to leave the reception early as Mary didn't want to leave Billy and Terry by themselves for too long. We said goodbye to everyone and I hugged Mam and Dad. Mam was smiling and I knew she was pleased that Mark and I had obviously enjoyed ourselves together. When we were on our own I said, 'I really enjoyed tonight Mark, did you?'

He put his arm around me and looked into my eyes. 'I did Ann, and I do love you, and I'm pleased we stayed together.'

That was the first time in years that I felt really close to my husband, and I hoped we could stay that way forever. We set off to walk home and giggled all the way down the hill. I was wearing high heels and kept stumbling. Mark laughed and took hold of my hand to keep me steady. He helped me all the way down and back up to our house, and I didn't want that night to ever end.

'Hi,' we both smiled at Mary. 'Have the boys been alright?'

'Yes, I've never even heard them, but I must get off home, now. Have you had a good night?'

'Yes, really good,' we both agreed, standing at the door and waving.

'Goodnight then.'

'Goodnight, drive safely,' we said before going up to bed quietly, so as not too wake the boys.

I was feeling really happy and we starting kissing and cuddling straight away. Mark always used contraception now but afterwards when I went to the bathroom, I was very wet and messy, which didn't normally happen. Suddenly I was worried about being pregnant again so soon, and when I got back into bed said, 'Mark, I think the condom might have been faulty or something.'

'It'll be okay,' he said, already nodding off. 'Go to sleep.'

I lay awake for hours worrying but did fall asleep eventually. When I woke up next morning I felt certain that I was pregnant. Mark was full of the joys of spring that morning but I felt sick with worry. Darren was only 10 months old and I definitely did not want another baby yet. Mark could see something was bothering me and asked, 'What's wrong?'

I replied, 'I'm pregnant, I just know I am.'

'Don't be silly Ann, you bring the worry on yourself thinking like that!'

We had such a lovely night at Andrea's reception and things were looking better for us. Why did this have to happen now? The last thing on earth I wanted right now was to be pregnant again. I tried to think myself into being happy, but only succeeded when I was with friends. I went along to see Brenda and Colin very often but never mentioned anything to them. Even when I went to Mam's I never told her either. I waited patiently for my period but it was a forlorn hope - I knew in my heart that I was pregnant. I just felt pregnant and had the usual signs: sore breasts and a sickly feeling all the time, and on 1st March my fears were confirmed. 'I'm late. I told you I was pregnant,' I informed Mark.

'We'll be okay, Ann. It'll be fine,' he replied with a smile and seemed delighted with the situation.

But I wasn't and still refused to tell anyone. Not even Brenda when she told me it was Lee's christening on 2nd May, and she was inviting the family back to her house after the church ceremony. It was like the Boxing Day party all over again, but even bigger as members of Brenda's family were there too.

Mark was buzzing and very chatty, and kept saying, 'I wonder who'll be next to have a baby?' before turning to grin smugly at me.

I never smiled back or said anything, but stared at him tight-lipped in an effort to shut him up. Brenda and probably others soon picked up the clues though. She kept looking at me and I'm pretty sure she knew, but never said anything at the time. The following day I was at her house with the boys, and Craig was busy playing on the floor. Darren and Lee were asleep and no other adults were present. Glancing at Craig to make sure he wasn't listening, Brenda whispered, 'Ann, are you alright?'

'No, I'm not,' I answered immediately, because I was so glad to at last reveal my secret to someone I trusted, and who I thought already knew anyway.

'What's wrong?'

'I'm pregnant again.'

'I thought you must be when Mark kept asking who was next. I could tell by your face.'

I was close to tears. 'Darren's only 11 months old Brenda, and he'll only be 18 months when the new baby's born.'

'Have you been to see the doctor yet?'

'No, I keep hoping the whole thing will go away. It'll be so stressful and such hard work with three babies in five years, and two of them under two years old. Just think of all that nappy-changing!'

Brenda nodded in commiseration and patted me on the arm. I felt trapped again, and thought I'd never get the chance to live the life I dreamed of, however desperate I might get in the future. Knowing I could leave if I got that desperate again had been like a safety-valve to me, but how could I possibly go with three little ones to look after and provide for?

'I haven't even told my mother yet,' I said despondently. 'I'll have to tell her soon.'

Brenda nodded again and looked at me with sorrowful eyes as I continued:

'And I'll have to leave my bingo job and I did so like it there, working and chatting with the other girls. It got me out of the house and kept me sane.'

That night I said to Mark, 'I've made an appointment with the doctor, and will ask my mother to watch the boys. I'll tell her at the same time.'

Craig was always excited about going to see my parents, but I was nervous as I got him and Darren ready and walked down the long hill. It was a lovely, sunny day and I waved to Mabel as I passed by her window.

'Ann,' I heard her call after me. 'Are you going to your mam's?'

'Yes Mabel, I've an appointment with the doctor and I want to ask Mam to keep an eye on the kids for me.'

'I'll be down in five minutes.'

'Hi Mam,' I called as I went in. Craig had run on ahead so she knew I was on my way.

'Hi,' she replied.

'Mam, can you watch Craig and Darren for me? I have an appointment with the doctor at twelve o'clock.'

'Of course I can love, is everything alright? Are you not feeling well?'

241

'I'm not feeling great Mam, and it's because I'm pregnant again.'

'Oh…are you sure?'

'I haven't had it confirmed yet but I think I'm nearly three months.'

'Oh Ann, it'll be such hard work for you with two toddlers and a baby.'

My mother was a wonderful person and wouldn't hurt me for the world, but that was not what I wanted to hear from her at that time.

'I know Mam, but what can I do?'

Mark was such a more reliable person since we had Darren and he got the maintenance job at the school, but life still wasn't great. He continued to have his tantrums and if things didn't go just as he wanted them to, I still got the blunt end of his tongue. I could have called it a day between us many times, but continued to stick it out. Yes, probably for the sake of the children, but also because the unknown scared me. I don't know the exact reasons why I carried on in a relationship I was no longer committed to, but I know I was not happy. I was 23 years old with two children and another one on the way.

There were some great people in my life and I loved my two little boys. They made everything worthwhile but in my marriage, there was no love or passion or even trust or mutual respect anymore. I watched other couples and wondered what their lives were like. I daydreamed about winning some money, so me and the boys could leave and be happy together without all the stress and worry, and living on a knife's edge because of Mark's moods.

I often found myself standing in the kitchen and just…thinking. Thinking about how my life could have been if

I'd lived it differently and made better decisions. It felt as if my thoughts were from a different part of my personality, and talking to me like a separate person. Sometimes it scared me when I realised how long I'd been standing there, staring into space and into my past, and maybe my future. I shook myself back into the present and got on with cleaning or cooking, or went to play with the kids to get my mind back to reality.

I know now that it was because I was depressed, and taking myself off somewhere else, at least in my mind, was my way of coping with it. I stayed strong for my children and my sanity, refused to let life beat me, and carried on.

A surprising thing is that I never confided in my parents about how desperately unhappy I was most of the time. Maybe I simply didn't want to burden the people I loved and respected most with my problems, or disappoint them with the knowledge that their daughter had made such a mess of her life.

Chapter Forty Six

Craig starts school

Although Mark and I hardly ever socialised, when we did he always told me I was the best looking woman in the room, and the best thing since sliced bread when it came to motherhood and being a wife. That was up to the point that some little thing upset him, which it invariably did, and then I was a fat, ugly useless bitch. After that came the prolonged sulk during which he always said that I didn't love him - and he was probably right. But he was the father of my sons, and a good father. He loved them dearly and I didn't feel that I could take his children away from him. I know I wasn't the best wife on the planet by any means, but I tried hard to be a good mother, and therefore to cope with whatever I needed to.

I was heavily pregnant again with another baby and did get very tired. I was hoping it would be a girl this time, and Mam said maybe it was because I was 'carrying differently'. To me it felt just like my previous two pregnancies but as it was only 18 months after Darren's birth, I thought it would be so nice if it was a girl, so they could have a similar relationship to me and my elder brothers. We were always good pals and still are to this day.

I never had any problems carrying my babies; one nurse joked that I was quite boring as nothing ever changed from week to week, which was a good thing I suppose. It had been a nice, warm summer with lots of sunny days. Craig would be five in October, so we were busy getting him ready to start school at the start of term: 6th September 1978, and our little lad looked all grown up ready for his first day. He seemed to have shot up so fast, especially after his younger brother came along. Mark was at work on the big day, so I got Darren dressed and we walked down to the school. Craig gripped my hand tightly as we met his teacher. He'd never been to nursery or pre-school as there weren't any around in our area, and he was understandably nervous. There was in fact a small, private nursery not too far away but we couldn't afford the fees. I looked down at his frightened face and said, 'It'll be okay, darling. Mammy will come back for you later.'

He looked up at me but did not smile, and I felt his little hand grip mine even tighter as we walked over to his allotted desk, where I was shown his name tag and a little drawer to put his books in. The teacher said, 'He'll be alright, Mrs Murdock. You can leave him with us.'

But as I let go of his hand and turned to leave, he cried out, 'Mammy, mammy.'

I hesitated but the teacher practically pushed me out of the door saying, 'He'll be fine, don't worry, they soon get used to it.'

She went back in but left the door slightly open and I could hear her saying, 'Come on Craig, everything's alright.'

My heart was breaking having to leave my little boy in there crying, but I remembered my mother saying that when she left me for the first time it was awful, but I was fine when she came to collect me after school. A friend, Elizabeth came by after bringing her little boy, John David in to start his second year. She stopped to chat and asked, 'How does he like his first day so far?'

'Not a lot,' I answered tearfully. 'He cried when I left him with the teacher.'

'They do,' she smiled. 'He'll be okay but it breaks your heart to leave them doesn't it?'

I nodded and sniffled.

'He'll be fine. Just wait until you come back for him. He'll be loving it by then, just you wait and see.'

I'd known Elizabeth since her eldest boy, Steven was born. Her daughter, Danielle was a bit younger than Darren. She eventually dragged me away from the school and invited me to her house for coffee. She was married to John, who'd lived across the road from my parents, so I actually met her years before but we became good friends from that first day at school.

After coffee and a long chat I called in to Mam's, where I stayed for lunch before going back to school to collect Craig. She and Elizabeth were right – he loved school and couldn't wait to go again the following day! We caught the school bus to Mirehouse shops and from there walked home, and that became our routine for years to come.

Chapter Forty Seven

Another member of the family

It felt like I'd been pregnant forever but at least it was only days now until the predicted date, which was 11th November. Craig had settled in well at school and was happy to go on the bus by himself. I walked him down to the stop and waited until he was safely on board. On the homeward journey he was dropped off just along the road, not far from our house, and I would meet him there. Sometimes I was a little late as Darren had a nap every afternoon and could be a bit grumpy when he woke up, so I'd hurry along but Craig was often already running to meet me. He didn't have any roads to cross so was safe, and it only took him a few minutes. I knew though that once I had the new baby, it would be even harder coping with daily routines.

On Friday 10th November, Craig had just arrived home from school when my parents called in to see us on their way back from town.

'Hello everybody,' Mam called as she came in through the back door.

'Hi Nana,' Craig said, already sitting in front of the television.

I was feeling agitated, anticipating that this new baby was going to be late like the others, and dreading the coming trauma. Mark had been off work all day and I heard him say, 'She's been like this all day.'

'Well maybe she's getting herself ready to have the baby?' Mam replied.

'Just talk about me as if I'm not here, why don't you?' I said angrily.

They all went quiet and I stormed into the kitchen for a drink.

'Well love, we're off home now,' Mam called through. 'We just popped in to see if you were alright.'

'Okay Mam, sorry I'm so grumpy.'

She just smiled and shook her head. 'Mark, let us know when she goes into hospital?'

He nodded.

'I don't think this baby wants to come, as usual,' I said as I waved them goodbye.

'It's not your date until tomorrow though, so the baby could still be on time.'

'Mm, maybe,' I smiled. 'See you both soon.'

That night Mark got the boys ready for bed and soon after they went up, so did we. We often went to bed quite early, as Darren woke up every morning about 6am so we were always tired, but at least he was always in bed by 6pm so we couldn't complain.

I tossed and turned in discomfort for hours, but must have fallen asleep eventually as I woke up needing the toilet. I noticed some blood in my underwear and still felt very uncomfortable. Mark was asleep so I nudged him and said, 'I think the baby's coming. Maybe you should go call the ambulance?'

Right away, he got out of bed and quickly dressed. One of our neighbours had given us a house key so we could use their phone to call an ambulance. When he came back I was already downstairs, lying on the latest sofa Mary had given us with a set of chairs, and was in considerable pain. He said, 'If you're going have the baby Ann, get down on the floor.'

I presumed he meant so I wouldn't make a mess on the new sofa, and laughed. He could be funny at times. The ambulance arrived quickly and as I was climbing into it Mark said, 'Let me know when you've had the baby?'

'Phone the hospital in the morning,' I called to him. 'It might not be for hours yet.'

'Come on love,' the medic said, giving me his hand to get into the ambulance.

I was quite proud that I'd managed to walk from the house unaided, but didn't want to hold things up. The medics were laughing and joking with me and it only took a few minutes to reach the hospital. As we pulled up outside the maternity ward, I felt a very strong contraction and winced in pain.

'Are you okay, love?' one of the medics asked.

'Yes I think so but please get me inside quickly. I don't want to have my baby in the parking area!'

They laughed again and wheeled me straight through into the lift, and as it came to a halt at the top I got another strong contraction. Again they asked if I was alright and I replied, 'Yes I'm okay, but I can't say for how long so get me outta this lift!'

They whizzed me to the ward where a nurse quickly examined me, and then it was all action!

'Get into that wheelchair quickly Mrs Murdock, you're going to have this baby any minute,' she said, rushing me around to the delivery room after I eased into it.

It was like a comedy film with people bumping into each other in their haste to carry out their allotted duties.

'Are you still alright?' the nurse asked with panic in her voice.

'Yes, are you?'

'We have to be quick. Can you get yourself up on the bed?'

'Yes thank you, I think I can manage,' I answered her bravely but as I positioned myself and lifted a leg, my water broke and it sounded like glass shattering onto the tiled floor.

The young nurse had left to get help but turned back at the sound of splashing water. 'Oh my God,' she cried and came running back.

I managed to flop down onto the bed and knew the baby was coming right there and then. The nurse's hands flew in all directions as she re-positioned me, and within minutes the baby was born. I don't know who was the most shocked: the nurse, the baby or me! It was one o'clock in the morning when I left home and I gave birth precisely fifteen minutes later, to Wayne David Murdock, weighing 9lbs 6.5oz. I was relieved that it was over so quickly and started to relax for the first time in days.

I knew Mark would be fast asleep but would want to know that we now had another baby boy, but decided to let him sleep as he had to work that day. Baby Wayne looked bewildered, probably wondering what had just happened to him. He had a little red blemish above his eye, which I was told later was a birthmark, but apart from that he was absolutely perfect. It was the quickest and easiest birth of the three, but the after-pains kept me awake most of the night. At one point I thought Wayne must be a twin, as I was convinced there was another baby inside me. My body was in shock and I felt ill, but was reassured to know that Wayne was fine and healthy.

A different nurse popped her head around my curtain later and said, 'Mrs Murdock, your husband has been on the phone to ask if you were alright, and if the baby was here yet.'

'Did you tell him?'

'Oh yes. I told him the baby was born five minutes after you arrived,' she smiled.

'What did he say?'

'He was very pleased. I told him you were both well and that he had a baby son.'

I smiled and said, 'Thank you.'

Mark, his mother, my mother, Craig and Darren all came to visit later that day. After looking at tiny Wayne, Darren looked like he'd grown so big overnight. Bless him, I thought. He's just a baby himself and Craig was only five. I was going to have my hands full alright, that was for sure with a five year-old and two babies in nappies. So I was glad of the break in hospital, and realised now why those women weren't in any rush to leave when I was in having Craig, five long years ago.

I became friends with a lovely girl also called Ann, whose little girl was a couple of days older than Wayne. Unfortunately Ann snored all night, and the baby cried for an hour or two before falling asleep exhausted. When Ann woke the next morning she said, 'Hello how are you?'

'I'm fine thanks,' I replied. 'And you?'

'Oh, fine. I had a really good sleep. What time is it?'

I looked at my watch. 'It's six thirty.'

She smiled. 'Haven't I got such a good baby? She slept all night without a murmur.'

I smiled and said, 'Well, she did cry a little, but then gave up and went to sleep.'

We both laughed and remained friends throughout our time in hospital. Mine soon came to an end when Mark's mother came to take me home. Mark stayed home with the boys and was apparently struggling, but at least they were excited to see me and the new family addition. On medical advice I decided to breast-feed Wayne, and felt like I never got a minute to even think of anything not related to childcare or housekeeping. We managed though and I consoled myself with the knowledge that Christmas, which I still loved and looked forward to, was only a few weeks off. We'd already bought most of the presents for the boys, and now added a few more for Wayne. We left it too late to get a turkey, so bought a capon which was very nice, instead.

Craig got a bike that year and Darren a little three wheeler, and we'd all been up for hours when my parents arrived. We had a quick cuppa together before Mam said, 'We'll go now love, we've promised to see your brother.'

I felt a bit deflated but thought they probably needed to escape the chaos of my house, and it turned out to be the worst Christmas ever. Mark did help me to prepare dinner, but Wayne was crying so I sat and fed him at the same time as trying to eat my own meal with the family, and whilst it was still hot. It felt like I was just going through the motions and not really involved or enjoying the day; certainly nowhere near as much as I'd hoped to.

Thankfully Wayne was a good, relatively easy baby to look after, but my workload increased and with it, the resultant traumas. A little relief came after doing the constant mountain of laundry one day, when I was drawing close to the end of my tether: We had a twin-tub, top-load washer and there was laundry spread all over the kitchen floor in various stages of the process, early on Sunday morning. The boys were all up and dressed and I'd already cleaned through the house, with some help from Mark. I was onto my third load of washing when the crazy machine decided to up and dance all around the kitchen! Built up tension gripped me and for a moment I broke down - standing in the middle of the kitchen I'd once loved so much, crying my eyes out and whimpering that I couldn't cope any longer. Mark came through and said, 'What's wrong?'

I pointed at the washer which was throbbing in the corner, like a boxer resting in between rounds. He switched it off and gave it a quick looking over, decided it was a goner and said, 'Don't worry Ann, I'll buy you a new one.'

True to his word, he did. We got a new automatic and my daily chores got significantly easier. Darren would sit in the kitchen and watch it whirring around for hours. It did amaze me too, I have to say!

The boys in our garden

The boys on Allonby Beach

Our holiday with Mark's parents

Darren (right) and Wayne

At Mark's brother's wedding

258

Chapter Forty Eight

Another health scare

I'm tempted to say that for the next few years things were alright, but that wouldn't be completely true. With three children aged five and under though, I didn't have much time to complain. My sister-in-law, Brenda, continued to be a much-needed friend, and often kept me going when I felt like throwing in the towel. We enjoyed some good times together and were always laughing about something or other, even if my laughter was a bit hollow. I still went to my mother's most days with the two little ones, and Mark and I still had arguments, like most couples do I suppose?

Wayne was four months old when I got my job back at the bingo hall, and they allowed me the same evening off. Mam looked after the boys on Thursdays when Mark was at work, and Saturday afternoon when he played football. She usually brought them to meet me after work and we all went to pick Craig up from school. Mark came home about 5pm, and I got the boys ready for bed before leaving for work myself. We were like polite strangers most of the time; too rushed or too tired to argue or even discuss anything, which if I'm honest is the lifestyle I preferred at the time. It kept the situation between us calm and allowed me to daydream about another life without being criticised or ridiculed.

Mark had a strange way of driving me crazy with his jokes whenever we tried to talk seriously, or he would lapse into a sulk for days on end so I never actually told him how I really felt. I also didn't want to hurt him with the truth though maybe I should have. Instead I just switched off and escaped to my own thoughts and fantasies. For the sake of the kids I never wanted to rock the family boat, so the less time Mark and I spent together was good for me and for the family as a whole. I knew that my marriage was in desperate trouble but honestly did not know how to fix it, or even if I wanted to.

Bingo finished around 9.15pm and I caught the first bus home, and was usually in bed shortly afterwards. One Thursday night though with the boys all asleep upstairs, Mark and I were watching television when I stopped dreaming and said, 'Mark, should we decorate the kitchen?'

The kitchen really needed sorting out and although I usually did all the decorating, I'd been feeling tired for weeks and thought it would be nice if we could do it together. I wouldn't normally ask Mark to help and didn't mind doing the wall-papering anyway, but the walls needed the old paper scraping off first, and that was the awful bit for me. He was a good grafter and I imagined us both working away together, and because we'd be busy and focused on what we were doing, might be able to talk about the things we needed to without him getting into a temper.

'Yes, we can do that now we have a bit more spare cash, with you working again,' he replied.

We went to town and chose some paper I was happy with, and I couldn't wait to get cracking. As I'd hoped, working together went really well and we had all the old paper off much faster than I could have on my own. The following day I did all the painting and then started preparing for papering. We'd been chatting whilst scraping the walls and after Mark finished his tea that day I said, 'Mark, will you mix the paste for me?'

'Okay, no problem,' he answered, and away we went.

I had the record-player on, Wayne was in his pram and Craig and Darren were in the living room. I was singing away to the music when suddenly Craig came through to the kitchen and said, 'Mammy, Darren is doing funny things.'

I jumped down from the chair I was standing on to reach the top of the wall, and Mark and I ran through to the living room. Darren's eyes were rolling back into his head and there was white froth coming from his mouth.

'I'll go and phone for an ambulance,' I shouted, heading for the door.

We still didn't have a phone, and there was no answer at any of the doors I knocked on as I ran back and forth across the street like a lunatic. I came to the last house and hammered frantically on the front window. Nothing happened and I was starting to panic, when a face appeared and said, 'Hello?'

I hardly knew the Hughes family but blurted to Mr Hughes, 'Can I use your telephone please? My son's having a fit.'

He quickly opened the door and said, 'Yes of course, come on in.'

I rang 999 and spoke at a hundred miles an hour to the call handler, whilst nodding and smiling my gratitude to Mr & Mrs Hughes, who stood behind me wringing their hands with worried expressions.

'Thank you,' I gasped. 'I must go and see if he's alright. Thank you again.'

The ambulance arrived very quickly and the medic rushed in. He checked Darren's pulse whilst looking at me and said, 'You look hotter than the lad does, are you okay?'

'Yes, I've been sprinting up and down the road looking for a damn telephone,' I answered.

He was wrong though, Darren had a temperature of 40.3 and we were very frightened for him. He was rushed to hospital where they stripped all his clothes off and pointed an electric fan at him. The windows were pushed wide open and I was soon freezing, and poor Darren said, 'Mammy, I'm cold.'

'No you're not darling, you're very hot and we have to cool you down,' I told him.

'No Mammy, I'm cold,' he repeated, laying there in this little cot, shivering.

My poor little boy, I thought, how can I explain this to a two year-old? We both continued to freeze and I remembered Mark was still at home with all the decorating mess, not knowing what was happening. I eventually got word to him and we were in hospital for three days. Darren had an ear and throat infection which caused his very high temperature. I had to leave him to go to work, as it was far too short notice to give and I didn't want to leave them in the lurch, but came back straight afterwards and stayed overnight with him.

Mark looked after Craig and Wayne and sorted the mess out at home. We seriously had our differences but he was always very concerned when any of the children were ill. Eventually Darren was well enough to go home but every time he got sick after that, which was quite often, we were immediately worried. Sometimes I over-reacted to minor symptoms and called the doctor, but when he checked him over, Darren was fine. That didn't stop me though because I refused to take any risks with my son's health, and called so many times that as soon as I stated my name, the receptionist would quote my address!

Other than that we were soon back in our routine and every day I got the boys ready, took Craig to catch his bus, chatted with the other mums for a few minutes and then walked back home or to visit my parents. I always had tea on the table for Mark coming in, and then got the boys ready for bed before going to work myself. I caught the 6.30pm bus which got me there just in time.

I still liked working at the bingo hall and loved chatting with the other women. I had my friends at work, my sister-in-law Brenda, my best friend Elizabeth and Mum, and my three boys who made life worthwhile and rewarding. Mark and I did have some enjoyable times I must admit. He could be very funny when in the mood, especially at family get-togethers where he was always the one that made everybody else laugh. He loved his boys and I believe he really did love me, too. We were still only in our early twenties and had been married for five years.

Chapter Forty Nine

A touchy subject

After a period of relative tranquillity we started going out socialising again, with Mark's football pals and their wives. One night I was sitting with the other girls and the men were up and down to the bar, and discussing football tactics. One of the women, Susan said, 'Should we have a bit of fun with the lads?'

'Yes, go on,' one of the other girls laughed.

'How do you mean?' I asked, hoping she wouldn't start on Mark.

She looked at me and said, 'Listen,' before shouting out, 'Look at Mark's hair.'

'Oh no,' I whispered to myself, as I saw Mark's face and realised he'd heard her.

I smiled at him but he turned away and my heart sank, knowing there would be some form of retribution. Mark's hair started to recede when he was twenty one, and he was really self-conscious about it. I knew that was the end of Susan's stupid game and sat there motionless, wishing she hadn't picked on Mark and particularly not his hair. He had a good sense of humour and anything else would have been fine, probably. I'd told him before that male-pattern baldness was caused by high levels of testosterone, and pointed out that we don't see many bald women and children about do we? Just grown up men so why was he so bothered and touchy about it? He could see the logic but still had problems accepting the fact of his changing appearance. We'd been having a lovely night but now I suspected it was over.

I stayed very quiet and didn't do anything that Mark could interpret as laughing at him, even though everyone other than me seemed to be having fun. Even Mark was chatting and joking with Colin and some other lads at the bar, but I noticed the high speed at which he was knocking the lagers back. Susan realised what she'd done and said, 'I'm sorry, Ann.'

'It's done now, Susan,' I replied quietly. 'Anything other than his hair would've been fine. He's very touchy about it.'

I watched the clock all night and also Mark from the corner of my eye, and wished the night was over so I could disappear into a dark hole somewhere, only to re-emerge into a different, much brighter world. I was distracted for a moment before realising that Mark *had* actually disappeared, though I couldn't see any gaping holes nearby. Colin came over with another of Mark's mates, Joe, and asked, 'Where's Mark, Ann?'

'Oh,' I flustered, ashamed that my husband had probably left me to make my own way home. 'I think he might have gone outside for some air.'

Luckily everybody was starting to leave, and I followed with my head down. Outside it was a warm summer's night and Colin turned to me to say, 'He's not here Ann, he must've forgotten about you.'

Everyone laughed except me, and Colin said, 'Come on, we'll walk you home, it's a nice night for a stroll.'

They all chatted along the way, though Susan was unusually quiet, and when we got to the end of my street I said, 'Goodnight everyone.'

Joe said, 'I'll come with you, Ann.'

'It's okay,' I replied. 'I'll be alright. It's only five minutes from here.'

Colin said, 'I'll come as well.'

I was going to speak but Joe interrupted, 'It's okay Colin, I'll take her home and make sure Mark got back alright.'

Colin's girlfriend, Elaine said, 'Go with them, Colin,' probably because she knew Joe was a bit of ladies' man, and took every opportunity to flirt with any female that stood still long enough.

The two men kept arguing amongst themselves so I walked off along the road, but both of them followed. When I got inside the house Mark was fast asleep in bed and I could hear him snoring. I turned to Colin and Joe and said, 'Mark's upstairs. He's asleep so I'm fine, you can go now.'

Joe said, 'I'm staying here in case he wakes up.'

I was a little shocked at that, thinking that although they were his friends, maybe they knew about his temper and were worried about me?

Then Colin said to Joe, 'If you're staying, I'm staying,' and they started bickering again!

Eventually I quietened them down and convinced them both that I was fine, and they should go home. They left and I could hear them still muttering away at each other all along the street.

Next morning Mark was eerily quiet so I said, 'Mark, I had nothing to do with what happened last night. It was Susan and the others.'

He didn't say anything and I asked, 'Why did you leave me on my own like that?'

'I knew you'd be okay with Elaine and Colin there,' he yawned with disinterest.

'Yes, I was. Colin and Joe came in to check you were home alright, and Joe wanted to stay.'

'What?' he asked, suddenly interested. 'Why did he want to stay?'

'Well, you know Joe. You tell me why he wanted to stay?'

He looked straight at me with tight lips and I could see his anger rising.

'You know it was only a joke, don't you?' I asked in an attempt to pacify him. 'They were going to say something daft about all of you.'

'Well, you should've told them not to say anything about my hair.'

'I didn't know what they were going to say. Susan just blurted it out like she does.'

By now the boys were all awake so we quietened down and carried on with the day's routines, and as usual, all was quickly forgotten.

Chapter Fifty

Journeys and jealousies

Mark was visiting his parents one afternoon. I was sitting in our living room, knitting away my boredom, Wayne was asleep and Darren was playing in the front garden. Craig had gone to play with his friend Austin, who lived just down the road. I heard Darren calling, 'Hello Daddy,' so knew Mark was back home.

I put down my needles and yarn and as soon as he came into the living room he said, 'Ann, my mam wants to know if we'd like to go on holiday with them?'

'Oh, that's nice of her,' I replied. 'Where are they going? And when?'

'Mam's trying to book for July, and they're hoping to go to Pontins holiday camp at Morecambe.'

'Oh I've been there and it's really nice. We went when Brian was very young.'

'Oh, right.'

'Yeah, they're great holidays for kids. Plenty for them to do,' I told him. 'And there's always good access for wheelchairs, for your dad.'

'Right, that'll be good.'

'So it would be a nice change and I'm sure the boys will be excited about going.'

'Mm, okay. What's for tea today, Ann? I'm starving.'

'I've made meat and potato pie. It's my favourite and the kids like it too.'

'Yes, they do, and I like your meat and potato pie as well,' he smiled.

The boys were a bit fussy about food, like me, but Mark would eat just about anything so was easy to feed. He seemed unusually happy this particular day, but that was probably because he was off work. I was the opposite in that I liked being at work, and when he and I were apart I knew that nothing much could go wrong, hopefully.

'Can you find out the date they're actually going?' I asked him. 'I'll have to ask for time off from work.'

It was half-term so the boys and Mark were all off for a week, which meant less running around for me taking the kids to school and nursery. Mark and I tried not to have the same weeks off, so we could split looking after the boys more easily through the holidays, but he hadn't much option when the school where he worked close down for the duration.

'Mam said she'd ring you to discuss arrangements before she booked.'

We had a telephone installed after the health scare with Darren, and were all sitting at the table eating when it rang.

I picked it up and said, 'Hello.'

'Hi Ann, it's Mary. Did Mark ask you about the holiday?'

'Yes he did and it sounds great. The boys are so excited. Have you a date in mind?'

'Yes, I thought the first week of the summer holidays. Is that alright for you?'

'Yes, that'll be fine. Just let us know when you get it confirmed?'

The house was full of happiness and excitement at the thought of an organised holiday, which was nice and I wished the positive atmosphere could last forever. Mark was teasing the boys, saying he was going to throw them in the swimming pool on holiday, and they were giggling. Why can't life always be like this? I thought to myself, and who was it that caused all the unhappiness? We had three wonderful children, a nice house and were all fit and healthy, but we didn't have much money and maybe that was part of the problem? Another factor was Mark's unreasonable possessiveness: I hardly ever went out with friends and never on my own, but problems still arose.

If I went into town even with the boys, Mark would always ask what time we'd be back, and it wasn't just because he wanted his tea on time. He made me agree to times that I couldn't stick to, even though I tried, but I'd inevitably bump into someone I knew and we'd start chatting. I loved talking to friends because Mark and I almost never discussed anything of interest. When I came home I always faced an interrogation anyway, whether I was late or not. These occasions really upset me as he would say things like, 'Who have you been out to meet?' Or worse, 'Who've you been fucking?'

He seemed to think I had men falling at my feet as soon as I stepped out the door, and even if I did consider fucking any of them, what did he think I'd do with the boys while I was at it? Maybe I'd just park them in the street while I popped down the nearest alley with some random bloke? I couldn't believe he could think such awful things like that about me, and if he did, how could he possibly love me as he said? I often felt like answering his ridiculous questions with, 'Yeah, I wish.'

Maybe I should have slapped him across the face like those brave women in American movies did, or maybe he should have slapped me; it would've been less painful than the mental torture he kept subjecting me to. Sticks and stones can break your bones but believe me, words can seriously hurt you, and take far longer to heal.

'Mammy,' I suddenly heard Darren saying. 'I'm tired.'

I'd been standing in the kitchen daydreaming again, and had no idea for how long. Darren was always tired early as he was awake every morning before six. We never needed an alarm clock! I quickly got a grip of myself, and changed him and Wayne ready for bed. I then put on my work overall before making the boys' supper. After they ate I took Darren and Wayne upstairs, kissed them both and told them I loved them. 'See you in the morning,' I whispered. 'Be good boys for Daddy.'

I cleaned my teeth and brushed my hair, went downstairs and put on my coat after kissing Craig goodnight.

'See you later Mark, I'm off to work now,' I called through from the hall.

No reply.

When I came home the house was quiet, the boys were all in bed and Mark was watching television. 'I've arranged my holidays for the week in Morecambe, Mark,' I told him.

'Great, my mam rang earlier and it's all booked.'

I was genuinely looking forward to the holiday, not least because there were never any real problems between Mark and I when his parents were present.

The schools opened again and things went along quite calmly, and soon the Easter holidays were upon us. I'd bought little holiday outfits for the boys and liked to dress the two youngest the same. The house was like a children's shop with all the new clothes and Easter eggs lying around! Mark and I both liked chocolate a little too much and soon cleared up whatever Wayne left. He never ate much chocolate. Wish I didn't.

Chapter Fifty One

Family holiday 1981

Easter was over in a flash and we all turned our attention excitedly, to the forthcoming holiday in July. Mark and I were back to our minimal-contact lifestyle and the days and weeks passed quickly and uneventfully. When the day finally arrived we were all packed and ready early in the morning. Mark brought his mother's car around and we loaded up our suit cases. As we set off Mark started singing:

'We're off, we're off, were off in a motor car,

Fifty cops are after us but they don't know where we are!'

The boys were howling with laughter and singing along, and we were like a perfect family off on our travels. Morecambe is further down the west coast in Lancashire, between Lancaster and the village of Heysham, where another nuclear installation was being built. We laughed and joked all the way and the journey passed quickly, and we soon arrived to the hustle and bustle of the holiday camp.

'It hasn't changed much, I still recognise it,' I said to Mark, remembering my trip there many years ago.

We waited in line for our chalet keys and then trooped off to find our home for the next week. I wheeled Wayne in his pushchair and Mark pushed his dad's wheelchair. There were bluecoats everywhere and all stopped to say hello to the boys, the sun was shining and I knew we were going to enjoy the holiday. It went well from the start, we really did have a lovely time and every day went without a hitch. Mark and the boys had a great time, so did Mark's parents, and so did I.

The following Saturday morning we all piled back into the car and set off back up the M6 to Junction 36, just east of Milnthorpe, then across the north coast of Morecambe Bay onto the A595 which took us home to Whitehaven. There were seven of us packed into that little vehicle, which would be illegal today if not then! We got home safely though and were soon back to our everyday lives.

All through the rest of the holidays I got things ready for Darren and Craig going back to school. Wayne was still too young and wouldn't even go to nursery until the following September. Craig was starting junior school and Darren the reception class, which is the first year of infants' school. I had enjoyed our holiday but was pleased to be back home. I'd missed everyone and especially my mother, so took the boys to see her.

Mam loved it when the kids came to visit and usually had a house-full of people. Margaret and her girls were often there as well me and mine. She taught all the kids how to play card games and gave them pennies to gamble with, but insisted they went to the corner shop to buy sweets and then play for them instead of the money. She declared, 'It's just not as much fun, playing for nothing!'

Dad shook his head and said, 'You realise you're teaching them how to gamble, Jessie?'

Mam just laughed and insisted it kept the kids occupied, but I think I'm a bit more like Dad - I didn't like to lose my hard-earned cash so wouldn't gamble it away on anything. A bird in the hand is worth two in the bush, was always my motto, even though I could never see what value a little bird might be? Mam was quite lucky and often won something at bingo. I had no luck at bingo, cards or in my personal life, I decided a long time ago. Mam said I must be lucky in love, because I wasn't in anything else. That's a laugh, I thought - love's exactly where I was most unlucky.

Soon the two eldest boys were back at school and Mark back at his job. He still worked as a caretaker and it never bothered me when he was off right through the school holidays. The long breaks were obviously a major plus-point to Mark, but I hated being off. Maybe one thing I was lucky at was having jobs that I liked? I found working directly with customers at the bingo-hall interesting, especially when I was calling the numbers out, and soon learned all about the two fat ladies and legs eleven etc. I made up a few of my own but won't go into that now!

Christmas was approaching fast again and was still the best time of year for me, except for one or two disasters. I loved even preparing for Christmas; hanging the decorations, setting up the tree and collecting gifts for loved ones, and most of all – seeing the joy on my sons' faces. This year the boys were all old enough to appreciate what was going on, so I knew it would be extra special. Christmas day was lovely and there were more toys in our living room than Woolworth's toy department! That might be a slight exaggeration I suppose, but we couldn't actually walk across the carpet for colourful, plastic items, and had to creep around the edges! We always made sure the boys had plenty of presents even if it meant we had to do without certain things, but we loved their excited happiness on Christmas Day and any small sacrifices were well worth it. When they were happy – we were happy, at least for a while.

The Boxing Day get-together was at our house again this year, which pleased the boys as they didn't have to leave their new toys behind to go visiting. Mark and I prepared a big spread of food and while I cleaned downstairs, Mark cleaned upstairs. He did a good job too and really was a great help. All the men: Colin, Mark, young Bill, Terry and Billy senior, went down to the pub while Mary, Brenda, Sylvia and me, sat down to chat over coffee and kids. Mark obviously enjoyed himself and was in a good mood when they all came back, and I don't think it was just down to the alcohol!

We all ate around the dining-table, apart from the kids who stayed amongst the sea of toys, and afterwards Brenda said, 'Come on Ann, we'll wash the dishes then we can all play Give-us-a-clue?'

We always had a great laugh playing this game and even the kids enjoyed it. We laughed until it hurt and Mark kept everybody's drinks topped well up, except his mother's as she was driving, and the day flew past. In the afternoon I realised that Mark had disappeared, and went upstairs to look for him. I guessed he'd had too much to drink because he was flat out asleep on the boys' bunk bed, and was cuddling the toy monkey that Darren got for Christmas the previous year. The others followed me up and laughed when they saw him lying there. Somebody produced a polaroid camera and took a picture of him cuddling the monkey, and even the kids thought it was hilarious. I didn't though. I knew Mark wouldn't like it and that as far as he was concerned, it would be my fault even though I didn't ask them up or take the photograph.

He woke with a start and without a smile, and was immediately sulky as everyone stood around laughing. They soon stopped though, the general mood dipped and everyone left. I started the big clean-up and Mark didn't speak for the rest of the night. We were all soon in bed and I consoled myself that tomorrow was another day. Mark usually forgot his anger quite soon and would apologise for being sulky, and we would try to laugh about it. But each new wound that he inflicted upon us joined an existing scar, and it was becoming harder to forget the pain. I could always forgive as it was the quickest way of moving on, but I could never forget, however much I tried. It seemed to me that Mark didn't actually like us to be happy and carefree, and normal, but maybe that was only my imagination?

Chapter Fifty Two

1982 and a new job on the horizon

The house always seemed quiet and sad to me after Christmas, in contrast to the hustle and bustle throughout the festive period. First day back at school was always hectic before setting off in the morning. After getting the boys ready and seeing Mark off to work, I put the breakfast dishes in the sink and left them there to soak, and we all buttoned our coats up tight as it was a very fresh, January morning.

The sun was still low in the east, casting long shadows across the street outside, but I knew it was cold as I'd been out in my slippers to put last night's rubbish in the bin. At least the ground was dry and not icy or frosty. I wasn't good with slippery conditions underfoot and often felt like an old woman on winter mornings, tottering around after a night on the drink! Mark said it was because I was unbalanced! Maybe he was right, in both senses. I'm still the same in the cold season but I wear more appropriate footwear these days.

I waved goodbye to Craig and Darren and said to Wayne, 'Well son, what should we, do today?'

He smiled and waved a plastic penguin at me.

'Should we go to see Nana and Grandad after we've cleaned the house?'

I interpreted another smile as a positive response, whizzed around the house with the vacuum-cleaner and then we were on our way, waving to Brenda as we passed her lounge window. Wayne held my hand and I chatted to him about all the things around us. He was a shy little lad and didn't answer much, but I knew he understood most of what I said. I heard an unfamiliar voice in my parents' house as we entered the front door and went into the living room, where Mam was talking to a friend she introduced as Mrs Johnstone.

'Hello, Ann and Wayne,' she said.

'Hi.'

'Happy New Year,' she added. 'Did you have a good Christmas?'

'Yes thank you Mrs Johnstone, but it's all over again now for another year.'

'Your mother told me about your situation with the children and work, and I just came around to tell her that there's a job going at the hospital that you might be interested in?'

'Oh yes, what is it?'

'It's an evening domestic. Cleaning and such, like your mum did when she worked there.'

'What do you think, Ann? I thought the hours might suit you better?' Mam asked.

'Mm, yes they might if they don't involve any weekends?'

'They don't. The money's quite good and there're no weekends or bank holidays either.'

'Oh good, that's even better.'

279

'The hours are four in the afternoon 'til eight at night,' Mrs Johnstone added.

'That sounds great. Yes I am interested. No more weekends and Mam, you could have your Saturdays back!'

We all laughed and suddenly there was a tap on the lounge door.

'Hello Jessie,' Mabel said with a smile as she pushed it open and came in.

'Hi Mabel,' I said.

'Oh, hello everybody, and hello Wayne, what did Santa bring you then?'

Wayne looked at me and I said, 'Far too much, Mabel.'

We all laughed again.

'Aren't we all guilty of spoiling our children,' said Mrs Johnstone.

There was always an easy-going, friendly atmosphere in my parents' house, which I missed so much at home. We all chatted away over coffee as Wayne played with the toys he kept there, and we were still chattering at lunchtime!

'I'll make us a sandwich,' Mam said.

'Okay,' I replied. 'But afterwards I have to go see Elizabeth before I pick the boys up from school.'

'Yes, I know, you just come round here to be fed,' she laughed.

We all knew she was only teasing. Mam had a lot of friends and was never lonely when Dad was out at work. There was always someone popping in, or she was out visiting or shopping. Elizabeth didn't live far away and I was soon knocking on her door. She was a lovely person and had an open house like my mother. I trusted her and could tell her anything, and she was like a true sister to me as Evelyn had been. My actual sister, Dorothy, was sevens year older so we never had a real sister-to-sister relationship, and she was married when I was only thirteen so I never saw much of her after that.

After a chat during which I told her about my continuing unhappiness at home, but also about the possibility of a new job, it was time to collect the boys. Elizabeth was always very sympathetic but like me, couldn't see a viable way out that was fair to all concerned. She lived right opposite the school which was very handy and Danielle, her daughter, was in the same nursery class as Darren. We continued discussing my problems and walked over together, and stood waiting for the final bell to ring as the school buses queued up at the roadside.

'Bye, Elizabeth,' I said as the kids streamed out. 'Might see you tomorrow and maybe we'll figure out a solution soon?'

'Bye,' she called back, smiling in commiseration.

Darren and Wayne were good pals and sat chatting away on the bus home. We got off at the shops just down the road from our house, waited for Craig's bus to arrive and then all walked home together. Lee was in Brenda's garden when we passed and Darren asked, 'Mammy, can Lee come to play at our house?'

'He'll have to ask his mum first,' I replied.

I often had a house full of children, which could be hard work but they always had fun and at least I could keep an eye on them all. Brenda's head popped out of her door and she said, 'Hi Ann, you okay?'

'Yes, I'm fine, Brenda. Can Lee come out to play?' I smiled.

'Yes, if that's alright with you?'

'No problem.'

Lee's dad, Colin, often took all the boys out on long walks along the coast, and they always enjoyed themselves without any bickering or arguments.

Lee joined us and they played happily for an hour or so until Mark arrived home from work, and Brenda called down for Lee to go home for his tea.

'Sorry Brenda,' I apologised. 'Can't stop to chat, I have to get ready for work.'

'No problem Ann. See you tomorrow,' she replied, dragging Lee away from his playmates.

'I was at Mam's today,' I said to Mark as Brenda And Lee disappeared up the road. 'And her friend, Mrs Johnstone, said there's a domestic job going at the hospital.'

'Yeah?' he replied, more interested in what was for tea.

'Yes, so she's going to put my name forward for it. She'll give me a good reference so I have a chance of getting the job.'

'Sounds okay. What are the hours like?'

'It's Monday to Friday, 4pm 'til 8 and no bank holidays.'

'That'll be much better,' Mark said with a smile. 'You'll be home a lot earlier at night than you are now.'

'Mam says she'll come up here to watch the boys until you get home, will that be okay?'

'Yeah, that'll be far better, Ann, and I don't mind having to make tea, either.'

We did work well together at times, and Mark often helped out with the boys and household chores. Our problems kept cropping up, invariably when the green-eyed monster of jealousy made an appearance, but we could be a really good team when things were going well.

Mark washed the dishes after tea and I got the boys ready for bed. They didn't go up now until after I left for work but I always got them bathed and into their pyjamas, then after getting washed and changed myself, I left for the bus. I still enjoyed my time at work and sometimes didn't want the shift to end. At work I could be myself and not have to be careful about everything I said. I could laugh and joke and smile at whoever I liked, without being told off like a naughty child. I got on well with all my colleagues and knew I would really miss them when I left. I liked the work because I was very much a 'people-person' and becoming a hospital domestic wasn't something I'd ever dreamed about, but beggars can't be choosers as they say. So I decided to switch jobs purely because of the shorter and more convenient hours, in the hope that Mark and I could manage our lives better.

When I arrived home after my last bingo shift, Mark was still up. He had the kettle on and made us both a cup of tea, before saying, 'You had a phone call from your mother's friend, Mrs Johnstone is it?'

'Oh yes, what did she say?'

'You have to go to the hospital on Wednesday, and ask for Winnie Joyce.'

'Winnie Joyce?'

'Yeah, she's the domestics' supervisor on the evening shift.'

'Oh right, okay.'

We finished our tea and went upstairs together. We always went to bed quite early but it was only because we were tired and needed sleep. Sex wasn't on our agenda which suited me fine, and Mark seemed to be okay about it though we never actually discussed the matter.

I asked Mam to have Wayne on Wednesday, while I called up to the hospital to see Winnie Joyce. It didn't seem as though she liked me very much, and I guessed it was because I got the job on Mrs Johnstone's say-so. Mrs Johnstone was obviously senior to Winnie and definitely gave me a good reference. I told Winnie that I had to give a week's notice to the bingo hall, and she gave me a start date of the following Monday. Mam was really pleased and though I had mixed emotions, consoled myself with the thought of having more time with the kids at weekends. I handed my notice in that night but was really sad to leave, though Mark was pleased and so were the boys.

I'd never realised just how big the West Cumberland Hospital actually is, until I walked around it and realised the immense amount of cleaning required. I soon got used to the work and the routines though, and met a lot of new people. Some of my colleagues knew my mother as she'd been a domestic there years before, and I got along well with them all right from the start.

At Easter we always dressed the boys smartly to visit both sets of parents, and usually stayed for tea with Mary and Billy. There would always be a houseful of people and everybody took lots of family photographs for their collections. After that, it was time to look forward to the summer holidays again, and I wondered if there might be any more surprises in store this year, pleasant or unpleasant.

Brenda and I were always out and about with the children during the good weather, and we walked for miles along the rugged coast or through the countryside which spread around us in all directions. I still saw my parents regularly, but they didn't have to look after the boys during the holidays as Mark was off with them. In September, Lee would start infants' school and Wayne would begin nursery.

Chapter Fifty Three

Horses, hounds and hiking

I was soon beavering away in my new job at the hospital, and enjoying the company of many new friends I made there. Getting home a lot earlier afterwards was a big bonus. The boys were easier to handle now they'd experienced some school discipline, and were all growing up fast. Mark and I had now been married for nine years though as many other people, we didn't do anything to celebrate our anniversaries. Our parents and relatives sent us cards but I never even received flowers from Mark, and he didn't get anything from me. It was just another day to us. We never went out anywhere at any time unless specifically invited, and when we did we always end up arguing, so I was content to receive cards from others and to wish each other, at least verbally, a happy anniversary. We got on with the task of taking care of our children, and getting through life with as little friction as possible.

Craig and Darren were excited on the last day of school before the summer holidays. We hadn't anything special planned but either Colin or Brenda and me, would take the boys out for the country walks that they loved. Colin was the boys' own Robin Hood as he led them through the woods, making bows and arrows and searching for sheriff's men to ambush. Usually it had to be innocent ramblers as sheriff's men were in short supply.

Craig had reached the age when he preferred to go off and play with his own friends from school or the neighbourhood, but Darren and Lee were still keen. On non-walk summer days Brenda and I would finish our housework in a rush, then sit out to relax in the sunshine. Having Brenda so close was essential for me. We talked and laughed about everything. One lazy morning before work, Brenda mentioned that Colin was taking the boys out at the weekend, and I said, 'It would be nice if Mark went out with them.'

'Yes, I know,' Brenda replied. 'Colin often wonders why he doesn't go along.'

It made me ashamed that Colin took our boys out but Mark couldn't be bothered to go with them. He preferred to stay home at weekends, watching the horse-racing on television or going down to the bookies to put a few bets on. Gambling on the horses was a curse, as it drained our resources no matter how much Mark convinced himself he was winning overall, and although he was fine after a win, he came home in a terrible mood when he lost, which was often. We didn't have money to squander on the horses or anything else, so his sneaky betting caused no end of rows between us. It was also embarrassing as he would beg, borrow and still steal cash from me, to gamble with, and I came to the conclusion that he must be addicted to it. It probably started years before we got married when Mark's father regularly gave him money to put on a horse, mainly because both Billy and Mary liked to have a few bets at the weekend. It was alright for them, they could afford to.

Mark suddenly developed a new interest when his brothers, Billy junior and Terry, acquired three young trail-hounds. These are dogs which for centuries have been cross-bred from mainly fox-hounds, to have longer legs and more speed for racing. Hound-trailing is a sport which still only takes place in northwest England and some parts of Ireland, and involves the dogs following an aniseed-mix scent trail laid over open country courses of up to around 20 miles. The hounds are fed and trained like athletes, and if successful are highly prized because of the large amount of gambling which surrounds trailing.

Billy and younger brother Terry came by some puppies and launched themselves into what they obviously hoped would be a prosperous venture. Mark was immediately attracted by the racing and betting involved, and helping to train the new dogs soon became a priority for him. Walking them at high speed took up all his spare time, and he was good at it because of his football fitness. He was suddenly willing to walk every day with the dogs, but still couldn't be bothered to go anywhere with his sons. He would even walk all the way to his parents' house to collect the dogs before taking them out, and also found time to accompany his brothers to the races.

Strangely enough, though Craig wasn't keen on going out walking with Darren and Lee, he became interested in the hounds and would go off with Mark when they were both free for half a day. Unfortunately hound-trailing was something else for Mark to gamble on, but I consoled myself with the peace and quiet at home when he was out. My real worry was that Craig would get himself even further involved in gambling alongside his father, after having already being taught how to assess betting odds by him.

During the holidays I bought school uniforms for the boys' following term, including the infants' class which also insisted on dress conformity. I bought some new clothes for Wayne too, as he was starting nursery. A new era was upon us, I thought, with all the boys at school and more time to myself. Getting everybody and everything ready on the first day back at school was chaos as usual, but at least Mark sorted himself out and left for work early. The boys and me eventually had breakfast and headed for the bus stop.

'Morning, Brenda,' I called when I saw her and Lee waiting for us outside their house, and we chatted on the way down for the bus. Wayne held my hand tightly all the way; he was obviously apprehensive as Craig and Darren had been on their very first days, even though he wasn't starting nursery until the afternoon session. That meant another trip later and by the time I got back, there wasn't much time before I had to leave for work.

Wayne cried when I left him at nursery, as I knew he would, but only on the first day and was absolutely fine after that, and soon got used to the routine. It didn't work out that I had much more time to myself, after factoring in the housework and taking Wayne to Mam's for lunch before nursery. I did manage an afternoon chat with my friend, Elizabeth though, most days before collecting Darren and Wayne. After that we came home on the school bus and waited for Mam to arrive to watch the boys, so I could go to work. Life was just as hectic as before and the days passed just as quickly. If I was feeling down as I often did, I shrugged my shoulders, picked myself up and thought: it'll soon be another day, and then another week, and there'll be lots more problems so why worry?

But there'll also be some good times, I told myself. Another Christmas was just around the corner and each year it was getting better, as the boys' excitement grew with their expectations. It reminded of me when I was little and like my parents, we always tried our best to make Christmas wonderful for the children. They appreciated our efforts and this year was another success in all departments. After Christmas and New Year we were back to the miserable, cold weather of January and February, but that passed and soon - spring was in the air.

One day just after the boys were back at school after half-term and the weather was improving, Mark came home early with a scowl on his face.

'What's the matter now?' I asked with a sigh.

'I'm being made redundant.'

'Oh no,' I gasped, a hand covering my mouth.

'I'm afraid so.'

'Why?'

'The damn school-board has decided to do away with assistant caretakers.'

'Oh no,' I repeated.

'Pat's due to retire soon and I was wondering whether to apply for his job?'

Pat was the current caretaker. 'Do you think you might get it?'

'I'd have a good chance but it'd mean moving into the caretaker's bungalow at the school, so I'm on call 24/7.'

I thought about that, seriously. The bungalow was nice but we really liked where we lived, we'd settled in well, the boys had their friends and I had Brenda and Elizabeth close by. We discussed the prospect for a week or so but eventually decided that the move wasn't for us. Our decision was reinforced by the fear of what happened to us if Mark lost the caretaker's job after moving. Council houses weren't as plentiful as they used to be.

After Easter Mark's job came to an end. We were immediately short of money as we didn't have a penny in savings, but at least it was easier for my mother, because she didn't have to trail up the hill to my house every day to watch the boys - I made sure that duty transferred to Mark. At least it might stop him borrowing money to throw at the bookie, but it wasn't so good for me because Mark was now at home all day again. He wouldn't let me go out because he got bored and ratty on his own, so I couldn't visit the friends that I desperately needed to talk to, and I grew to absolutely hate him slouching around the house all day. I started wishing I could work all day and half the night and even though it was only cleaning, I found more enjoyment being at work than in my home, and dreaded finishing time.

I thought how terribly sad my life was and had been for years, and then was gripped by the fear of how unbearable it would be when the boys grew up and left home, leaving Mark and I on our own – for yet more years. If I could have provided for the boys well enough, I'd have up and left with them there and then.

After the initial black period resulting from our drastic drop in income, Mark realised that he could spend more time with the hounds, and having his absences to look forward to also lifted my spirits a little. I'd just started seeing my friend old Lynda again, after bumping into her one morning at the bus stop with Wayne. She'd moved back into the neighbourhood and invited me round to her house for coffee. Her home was expensively furnished and she still only had one child: Jonathan.

'How long have you lived here, Lynda?' I asked her.

'Only about four months but we're moving again, soon.'

'Oh, really?'

'Yeah, we only took this house until our new one's ready. We're buying one on Hillcrest.'

'Oh wow, lucky you. Is James still working away from home?'

'Yes, he's over in Norway at the moment, on the oil rigs and he only comes home every six weeks.'

'Don't you ever get lonely, Lynda?' I asked.

'No, it's great having my own time and space, I love it,' she replied with a grin. 'And he earns really good money!'

We exchanged phone numbers and she promised to give me a call when they settled into the new house.

'You and the boys could come over for a little house-warming party one day?'

'That would be nice.'

'We'll be moved in time for the summer holidays, so you could even come one day through the week.'

'Yes that would be great but I'll have to go now, Lynda. Mark'll be wondering where I am and Wayne goes to nursery soon, but please keep in touch.'

Marks face was like thunder when we finally got home and I went through to the living-room.

'Where the hell have you been?' he shouted.

Despite being nervous, I kept calm and said, 'Can you remember my friend, Lynda?'

He continued to glower at me but didn't answer.

'Well, I met her at the shops today and she invited us round for coffee. Isn't that right, Wayne?' I said, asking my infant son to corroborate our movements to my husband.

'Yeah,' Wayne replied with disinterest.

'She's invited me and the boys round on the day she moves to their new house, at Hillcrest.'

Mark turned back to the televised horse-racing.

'They're buying a brand-new house there,' I added, rubbing in the fact that James could afford a new house and his wife didn't even have to work.

I knew I was being a bit cruel and he definitely wasn't amused, but felt that I'd actually stood up to him and his stupid, possessive temper, and was surprised at how good that made me feel.

Chapter Fifty Four

More canine capers

Wayne was well settled into nursery and I missed him not being at home with me through the day. He was a good if disinterested listener and I chatted away to him all the time. He didn't contribute much to the conversations but it made me feel better than daydreaming and talking to myself, as I had for years. I actually had less unoccupied time than ever now, and seemed to be always either getting the boys ready, taking them to school or picking them up, and fitting everything else in between. Mark walked over to his parents' house every day to take the hounds out, and told me more than once when he came back, that his mother wasn't happy with the kennel that he and Terry had built for them. I didn't blame her, knowing something of Mark's carpentry skills, and wouldn't have been happy either. The dogs were very friendly with lovely, intelligent faces, but they were fed on scraps and leftovers and never washed, and the 'kennel' was never cleaned properly.

Mary complained so much and for so long that one evening when I arrived home from work, the dogs were there to greet me. They were really still puppies and Mark put them in a cupboard near the back door, which was originally the coal-house before central-heating took over the world. I decided to make a stand again and told Mark that the coal-house was nowhere near big enough for three growing dogs, and that if he intended to keep them he better get a job so he could feed them right and build proper kennels. We didn't have them long after that and after questioning him at length, I believe he found a more suitable home for them with a more able, hound-trail enthusiast. They could become quite valuable animals so I don't think any harm would come to them, and I don't think Mark was cruel enough to allow that to happen.

He still went to the trails and probably had a bet or two, but he didn't have the dogs to walk anymore. I wondered whether I'd done the best thing as he stalked around the house getting under my feet again all the time, and the boys really missed playing with the dogs. 'We love them,' they all said. 'When are they coming back?'

'They've gone to live with a man who knows how to look after them properly,' I said.

'Can't we see them ever again?'

'Maybe, and…maybe we might be able to get a little dog of our own some day.'

'Wow, honestly Mam?' said wide-eyed Craig. 'That would be brilliant!'

'Well let's see what happens and how well you all behave in the meantime.'

One morning shortly afterwards at about eleven o'clock, there was a knock at the front door and when I opened it, Terry and Billy junior were standing there with strange grins on their faces. 'What are you knocking for lads? The back door's open,' I said.

'Hiya Ann,' Billy said and then started talking to Wayne who was playing on the floor with his toys.

I stood there wondering what was going on and eventually he continued, 'Ann, we were having the craic with Mark, and he said you might like a little puppy of your own?'

'Oh, well we did discuss it a while back, why?'

'We have a marra who has a little border-collie, and it's going free to a good home.'

'Oh, right. Is it a girl or a boy?'

'Er, I'm not sure. Which would you prefer?'

'A girl if possible, if we decide to have one that is.'

I invited them in, and made a pot of tea whilst chatting and saying I had to take Wayne to nursery.

'We have to be off anyway,' Billy said, gulping his tea and burning his mouth on the hot mug.

'I didn't mean this very instant!'

'It's okay,' he said, licking his lip and nodding to Terry. 'Bye Wayne, we'll see you soon.'

'Bye Wayne,' Terry added.

I didn't think much more about the surprise visit, not wanting to rely on Mark's brothers for anything, but the very next day at exactly the same time, there was another knock at the door. I opened it to see Billy and Terry standing there again, but this time with a third visitor. They had with them a beautiful little black & white puppy, which I found absolutely adorable from the first moment.

'Is it a girl?' I asked, looking into the pup's deep brown eyes, which looked hopefully back at me.

'Ahh, no sorry Ann, it's a boy I'm afraid.'

I felt a slight pang of disappointment as Terry let go of the pup, but it looked so incredibly cute wandering into the house, sniffing everything in sight before taking a leak on the carpet. I would have thought I'd be furious about that but heard myself saying, 'Well, he's made his mark here already.'

Billy and Terry laughed and again surprisingly, so did I! The pup's little tail was wagging like a faulty windscreen-wiper as he looked to me again, and I knew there and then that he'd found himself a new home. I moved Wayne away from the dark stain on the floor, cleaned it up the best I could and got him ready for nursery. Mark came in, looked at the dog, the stain, and then me. I said, 'We'll call him Benjie.'

'Oh, he's staying then, is he?'

'He's staying, so can you watch him while I take Wayne to school?'

'Yeah, no problem.'

'And if he makes another mess on the floor you could always clean it up?'

'Yeah, maybe.'

I came straight back from nursery to make sure all was well between Benjie and Mark. Everything was fine and I was soon playing on the floor with the new addition to our family. Mark could see I was enjoying myself so said, 'I'll go and pick the boys up, Ann, seeing as you're having so much fun.'

'Thank you,' I laughed but went to collect Wayne myself. I met Brenda on the way back and told her about the puppy, and she came along to see him.

'Would you like a cuppa, Brenda?' I asked as Wayne patted the pup.

'Yeah, go on, I have time for one.'

'Mark's going to pick Darren up so he can easily get Lee at the same time?'

'Oh, would you Mark? That's great, thank you.'

Mark smiled and nodded as he pulled on his shoes, and Brenda and I sat talking over tea as he went to collect the kids.

Benjie and Wayne lay fast asleep on the freshly-cleaned carpet, and the house was so quiet and peaceful. It didn't stay that way for long though, as all too soon the boys were bustling in through the door. Mark had told them about the dog and they were very excited. Poor Benjie was initially frightened by the sudden noise but was soon running around the house, chased by all three howling boys. We laughed and laughed until Brenda said, wiping tears from her eyes, 'Ann, I'll have to go. Gary and Andrea will be home from school by now.'

'Okay Brenda,' I replied. 'And if they want to see the puppy just send them down.'

'Okay, bye,' she called on her way out.

Ten minutes later the door opened again and Craig came in. I said to the pup, 'Here's our Craig, Benjie, someone else for you to meet.'

Craig's eyes lit up and he said, 'Is he ours, Mam?'

'Yes, he is,' I answered with a big smile. 'And we're calling him Benjie.'

Craig was straight down on the floor with Benjie licking his face, when all of a sudden Craig said, 'Mam, Benjie hasn't got a winky!'

We all got down on our hands and knees to have a look, and the poor animal must have wondered what was going on. Mark and I burst out laughing. We'd been with the puppy all day and hadn't noticed once that he was in fact a she!

'Well, it's something when a nine year-old knows the sex of our dog better than a houseful of adults,' I said to Mark.

'I never even thought to look,' he laughed. 'Trust our Billy to pull a stunt like that on us.'

'Well,' I said. 'Let's call her Tessa instead?'

Everybody agreed and although I'd loved Benjie, I was pleased because I'd originally wanted a female. I'm not really sure why; probably just because I was one too. Tessa would soon become a wonderful new member of our family who we all loved to bits.

Later that day Brenda came back down with Andrea and Gary to see the new puppy. 'Come on in,' I smiled. 'Come and meet our Tessa.'

Brenda looked confused and I said, 'Don't ask why, but Benjie is now a girl called Tessa.'

As I was home the most, Tessa and me formed a very strong bond. She followed me around the house when I was doing my chores, and snuggled in my lap when I stopped for a break. She brought me some happiness just being around and looking up at me with those big beautiful eyes, and I'm certain she knew what I was thinking most of the time. My life could have been wonderful - I had three healthy sons and a nice home, a job that I liked and lots of friends and family around me, I was fit and well most of the time but something major was missing - there wasn't any real love between Mark and I.

I still daydreamed about what it would be like to have a husband who I truly loved, and knew that I hadn't given up on my dreams just yet. When I was with Colin and Brenda it was plain to see that they had a strong bond between them, without being embarrassing or too lovey-dovey all the time. Mark and I were never like that now. I always felt tense and on my guard against what he might do or say or even think, at any moment. He still told me that he loved me, but I was now quite sure that he didn't, at least not in the way I needed to be loved and cherished.

Maybe the fault was all mine; I'm certain some of it was, but we never built on our early successes or progressed as a couple, because he pushed me away so many times with his destructive moods. I was hurt so often that I built up a defence against him. I switched off and adopted an indifferent attitude against his cruel words, and that became the way we lived. I didn't get hurt as much and even when I did, I'd do my utmost not to show it.

Eventually my defences became so strong that Mark couldn't penetrate them whatever he did. I'd eclipsed him from my emotional life. His opinion didn't matter anymore and couldn't reach me. I realised that I didn't need or want him and hadn't for a long time, and that if I stayed with him I was sacrificing any happiness I might find with someone else. I was wasting my life and would prefer to be on my own with the sons I loved so much, and now with little Tessa to share our lives. I knew my marriage was effectively over; the only problem was getting my husband to realise and accept that fact.

Chapter Fifty Five

Yet another health scare

I was at Brenda's house one afternoon when she told me she'd found a lump in her breast. She was worried and I tried to reassure her, 'You'll be fine, Brenda love. It'll be like the one I had which was just a blocked duct, and it was sorted in no time.'

'I'm going to the doctor's in the morning,' she said quietly, obviously unconvinced. 'I'll let you know what she says.'

Next day Mark went to the shops and came back to say, 'Ann, you need to go see Brenda. She has to go into hospital tomorrow and is real upset about it.'

'Oh no,' I said, pulling my coat on.

Within three days Brenda saw her GP, was admitted to hospital, had the lump removed and then told she had breast cancer. She cried and cried, and I cried with her. Soon afterwards she had a six-week course of radio-therapy at the famous Freeman Hospital in Newcastle. We all pitched in to help out with the kids and it was a very distressing time for all concerned, and especially for her family.

She went in on Monday morning and stayed until Friday, as it was too far to travel west coast to east coast every day, and this went on for several weeks. I missed her once-cheerful presence through the week, but Mark and I took turns going with Colin to collect her at weekends. Her indomitable spirit stayed intact though, and even though she was still very scared about her future, we always managed to laugh about something.

The summer that year was really hot by Whitehaven standards, and Colin regularly took the three boys off for long walks while I sat with Brenda. We talked about her ordeal, and she told me about the children from all over the country with cancer, that she'd met in the Newcastle hospital. 'We don't realise how lucky we are, even me,' she said. 'At least we have healthy, happy children.'

'I know,' I whispered.

'It brought tears to my eyes, seeing those poor little kids over there, playing and chatting and laughing as though they hadn't a care in the world. It's tragic.'

'Some of them will pull through though.'

'And some won't.'

I knew how lucky we were to have our kids, and it was horrible to think about children that were seriously ill. Hopefully I would never encounter such drastic problems in my own family. It started me thinking about the value of families and I wondered if I had enough in life already, without wishing for more? Was I being greedy wanting personal happiness?

I woke next morning hoping the coming day would be better than the last for my husband and I, and was actually hoping to fall back in love with him. I was waiting for the ever-present cloud over my life to show its silver lining; the one that my mother so often told me was waiting for me, because every cloud has a silver lining, doesn't it?

Wayne was starting full-time infants' school in September, which meant there would be more hours in the day with just me at home with Mark, who still hadn't found a job. I hadn't yet fallen back in love with him either. We'd managed to save a few quid from my earnings, and bought ourselves a little car so Mark could look further afield for work. I'd been learning to drive but hadn't yet been successful in passing the test. After a few failures I lost confidence and packed driving in altogether, and wondered if I'd done that too soon in other areas of my life? I flunked four tests and felt a complete failure both at driving, and in my life generally. I was despondent and decided that all my clouds were grey and not even one had a silver bloody lining!

Mark had been driving for years and this particular day I watched him zoom off in our car. He drove south towards St Bees and Egremont, and I didn't care in the least where he was going. I watched as he chugged down the long hill and out of sight and as he disappeared, I felt strangely comforted. It was partly because Mark had gone but also the ease and freedom with which he'd done it. I was jealous and hated the fact that I didn't have that freedom, and decided that I'd pass that damn driving test whatever it took.

Chapter Fifty Six

Blissful biscuits

Life continued though I could never quite shake the feeling that it was passing me by on the blind side. Brenda's cancer treatment seemed to be working; she was cheerful and looking well. One morning walking back from the bus stop she said, 'Should we go into town later?'

'Yeah,' I answered. 'That'll be nice.'

It was early September and still quite warm, and we were both puffing a little as she plodded up the steep hill to the close.

'I'll just tidy round at home,' I said. 'And tell Mark we're going into town.'

I knew he wouldn't be happy about it but he did like me being friends with Brenda, and if she needed company I wanted to be there for her. Tessa came to greet me with her tail wagging as always, and I stopped to give her a cuddle. I'd half convinced myself she understood most of what I told her, so said, 'I'm going into town now, Tessa. You stay with Daddy and I'll bring you a treat back.'

Mark gave me a hand with the quick tidy-up. He was always willing to help with the housework and liked the place nice and tidy as much as I did. He said he'd go up to see his parents while we were out, and give Brenda and me a lift into town on the way. 'Thanks Mark,' I said, picking up the phone to call Brenda.

When she answered I said, 'Hi Brenda, it's just Ann. Mark will give us a lift into town as he's going to see his Mam and Dad.'

'Oh that's good of him,' she said.

'See you in about five minutes?'

'Okay.'

I was keen to tell her about any of my husband's good deeds, and to be fair there were a few, to balance up the shame I felt about some of his not so good deeds; particularly his failure to go out walking with Colin and the boys. It put me in a better mood and I felt quite buoyant as we set off in our little car. In fact I always felt relaxed and happy when I was out and about with friends, family or colleagues, or even on my own I'm afraid to say. At home with Mark I was nearly always depressed, though I tried hard to never let anyone know that. I'd smile and pretend to be cheerful, and carry on with the charade that had become my life, like nothing was wrong in our little world.

In town I met Susan, a friend from Woolworths who'd also been bridesmaid at my wedding. I hadn't seen much of her since her own wedding and she said, 'Hiya Ann, you okay?'

'Hi Susan. Yes, I'm fine. How are you and how's married life treating you?'

'Oh, alright you know. We have two children now, a girl and a boy, and I'm working at the Co-op on the twilight shift.'

'Well I'm glad to hear it's all going well.'

'Are you still working, Ann?'

'Yes, I work at the hospital as a domestic.'

'A domestic?'

'Uh-hum.'

'How do you like that?'

'Well, it's okay. Keeps the wolf from the door, as they say.'

She laughed and then fell quiet as if thinking something over.

'Why do you ask?' I said, to break the silence.

'Oh, it's just that there's a job available at the Co-op.'

'Oh yeah, doing what?'

'Just stacking shelves, on the twilight shift, but you'd be working with me if you were interested?'

'Stacking shelves?'

'Yes, well you'd be packing biscuits to be exact, and I'm in another department but we'd be on the same shift.'

'What're the hours?'

'It's Monday to Friday with no weekends.'

'What about bank holidays?' I asked, comparing the hours to those I worked at the hospital.

'No bank holidays. The stores don't open on holidays so nobody works.'

'No, of course not,' I said, thinking that although I didn't dislike being a hospital domestic, working in a shop like I used to would surely suit me better. 'Do I need an application form?'

'I can ask Jean, the supervisor, to have a word with Ian, the manager?'

'Okay.'

'Alright,' she said with a smile. 'I'll do it tomorrow and give you a call?'

'Fine,' I replied, and we exchanged telephone numbers.

It was nice to see her again and I knew I'd like working with her. I felt a bit disloyal to my colleagues at the hospital, but knew that not one of them would hesitate for a moment if offered a job they fancied better. The more I thought about it that day, the more it appealed and I began hoping Sue would call to say I had an interview. I'd always been quite lucky in getting jobs that I applied for, so far anyway.

'I hope I get the job, Brenda,' I said as we strolled through Whitehaven's bustling shopping district.

'I didn't know you were looking for a change.'

'I wasn't. The girls at the hospital are lovely but cleaning's not my favourite job in the world. I do enough of that at home.'

As we sauntered along we bumped into Lynda, another old friend who I'd spoken to a few weeks before.

'Hello Lynda,' I said. 'Have you moved to the new house yet?'

'Yes, I have Ann. I was going to call to invite you and the boys round, but I've lost your phone number.'

'Oh right,' I said, and wrote my number on a piece of tissue from my bag. 'Give me a call anytime.'

'I will. James is home next week but I'll call you when he's gone back to work.'

'Okay, see you soon. Bye.'

Our shopping was done by then so we carried on walking towards the bus station. I'd bought pies to take home for a late lunch and also included one for Mark. We got to the bus station with only a few minutes to wait. In less than half an hour I'd be home, and could feel the sadness creeping back over me like a blanket. It blocked out the light and the air, and my short taste of happiness. It was as if I'd been let out of a dark place but now the release was terminated, and I had to go back to my life of misery.

As we trudged up the long hill I could see that our car wasn't parked outside the house as usual. 'I'll just check that Tessa's okay,' I said to Brenda. 'Then come and have lunch with you?'

Tessa was fine and I left Mark a message saying I was at Brenda's, and to call if he needed me. Coming home to an empty house reminded me of when Mark had a job, and I thought how much better life might be if he had one now. I hated him not working and lazing at home all day, and still sneaking down to the bookie's shop. Sometimes I thought Unemployment Benefit was a curse, as it allowed him to cruise through life without a care, but we couldn't have survived without it.

I heard a car going past Brenda's and jumped up to look out the window. It was Mark. 'Well, he's home, suppose I better go,' I said. 'Oh and don't worry, we'll collect Lee from school for you.'

'Thanks Ann,' she replied. 'See you later.'

I went home, finally got past Tessa's whirring tail and asked Mark, 'Are your mam and dad okay?'

'Yes they're fine,' he replied as I noticed it was nearly time to collect the boys. We had to set off earlier now as Wayne, Darren and Lee were all at the same school, but Craig was now in the juniors. We did the round trip together, and came home with a car-full of schoolboys. Straight after tea I got ready for work, and Mark volunteered to drive me in and take the boys along for the ride. I walked home after the shift and when I arrived, the boys were all in bed.

'Hi, everything okay?' I asked Mark, missing saying goodnight to the boys.

'Yes, everything's fine, and you had phone call from your mate, Susan.'

'Oh yes, what did she say?'

'She asked if you'd call her back.'

'Right, I forgot to tell you - Susan was going to put my name forward for a job at the Co-op shop.'

He frowned at me. 'Why do you want to work there when you've got a job at the hospital?'

'Yes, I know I have, and I like it but I'd rather work in a store again, than cleaning at the hospital.'

The frown remained.

'Is there something wrong with working at the Co-op, in your opinion?' I asked, resisting the urge to place both hands on my hips in a defiant stance.

'I don't know why you have to work at all?'

'Well one of us has to,' I replied, a little too quickly and loudly.

Mark turned his back and walked away and once again, I felt like I'd stood up to him and won. I hated being nasty to him but the point had to be made. I liked being at work, it got me out of the house and away from Mark for a while, which in turn saved my sanity. I knew he wasn't happy about it and still didn't like me being anywhere there might be other humans, particularly any males of the species.

'What is the problem, Mark?' I asked with a little more control. 'It's a job. I'll be working. What the hell do you think I'll be doing at the bloody Co-op?'

He stomped outside and drove away in the car. Alright for him, I thought. I'd already decided that our tiffs and arguments would continue whatever I did, and the best thing for me to do was to just ignore them. They were always about something stupid anyway.

The following week I got the Co-op job after a short interview, and felt straight away that I'd done the right thing, at least for me. I liked the girls at the hospital and we did have a laugh together, but I was also so pleased to be working in a busy store again.

I packed and stacked biscuits merrily and enjoyed every minute of it. We started work at 5pm and the store closed an hour later, so there weren't many customers involved. All my workmates seemed friendly, and there was a positive atmosphere between them and the managers. The under-manager was a young lad called Les, with whom there was always some light banter going on, and the manager was Ian. I liked Ian right away but noticed that he flirted with some of the girls, so kept a reasonable distance. Not that I was a prude or anything like that, but I didn't know the lie of the land yet and couldn't afford any dubious tales finding their way back to Mark. Ian did tell one of the other girls that he thought I was very attractive though, and for the first time in years I felt alive and like a woman; an attractive woman and not just my children's mother or Mark Murdock's wife.

I never took time off work even if I felt ill. I would go in and always felt better when I was there. The White-haven Co-operative store became my own true little haven, from married life, and I loved it.

Chapter Fifty Seven

Pirates and parrots

I took the boys to Lynda's quite regularly now, as her posh new house had become another treasured sanctuary for me, where I could relax and be myself. The boys loved it there and she always had lots of pop and crisps and sweets for them. Unhealthy I know but it wasn't too often. They thought she was rich and compared to us – she was. Lynda and I sat and chatted for hours while the children ran riot around the house or in the big garden. The house was really nice but she never interfered with the kids' games or worried about any mess they caused. I first started drinking coffee at Lynda's, and remember going home with a splitting headache after being there all day, one weekend. She was a declared caffeine addict and I willingly followed where she led. Lynda definitely brought out the rebel in me.

So life was now split between Lynda's, my mother's, Elizabeth's and Brenda's, but the only place I didn't take the boys with me - was work. So I never felt as if I was neglecting my parental duties at all, and the house was always clean with good meals on the table at the right times. I suppose Mark might have felt a bit neglected, but only during the hours he should have been out at work anyway. It didn't seem to me that he ever intended to get another job.

In 1984 Craig was at senior school, Darren was in the juniors with Wayne still an infant. They all attended without a hitch and never gave us any problems. Craig started playing rugby-league and this also gave Mark an interest, and he'd often drive him to Hensingham for training. He told me that Craig was a really good player, and that the coaches were really impressed with him. There was a long-standing rivalry between Hensingham and Kells, which were both good teams, so training was always hard and dedicated. I was happy that he had a healthy interest and life passed relatively smoothly around this time, but that was undoubtedly because Mark and I lived almost separate lives.

We were looking forward to Christmas at work, and all the girls talked about the big party, which was to be a fancy-dress affair. Apparently the parties were really good and all paid for by the company, and one afternoon Susan came across to where I was working and asked, 'Are you coming to the Christmas do, Ann?'

'I'd like to,' I replied. 'I believe it's fancy-dress?'

'It is. It'll be a right laugh.'

'What are you going as?'

'Me and Linda are going as Grandma and Grandpa,' she laughed. 'I'm Grandma with a big apron on and curlers in my hair!'

We both laughed but I was thinking about possible tantrums at home if I decided to go. Suddenly I said, 'I think I'll go as a pirate with a parrot on my shoulder like Long John Silver!'

We both burst out laughing again and I felt that little surge of freedom bubbling to the surface. I loved dressing up whenever I got the chance, which wasn't often, and decided that I'd go to the party, and would go as a pirate! I didn't tell Mark straight away but Brenda & Colin made me a pirate's knife and a hat with skull & crossbones motif. I was a bit nervous about comebacks from Mark, but had made my decision and would stand by it.

I hadn't been on a night out anywhere for so very long, and even longer without Mark, and was quite excited when notices were put up in the shop, telling customers that the store would be closing early that day. We had to be there for the same time that our shift would have started, so after collecting the boys from school and making sure they were all fed and watered, I got ready. I'd told Mark the week before that I was going, and he seemed surprisingly okay with it, but I was still a bit nervous. He didn't like me wearing make-up so I didn't put any on, but drew a beard on my face with an eyebrow-pencil I'd bought specially for the job. I thought I looked the part and the boys laughed when I came downstairs. I think even Mark had a little smile on his face as he volunteered to drive me to the party. That also made me smile and the boys came along too.

Everyone had obviously taken things seriously; there were some brilliant costumes on show and the atmosphere was terrific. We had our meal and then played bingo, believe it or not, but there were some really useful prizes like microwaves and televisions! I could never win at bingo but I won a raffle, so was quite happy. As I sat smiling at my prize, which was a bottle of something expensive, Susan leaned over and asked, 'Ann, are you coming into town?'

'Oh, not sure,' I answered. 'Are you?'

'Well I'd like to but Linda's going home, so maybe we could go together?'

We did, had a great night out, and caught a lift home with Susan's brother. I'd never felt so happy and alive for years, but never told Mark we'd been around the town's nightspots having innocent fun. My friends and I often laughed about the parrot that sat on my shoulder, with its little head turned in as if it was talking to me. Good job Mark wasn't there, he'd probably have punched it!

It's one of the good memories I have, some of which even include my husband, but at the time I preferred being just about anywhere to being at home. Whenever the boys and I were out visiting I was at least content, and after all the years of practice I was able to conceal my true feelings from Mark. Perhaps I should've just told him the whole truth and accepted the consequences, but I was far too afraid of how that would affect the children. So we carried on as if everything was fine, even if for me it definitely wasn't and probably never could be again.

Me and my parrot

Chapter Fifty Eight

The final whistle

Mark still went to the hound-trails two or three times a week during the racing season, which apart from the gambling was good as it gave him an interest, and he walked for miles with the dogs which was better for his physical and mental health than hanging around the house. But I noticed him limping slightly one day and asked if he was alright.

'My leg's been really sore,' he said.

'Whereabouts?' I asked.

'The back of my knee, and there's a lump.'

I had a look. It was a big lump and caused me real concern.

'You should get that looked at,' I said. 'It might be something nasty.'

'I know,' he answered but then went quiet.

'Should I make you an appointment?'

He stayed silent for a while and then said, 'I used to play football with this lad, Ann. He had a tumour on the back of his knee. He ended up losing his leg and then he died.'

Oh my God, I thought. Realising that he was really worried and afraid to discover a truth he didn't want to know.

'That's not going to happen to you, Mark,' I smiled and tried to look convincing.

I know we had our differences but I would never wish him any harm and certainly didn't want him to die. The fear became overwhelming and we both had a couple of terrible weeks worrying about it, and keeping it from the boys. He eventually saw our GP and an appointment letter arrived soon after, arranging for him to go into hospital and have the lump removed. On the evening after his operation I went up to see him, and he smiled when he saw me walking down the corridor.

'Hi, how are you feeling?' I smiled back. 'You're looking well.'

'Yes, I think I'm okay. The consultant's been to see me and says everything's going to be fine.'

It was a genuine relief. 'Oh Mark, thank heavens for that. I've been really worried.'

'So was I, but apparently with me being so fit, the muscle at the back of my knee is so strong that it snapped out of its protective sac.'

'Really?'

'Yeah, but he's put it all back together and stitched me up so I should be fine, but he says it could easily break again.'

'Well you'll have to be very careful from now on, but that's great news, Mark. Have you told your parents yet?'

'No, not yet but they're coming in to see me tomorrow.'

'They'll be on the phone tonight Mark, to see how you are. Should I tell them, or do you want to tell them yourself tomorrow?'

'No, it's okay, you tell them and then they won't be worrying all night.'

Mark was a very physical footballer and always getting bad knocks, but it would make him so unhappy to give it up. Football was a major part of his life and had been ever since he was a little kid. It had caused us many fall-outs, when he came home in a nasty mood after a bad game, but I'd hate to see it taken away from him. On one occasion following a debatable decision by the referee, Mark told him to fuck off home and get some new glasses. He was suspended for several weeks and then had to go to a disciplinary hearing, and the atmosphere in our house was awful. I said, 'Well you shouldn't have sworn at him.'

'He deserved it,' Mark replied. 'And he shouldn't be refereeing if he can't see properly!'

Mark always had a quick temper and lost it often, and I was always at the sharp end trying to patch up the damage. Not long after his knee operation, he was playing again and twisted it badly going for a 50/50 ball. He tore all the ligaments in his knee, which were still weak after the operation, and that was the end of his football career. The doctors advised him to give it up altogether after his leg continuously swelled up with the slightest knock. Great, I thought, he'll be like the proverbial bear with the sore head now, and spend more time sulking at home. I did however feel sorry for him, knowing how important football was to him. I sometimes wondered if he considered football to be his true calling in life, and that's why he couldn't take an ordinary job seriously. His father was a talented boxer and might have unintentionally planted in Mark's mind at a young age, that sport and not work was his real destiny?

Thankfully, Craig was playing so well at rugby that Mark went to every match in support, and that gave him something to focus on. Craig was like Mark in so many ways. He loved rugby, and football and just about all sport, including horse-racing of course, and they would watch it on television together for hours.

Craig stayed at my parents' house when Dad was on night-shift at Sellafield. He liked to keep his gran company as she hated being in the house alone, and he'd done so for a few years. Mam laughed when he was young because he knew exactly when the night-shift came around. 'He must keep a timetable,' she said.

The boys and I would usually go down with him and on one particular day, Dad was laying on the couch watching telly. 'How's Mark?' he asked.

'He's okay, thanks Dad. He's feeling a lot better and is off out to the trails tonight.'

Even after all that had gone on between Mark and I, Dad never called him, or anyone else for that matter.

'Good, that's good,' he said, turning his attention to Craig: 'Would you like to go to Wembley, to watch the rugby final with your old grandad next year, Craig?'

'Oh yeah, that would great, Grandad,' Craig replied, smiling like a Cheshire cat. 'Can I go, Mam?'

'How much will it cost, Dad?' I asked fearfully.

'It won't cost you a penny, Ann. I'll pay for our Craig.'

Darren and Wayne didn't seem bothered that Craig was going away with Grandad, as they were always doing things with Colin when Craig wasn't involved. I gave them both a kiss and said goodnight. 'Come on you two,' I called Darren and Wayne. 'We'll go back home and see if Daddy's back yet.'

318

I missed Craig when he stayed at my parents' but it was only for two or three nights, and was so much easier for me with only two boys at home. No matter which two it was, two were always much easier to manage than three.

Chapter Fifty Nine

Sun, sea and sadness

Christmas came and went again and I enjoyed it as usual, and was looking forward to the New Year. Mark had been out one afternoon, and when he came home I was busy in the kitchen making tea. He had a bright smile on his face and said, 'Ann, listen to this: I was talking to a bloke today, and he said if I've paid into a works' pension like I did at Sellafield, but am not working there anymore, I can claim all the money back.'

'You sure?'

'That's what the guy says.'

'Well it's worth looking into. I'll call my dad. He'll know if you can claim or not.'

Dad found out that Mark could claim back his contributions, plus however much the fund had made on top, and got us the paperwork needed. We filled in all the details and a few weeks later, received a nice fat cheque for an amount we'd never seen before. We discussed what to do with it and I was anxious that none should go to the betting shop, so we decided to book a family holiday. We'd never been abroad before so went into town the very next day for some brochures, and had fun showing the boys all the pictures of families having fun in the foreign sun. We decided on Ibiza and arranged to go on 1st May 1986, which was about three months off.

We'd never been on an aeroplane before either, so that was both frightening and exciting at the same time. I'd also started taking driving lessons again after five years, but it was so much better this time as Mark let me drive our car when he took me to work, so I got some practice and was much more confident.

After I failed four driving tests years before, I refused to drive ever again but I think that was my embarrassment and indignation talking. I realised it was something I'd have to stick at and persevere with if I wanted to succeed, and decided to start learning again. I refused to go with the instructor I'd used previously, because he obviously put me in for the test too early and I associated him with failure. Instead I arranged lessons with *Matt Graham's School of Motoring*.

I loved learning to drive this time around, and took to it like a duck to water on a rainy day. Obviously I was more ready for it now with not so much else to worry about. So now I had another major interest and the days really did fly past. I was busy learning to drive, going to work, getting things sorted for our holiday, and the usual, everyday chores. Life ticked along nicely but Mark and I didn't get any closer together. It was more like we were mates that bickered a lot than man and wife. We were both fully functional 31 year-olds but didn't have even the glimmerings of a love life, and neither of us seemed to miss it. Maybe we were always too tired, as they say? We always worked well as a team though, keeping the house clean and tidy and making sure the boys were happy, and that's how our life was. We got by day to day and perhaps that was enough for Mark? We never discussed the matter but it certainly wasn't the married life I'd hoped for and dreamed about. I plodded along in my own little world, enjoying the things I could, keeping the peace whenever possible, and putting aside the fact that I really craved something much better.

We arranged for Tessa to stay with my parents, bought our train tickets from Whitehaven to Manchester airport, and were all set for our first ever foreign holiday. I was definitely looking forward to two weeks in the Ibizan sunshine, and had lost a few pounds to look my best around the hotel pool.

Elizabeth's sister let me borrow some of her summer clothes and they fitted me perfectly, so I didn't need to buy anything extra. I got a few things each week for the boys and Mark, and it was soon time to start packing it all for the trip.

Tessa knew something strange was going on but I kept telling her, 'Don't worry Tess, we're coming back and you'll just be staying with Grandad for a fortnight.'

I don't think she understood because she still looked worried. Dad said we should let her sleep at home at nights, so he and Mam stayed at our house so the dog wasn't upset too much, which was really helpful of them.

We had a night-time flight and travelled late afternoon to the airport. The kids were even more excited when we arrived and they saw all the big planes parked up. It was a wonderful day just being there in the holiday atmosphere; Mark kept the boys laughing with his scary jokes about plane crashes, and everything looked good.

On the plane my ears hurt and popped with the pressure changes, and everything seemed very loud, but I enjoyed the journey. Mark was a bit disappointed because it was dark for most of the flight, and he couldn't see anything but tiny flickering lights out of the little round windows. It was dark when we arrived in the early hours of the morning, but the heat build-up through the day meant it was still warm outside as we trooped into the arrivals building.

Things began to sour a bit as we waited for our luggage, and watched the very last cases disappear from the conveyer belt without us having even one of ours. My heart sank as I watched the final passengers from our flight carry their bags towards the customs' desks. There was hardly anyone around at that early hour as we looked for a holiday rep, but they'd all disappeared as well. Mark went looking for one and discovered that we'd also missed the coach taking us to our resort. Now I was really worried. We wandered around and managed to find a security guard who had a big pistol strapped to his hip, and spoke hardly any English. This was turning into a nightmare, I thought, and when he questioned us it felt like we were criminal suspects. But he did understand our predicament and took our details, then found our luggage and eventually a taxi turned up.

Even then I was frightened as the driver didn't speak English either, and we sped off into the darkness without a clue as to which direction we were supposed to be going in. He could be taking us anywhere, I thought. How would we know? The boys were quiet and I think Mark knew we were all nervous. He took hold of my hand and whispered, 'Don't worry, we'll be okay.'

I felt close to him then and squeezed his hand. I was so pleased he was there to protect us, and had no doubt that he would have if necessary. All was well though and we finally reached our hotel. It was still dark, we were very late but the receptionist was waiting for us, and thankfully the lovely lady spoke quite good English. She checked us in and called a porter to show us to our rooms - one with twin beds for Mark, me and the kids except Craig, who had his own room but it was a long way down the corridor. As we were unpacking and settling in I said, 'Mark, I'm not letting Craig sleep down there. It's too far away from us.'

'Okay, I'll sleep in Craig's room,' he said after a little grumble. 'And all the boys can sleep with you?'

'No, that's not fair on you,' I replied. 'We'll make do with all of us in this room.'

So we arranged four beds for us all in one room, and left our empty cases in the spare one. It was now 3.30am Spanish time, which is an hour in front of the UK. We were all tired after the journey and the airport hassle, and soon fell fast asleep. It only seemed like a few minutes later when I heard Mark say, 'Look at that blue sky.'

It was morning and he was right – the sky was bright and very blue with a wonderful big round sun shining down on us. Mark and Craig used the other room to shower and I got Darren and Wayne ready, and after a very welcome shower myself, we all went downstairs for breakfast.

There were a lot of older people in the dining-room which felt a bit weird at first, but then I thought it might be a good thing as it would probably be quieter and less rowdy than with a bunch of teenagers on holiday. The ones who noticed us smiled, and I was glad we were all dressed smartly. I'd been told that Mark and I both looked young to have three children, with the eldest being twelve, but I liked the approving glances from people seeing a smart family out and about.

By the time we finished breakfast the weather had changed, and was a bit overcast with grey clouds. It was still very warm though and we were cheerfully expectant as we went to meet the rep for our Welcoming Day, and to let her know that our biggest suitcase hadn't arrived with the others. Maybe the scary taxi-driver had nicked it? Our sun-cream and Mark's shorts were in the case, and most of our toiletries so we needed to go out and buy some. They were expensive and we made a big mistake by forgetting to buy sun-cream that very first day. Sadly, Craig was burnt by the scorching, Mediterranean sun and was in pain for days, but refused to stay indoors so we lathered him in lotion and bought him a sombrero. We went to the water-park and the beach, and the sun shone brightly all day, every day.

One morning we went on a boat trip and stopped off at San Antonio, which was so packed with people it was like a glorified Blackpool with sunshine but no rain or sticky rock. It was crowded and hard to keep an eye on the boys, and I was pleased when it was time to get back on the boat.

The first week passed, Craig's red skin turned brown and the pain eased up, but there was still no sign of our missing suitcase. We managed without it but I was starting to miss everyone at home, especially Mam, Dad and Tessa. I phoned Mam and the dog recognised my voice. She went crazy and Mam laughed saying, 'She's trying to climb up on my knee and lick the phone!'

The boys were in stitches when I told them, and I think they'd started to miss her too. Amazing what effect dogs and probably other pets, can have on your life. Mark had never been a big fan of exotic night-life, and after being outside in the heat all day, we were usually too tired to venture out anyway. There were various shows on each night but we only went a couple of times, and were back in our room most nights by 9.30.

We were always up and off down for breakfast early, with the boys ravenous and keen to get outside, and they soon nodded off after our evening meal. Mark managed a drink or two but fell asleep as soon as his head hit the pillow. It took me longer so I'd put the bedside light on and do my code-breaker puzzles to pass the time, and then I'd just lay there and think.

Even on holiday in a hotel at a big resort, surrounded by people and my family - I felt lonely. I looked over at the boys sleeping soundly, and Mark too, and the tears ran down my face. I switched off the lamp and eventually fell asleep, and woke the next morning to carry on with the holiday I'd looked forward to so much.

By now I was wishing every day would pass quickly, so I could be at home with my friends and go to work, and get back into the daily routines that took my mind off the unhappiness that plagued every part of my life.

Craig, Darren and Wayne in Ibiza, 1986

Me and the boys, on the beach in Ibiza, 1986

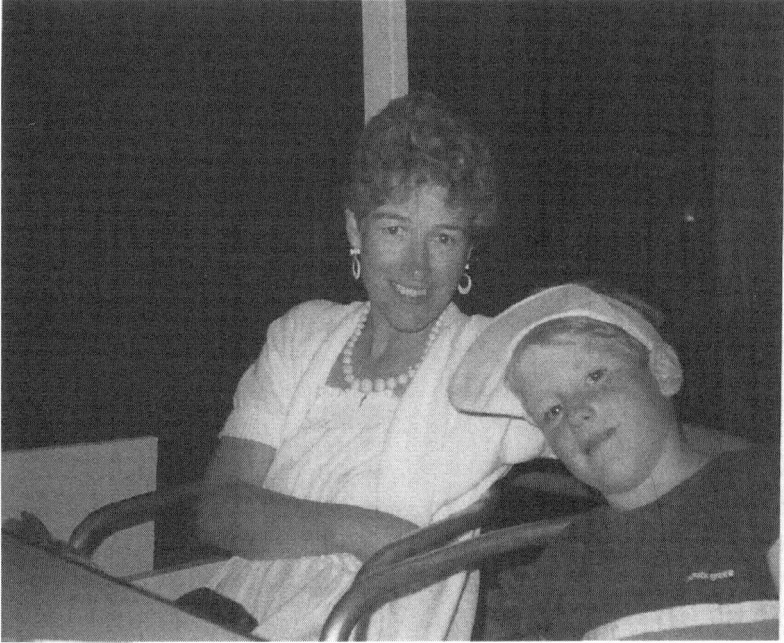

Darren and me in Ibiza, 1986

Chapter Sixty

A welcome return

We were walking back to our hotel on the Friday before leaving for home on Monday, and dozens of new holidaymakers were just arriving. A big coach came slowly along the road and hawk-eye Craig shouted, 'Mam, there's our case.'

I looked around quickly and he was right, there it was sitting on the front seat of the coach like it was on holiday all by itself! Rejoice, we now had clean towels and a stack of cream and toiletries, and Mark had some shorts to wear. The boys thought it was hilarious when he put a pair on, as his legs were so white compared to the rest of him. Our case had apparently taken itself off on a world tour, and had tickets stuck to it from every country it had been to!

I was counting down the hours now to when we would be heading for the airport and flying back home. It was another awkward flight at 2.30am, and we weren't being picked up from the hotel until midnight. We had to vacate our rooms by

10am Monday morning though, so I asked for another room that we could use for the day. The hotel obliged but all the room had was a bed with a bare mattress. Not the height of luxury but it meant the boys could have a lie down when they were tired, even if it was a bit crowded.

On the last day of our holiday the weather was cloudy and windy but still hot. I was so looking forward to getting home and back to our normal life that I didn't care anyway, and the day dragged for me. Midnight finally arrived and we boarded the coach, this time with all our luggage. I was exhausted after the long day waiting around, and flopped gratefully into my seat as we set off for the airport. In truth, I think we were all relieved to be going home to the grey skies and green fields of England, and there was definitely a more relaxed atmosphere amongst us.

'Did you have a good holiday?' Mark asked the boys.

'Yes,' they replied in unison, and started chatting about the things they'd enjoyed the most.

'What about you, Ann?' he asked me with raised eyebrows, not too sure what my answer would be.

I smile and said, 'Yes of course, the holiday was great. Did you enjoy it?'

'Yeah, it was a good holiday and the weather was great. Shame our case got lost but we did get it back in the end.'

As I stared out into the darkness I wondered if Mark ever got fed up like I did. He didn't seem to and maybe he was happy that we were still a family, and still together. I never asked him and we never discussed it. Perhaps I was selfish but I just carried on with the routines that allowed me to survive, but always hoping and praying for the silver lining, that Mam had promised me.

There was a lot of hustle and bustle at the airport, with hundreds people chattering as they queued in long lines at the check-in desks. Eventually we got through passport-control and customs without a hitch, unlike entering the country when I was embarrassingly stopped and searched. That was probably because I looked so nervous and we were completely on our own at the dead of night.

We found a café that was still open, and all had cool drinks around a table as we waited and watched for details of our flight on a big screen. Should've brought drinks and snacks with us, I thought as Mark said, 'You look real brown, Ann. You've definitely caught the sun.'

'Do you think so?' I replied, looking at my arms. They hadn't looked very brown in daylight but yes, in the subdued light of the airport lounge I did look quite brown. Funny how such small, insignificant things could cheer me up. I looked at my boys and loved them so much all over again now we were on our way home. We all looked tanned and healthy and even Mark had coloured a little, apart from his legs. He didn't have the complexion to turn brown, he just went red but he did look well.

It had been a long day and we were all tired, but at least there wasn't long now until our take-off time. Suddenly the tannoy system crackled into life: 'Attention, attention. Passengers for the flight that is due to leave Ibiza for Manchester at 2.30am - this flight is delayed until 4am.'

Oh no, I thought, as dozens of other passengers groaned and complained. The boys looked as deflated as I felt, but fair play to Mark, he tried to cheer us up and said, 'Never mind, the time will soon pass. Let's try and get some kip?'

Wayne soon fell asleep across a couple of chairs, and Craig and Darren's heads slumped to the table. I looked around for more comfortable seats but in the end, Mark and I just snuggled into the café chairs as best we could. Throughout the night there were two more information announcements, telling us that our flight still hadn't arrived, and it turned into one of the most uncomfortable nights of my life, excluding pregnancies. The plane finally arrived after a reported turbulent journey, and we were back up in the air by 6.30am. It had been a long, gruelling wait but at last we were all safely on board and heading for Manchester.

The flight was smooth, we all dozed for an hour or so, and were soon on the train heading for Carlisle, feeling slightly more refreshed. Mark called his mother, told her we'd been delayed but would be in Carlisle around lunch time. Mary said she'd pick us up, which was a great relief, and as we exited the train station the boys saw her and Billy waiting for us. They all ran for a hug before piling into the car.

'Have you all had a good holiday?' Billy asked.

'Yes, it was great,' they answered, the misery of the last twelve hours forgotten as they reported everything they'd done.

There was a joyous atmosphere in the car, and I think the main reason was because we were now trundling home to Whitehaven. We weren't as tired now and the journey passed quickly amid the excited chatter and questions about how Tessa was. We were all eager to see her and I couldn't believe just how much I'd missed her. I felt guilty about leaving her behind!

When we arrived home, the house was in turmoil. The council had started refurbishments while we were away, which included the installation of gas central-heating, yippee! Thankfully they were nearly finished at our house and Tessa came up to each one of us in turn, sniffing to confirm our identities and wagging her fluffy tail. But then she went and lay down and was apparently in a sulk for a few hours.

'Come on, Tessa,' I kept saying, but she was completely un-amused that we'd left her for so long.

I think she'd lost some of her trust in us, and was cautious because she feared we might up and leave her again at any moment. I called my parents: 'Hi Mam,' I said when she answered. 'It's Ann. We're back safely, is everything alright?'

She gave me the run-down about the council and how many miles Dad had walked with Tessa.

'Yes, I can see that, Mam. She's looking very slim and fit. Tell Dad thank you for looking after her and the house.'

I'd previously arranged to go to Elizabeth's that night. One night every month a group got together for drinks and a catch-up. There were usually four of us or sometimes five, and I couldn't wait to see everyone.

Mark drove down for chips from the local shop and they tasted so good, even if they weren't as healthy as the Mediterranean food. I only had a few to put me on until evening, and ate them with a nice cup of English tea. Everybody piled into the car to drop me off at Elizabeth's, and we called into my parents' on the way.

'Hello everyone,' I called from the hallway.

'Hi Dad,' I smiled. 'Thank you for looking after Tessa and the house so well.'

'Did my best, Ann. The council are back tomorrow to finish off the work.'

'Okay, thanks Dad. Was Tessa alright?'

'Yes, she was no bother at all.'

'Hello love,' Mam said as she came through. 'Did you all have a nice time?'

'Yes, it was really good,' I lied.

'Well you look well and you've got a nice tan on you.'

'Yes, it was really hot and sunny. I can't stay long, Mam. I'm going to Elizabeth's but I'll catch up with you tomorrow.'

'Okay love, have fun.'

'Bye Mam, bye Dad. Thanks again and I'll see you both tomorrow.'

Mam came out and said hello to Mark and the boys, still waiting in the car.

'You all look well. Are you pleased to be home?' she asked.

'Yeah, it's nice to be back but we did have a good time,' Mark answered.

'We'll have to go now, bye Mam,' I said again.

'Bye love,' she called, waving as we drove away.

I was so pleased to see my parents again, and my friends and we laughed all night about the holiday and things they'd been up to. Afterwards, Carol, Lynda and Elizabeth walked along home with me. It wasn't late but I was really tired. Tessa greeted me as I went into the house. 'Shh,' I said to her. 'Everyone's asleep.' I think I'd been forgiven for leaving her and she'd had a great time with my parents. The next day she was fine and full of beans again, the boys were all back at school, and all was as well as it could be.

Chapter Sixty One

Success at last

I had mixed emotions after the Ibiza holiday. I was really pleased to be home where I wasn't lost and lonely, with work to occupy my mind and friends for company. The boys were all busy, with Craig back at rugby training and also looking forward to his Wembley trip in August. Wayne was ready for his first Communion at church and a classmate had waited until he returned from holiday, so he didn't have to do it alone. The rest of the class had already partaken of the bread and wine while we were away. So the following Sunday we all went to church to witness Wayne and his friend do the same. I don't think Wayne thought about it too much, and probably neither did any of his friends at that age. He always took things as they came at him and never really complained about anything.

I was beginning to miss the sunshine we enjoyed every day on holiday, but also preparing for my driving test which was certainly concentrating my thoughts. It was booked for 5th September and Mark said, 'You'll easily pass this time so don't worry. It'll be a nice birthday present for you.'

I read the Highway Code back to front and upside down, and Mark asked me random questions on it which I was usually able to answer. I drove all the time when we were out in the car together, and gave lots of people lifts whether they wanted them or not, so I got used to driving with different people in the car. It helped me stay calm in different situations and get varied feedback on my progress. All through summer we took the boys and Tessa down to the beach and I would always drive. I drove to work and when Mark picked me up I drove back home, so I got lots of practice and built up my experience.

The council contractors had finished work at the house, but were still installing the gas pipe along our road for the new heating. They saw me venture out with L-plates attached every day.

'I hope they're not still around when I take my test,' I said to Mark one bright morning. 'It'll be awful if I come unstuck again for the fifth time, and they see Matt bringing me home like a total failure.'

'You'll be fine,' he said in his unruffled way, but I was dreading failure yet again.

It was a fine, dry day for the test, the boys were off school and playing outside, neighbours leaned on fences and gateposts like hungry vultures and yes, the council guys were still around. My stomach churned as I awaited the appointed hour.

'Try not to worry,' Mark said with a limp smile when Matt sounded his horn outside the house.

Keep quiet, don't alert everybody, I silently willed the instructor as I got to my feet and pointed them towards the door.

'Bye Mammy and good luck,' the boys shouted.

'Yeah, good luck Ann,' added Mark without looking up from the racing pages. 'Just drive like you always do.'

'Bye,' I answered softly, and tottered down the front steps which hadn't seemed so steep since the first time I saw them.

'Good luck,' the council guys called out, waving with beaming smiles and shovels.

'Thank you,' I said with a sickly grin, wondering how they knew it was the big day.

I bet it was Wayne, I thought, he's always talking to the workmen and loved watching them digging with their spades and loud jack-hammers. It would be an hour until the test after my final lesson, I knew, opening the driver's door of Matthew's car. He'd told me I was ready, and this final session was just a warm-up in case there was anything I wanted to ask.

'Hello Matt,' I said nervously. 'So this is it, then.'

He nodded and smiled. 'Just remember to take it easy, Ann. And if you do anything wrong, ask if you can do it again.'

Oh God, I thought as my stomach did somersaults. I kept telling myself that if I passed, great but if not – I'd try again until I damn-well did. The practice session went smoothly but sitting in the test centre waiting for my name to be called, was awful. I was drifting into a comforting daydream again, when I heard someone call out, 'Ann Murdock, please.'

I stood automatically and said, 'Hello,' to a man standing looking at me with a big clipboard in hand.

He nodded towards the door and said, 'Shall we go?'

If we must, I thought shakily, but my examiner was really nice and encouraging in his manner if not his words. I don't think they're allowed to offer encouragement but he did speak generally, which eased the tension. I felt more relaxed, especially when I set off successfully and noticed him nodding out of the corner of my eye, as I used all the mirrors and indicators correctly. After that I drove around the test route confidently, and knew I'd performed reasonably well.

He told me to pull the car up to the side of the road, which I did after signalling, and applied the handbrake after selecting neutral. He asked me some questions on the Highway Code, and I answered the best I could. His stern expression never changed as he jotted things down on his forms, for what seemed like an eternity. He then fell silent and I'm sure he must have been able to hear my heart thumping.

Eventually he shuffled his paperwork and I noticed a pink form in his hand. My heart sank to the depths of despair and my head dropped to my chest. I felt tears welling in my eyes and turned away to gaze out of the window, at ordinary people passing by in their cars - people who could drive properly and weren't failures. The examiner stuffed the wodge of paper in his briefcase and turned to me. 'Well, Mrs Murdock,' he said. 'I'm pleased to tell you that you've passed.'

I let out a big breath of air and said, 'Thank you so much.'

He handed me a white form, asked me to sign something or other and added, 'Just wait here for your instructor. He'll see you if you stay parked by the side of the road.'

When Matt got in the car he said, 'Well then, how'd it go?'

'I passed. Thank you so much Matt, for all your help.'

'Don't mention it, Ann. I knew you'd pass alright.'

'Thanks, but will you drive home, please Matt? I'm so excited I'm trembling.'

I chattered nervously all the way home as my pent-up tension released, and when we pulled up in our street the pipe-layers where still there.

'Bye Matt and thanks again,' I said, jumping out of his car and actually running up the precipitous steps to my front door.

The boys had heard the car and were lined up waiting in the front room with Mark. 'Well,' he said. 'Did you pass?'

I smiled and said, 'Yes, I did.'

The boys cheered and Mark gave me a kiss on the cheek. I kissed him back and was so pleased I'd have kissed the whole the street, including the pipe-layers.

'We thought you'd failed, Mam, because you didn't take the L-plates off the car when you got back,' Craig said.

'Oh yeah, never thought of that,' I said, glancing out the front window at our car, still parked at the kerb with the L-plates fluttering in the breeze. 'I'll go and do it now.'

I went down and took the plates off, and the gas-pipe guys started clapping and cheering. 'We thought you must've failed,' one said, white teeth showing brightly in a dust-blackened face.

'I didn't think you'd be interested,' I answered. 'And I wanted to tell my sons and husband.'

'Well done anyway,' he said. 'There'll be no stopping you now.'

You could be right there, I thought, because passing the test after it had beaten me so many times, immediately gave me an inner confidence I hadn't felt since being a teenager. I didn't need to rely on Mark anymore to take me anywhere, now I could now drive myself. I could whiz off to Lynda's or Elizabeth's; I could take my parents to Carlisle to see Dorothy, and the boys and I could go for trips to just about anywhere we chose! I felt more free and alive than I had for years, and I was determined to never give up that freedom again. I would go out with friends or even on my own if I felt like it, and I'd be myself and talk to new people if I wanted to, as Mark wouldn't be there watching me or asking who I was smiling at or talking to.

That kind of behaviour enraged me because the simple facts are, that I like people and I like smiling. I'd always been a smiler whether I had anything to smile about or not! Mark's uncle Joe said when he first met me that I lit up the room with my smile, and the reason I got on so well with customers and colleagues, is that I smile at everybody and they smile back! Even when I'm sad and breaking up inside, I keep on smiling. When I was growing up Dad would sing: 'Stop crying as you bring on the rain, but smile and the world smiles with you,' and I believed him.

My routine didn't change much to start with. Every day I took the boys to school and then called at Elizabeth's for coffee, then I'd pop over to see Mam before heading back home. I did the laundry and cleaned the house, and rushed back to school for the boys. After tea I got ready and went to work, and still enjoyed being with my colleagues as I always had. Nothing actually changed except in my mind. I felt different and thought differently, and knew something would change for the better eventually.

After a few months my routines began to alter a little, when some nights I called in to see Lynda after work or on my days off. I always came home to make the boys' supper before going anywhere though, so Mark didn't have to bother himself and had no cause to complain. Getting around was so much easier now I was fully mobile.

One night at Lynda's, after putting her children to bed she said, 'I have a new friend, Ann.'

'Oh yeah, that's good,' I replied nonchalantly. 'Who is it?'

'It's a man.'

'A man?'

'Yes, a man friend, and we meet when I take the dog for a walk.'

I was shocked. 'Really?' I spluttered, mouth open and eyes wide.

'Yes, really. He's called Raymond.'

'Raymond?'

'Yes, and I'm meeting him tonight.'

'Tonight?' I gasped again. 'When, exactly?'

'Right about now so do you want to come with me?'

I was more than a little interested. 'Won't he mind?' I asked.

'No, I told you, we're just friends,' she smiled.

I thought about it, but only for a second. 'Okay, I'll come.'

We walked partway around the block and I saw a young man coming towards us. Lynda gave me the dog's lead and said, 'Just wait here a minute.'

She went ahead on her own and started talking to the bloke, and then they both walked back to me. She was laughing and giggling as she introduced me to Raymond.

'Hello,' I said, and we all started chatting right there on the footpath.

It seemed quite normal and he appeared to be a really nice man. We were there about ten minutes before Lynda said, 'I'll have to get back now,' and I turned to leave with the dog, Sandy.

We walked a few yards and I looked back to see them kissing, and not in a 'just friends' way. I carried on and she caught up with me. 'So what you do think?' she asked.

'Yeah, he seems nice enough. Have you known him long?'

'About six months.'

I never asked but wondered where and how she met him. Maybe just out on the street walking Sandy? I was shocked at first but soon realised that I was also a little envious. Her husband had a good job on the oil rigs, he gave her everything she wanted including a nice new house, like me she had three lovely children - and now a boyfriend! Was she being greedy and ungrateful, or was she really as unhappy as me and desperately searching for true love?

Lynda and I became even closer after that night, and she confided in me about what she'd been up to over the years. Raymond was just her latest interest. She made it all sound so exciting but I wasn't tempted. 'I just couldn't cope with all the conniving and deceit,' I told her.

'How do you know?' she shot back. 'You haven't tried it yet.'

'True,' I conceded. 'But it's easy for you with James working away all the time.'

'Yes, there is that I suppose. Lucky aren't I.'

I began to wonder what it would be like to have a secret boyfriend, but then dismissed the notion as a silly daydream. The daydream never went away completely though, particularly as Mark and I were arguing more than ever over my new-found freedom. It was a vicious circle: I went out and we argued, and the more we argued the more I went out to get away from it all. We were in a downward spiral and I think Mark was probably lonely with me being out so much, though he never admitted it and still related well to the boys. We still went to family parties together and I tried my best to portray us as a happy family, and nobody, not even Lynda had any idea exactly how unhappy I was.

Mark's cousin, Elizabeth, got married to her fiancé, David, at Workington, a few miles down the coast, and the reception was held at a hotel owned by her parents: my aunty Kathleen and her husband, Harry. Kathleen's brother, Joe lived in and helped run the place. A private bus was arranged as there were quite a few relatives going from Whitehaven, and I asked Mam if she'd have the kids. She said she would and took them to her house. I was looking forward to a night out but mainly because Brenda and Colin would be there. Brenda was doing okay and seemed quite healthy in the circumstances, and had been told that everything looked good for the future.

Another of Mark's cousins, Lawrence, was there with his wife, Ann. I got on with her really well which was probably a good thing, as we shared the same name. Mark and me sat at a table with Colin & Brenda, Lawrence & Ann, Billy & Sylvia, and Mark's youngest brother, Terry. We laughed and joked for hours and the craic was excellent. Brenda, Ann, Sylvia and I were up on the dance-floor most of the evening, and we all had a great time. I was pleased that Mark seemed to enjoy himself too, though he did knock the drink back a bit quick.

We all piled back onto the bus at the end of the night to come home, with everybody still laughing and joking. Mark had all his brothers and cousins around him and it was nice to see them all together, having fun at his aunt's hotel and welcoming a new member to the Murdock family. Suddenly though, Mark snapped something at me. I didn't hear what it was because of the noise, but I could tell by his snarling face that it was something horrible. I knew better than to respond but he kept on at me anyway, hissing insults and growling all the way home until Lawrence, who was sitting right in front of us, turned around and said, 'Mark, will you leave the lass alone and shut the fuck up.'

Mark was stunned and Lawrence continued, 'She hasn't done anything wrong so what the fuck's the matter with you?'

Mark still didn't respond and Lawrence finished up with, 'Just give her a break for Chrissake.'

I was so pleased that Lawrence stuck up for me, and to know Mark's own family had heard his ranting and that it wasn't just me making things up. But I was also embarrassed and feared that he'd take it out on me worse than ever when we got home.

To everybody's surprise and my further embarrassment, Mark stood up without a word and got off the bus at the next stop, leaving him a long way from home.

'What is wrong with him?' Colin asked me.

'Just the same as always, Colin,' I answered. 'Me, I suppose is the answer, and I have absolutely no idea what to do about that.'

Lawrence said to Colin, 'He was talking to her like she was a dog, and there's no need for it.'

I silently wondered what terrible thing I'd done this time, to be treated that way, and thinking that I'd go berserk if anybody spoke to my dog like that. We'd had a lovely day and evening but that was never enough for my husband. I knew I didn't have to do anything much for him to turn nasty so why was I always surprised? I also knew that when he sobered up he'd tell me how much he loved me, but that wasn't how you behaved towards someone you love. I was completely sick of the insults and embarrassment, and had definitely had enough of both. Things had to change and this time, I was determined to make sure they did.

Chapter Sixty Two

Patrick

I got off the bus and walked dejectedly along the road with Brenda & Colin. 'Why can't Mark be more like you, Colin?' I asked to break the awkward silence caused by my husband's latest public tantrum.

Colin shook his head and frowned.

'He's been like this ever since I first met him,' I continued, now the floodgates were open.

'Honestly?' he asked in disbelief.

'Oh yes, Brenda knows all about it, don't you Brenda?'

'I know you've had a lot of arguments because you told me so, and I know you've been very upset quite a few times.'

'Thank heavens you don't mind me off-loading all my troubles onto you.'

'Who says I don't mind?' Brenda laughed.

Colin laughed as well and Brenda said, 'Oh yeah, you think Mark's wonderful don't you?'

We all laughed then.

I'm sure I would've cracked up altogether if I didn't have my friends around me. I never told Mam everything as I didn't want her to worry, but when I did tell her anything she would always say, 'It'll be better tomorrow, Ann. I could've left your dad many a time when I was fed up, you know?'

But my dad was nothing like Mark. He was always calm and went to work every day and didn't gamble, and loved my mother more than anything. He always had since they first met.

I said goodnight to Colin & Brenda and carried on to my house, two doors away. I knew Mark wouldn't be in yet and the boys were all at my parents', so I hoped he'd sleep in one of their rooms. To make sure he didn't get in with me, I sat downstairs with a cup of tea until he arrived. He came in quietly, didn't even look at me and went straight upstairs. I was relieved as both of us had been drinking all day, and I did not want another drunken confrontation; I'd had enough on the bus. All I really wanted was a peaceful life and to be happy, but doubted that was possible in my current situation. I gave it a few minutes before creeping upstairs, and Mark was already asleep in Craig's bed.

Next day we carried on as normal as we always did after a row, but the effects didn't go away; they lurked in my heart and mind and festered there. I went to Mam's to pick up the boys and at least they were happy to see me.

'Hello love,' Mam said. 'Did you have a nice day at the wedding?'

'Yes, it was lovely, Mam. The wedding was really nice, and Elizabeth looked gorgeous.'

'Oh good, that's nice.'

'Come on then boys, say thank you to Nana and let's hit the road.'

'Bye Nana,' they chorused.

347

'I'll see you tomorrow, Mam.'

Mark was up when we got back and asked if the boys were okay.

'Yes, they're fine,' I told him without making eye-contact as I washed dishes in the kitchen sink.

'We were playing bingo for *Polos* last night,' I heard Wayne announce in the living-room.

'Grandad was going mad with Nana,' Darren added. 'He said she shouldn't be teaching us to gamble.'

'Well, it was only for sweets, Darren,' I commented.

Wayne came running into the kitchen shouting, 'Mam, Dad says we can all go to the beach with Tessa.'

'Yes alright, that'll be nice, and Tessa can have a long run off the lead.'

And that's what always happened – we'd do something with the boys and the bad stuff was never mentioned again. But it was not forgotten, at least not by me.

The boys were having a whale of a time at the beach and Mark was throwing a stick for Tessa, when suddenly she yelped and ran to me. Her mouth was bleeding so we took her into the ladies' toilets, where we cleaned her up and gave her some water. She was alright after that and the drama was over, and it got Mark and me speaking to each other again. And that's how it always worked out - life and practicalities took over. We headed back home like a normal family and carried on with life.

A couple of weeks passed peacefully, mainly because I didn't go out on my own, or did anything that might just upset Mark for some obscure reason. Even when I went into town shopping, I went with Brenda so he wouldn't accuse me of smiling randomly or talking to any stray men. Eventually though, I plucked up the courage to resume my life and hard-won freedom, and sneaked up to Lynda's house one afternoon when he was out. While we were talking Lynda said, 'James is coming home on Saturday, and there's a rock group playing at Gallagher's on Tuesday night. Do you fancy going?'

'Yeah, I'd love to, but Mark won't be too keen.'

'Oh no, I didn't mean we should take the men. I meant James would be here to look after the kids.'

'Oh.'

'So let's go on our own?'

'Yeah right, you know what Mark's like, he'll kick off big time.'

'Well don't tell him. Just say you're coming here.'

Mark was still a bit sheepish about his tantrum on the bus, so I thought I might get away with that. He knew I liked going to Lynda's, so it wouldn't be out of the ordinary and shouldn't arouse his suspicions.

'But how could I get dressed up for a night out if I'm just coming here for coffee?'

'You can borrow some of my stuff. We're the same size and I've got wardrobes full of clobber I never use, so just come over in your scruffs and get changed here.'

She'd obviously thought about it and I loved being around her. She always made life seem dangerously exciting, but compared to sitting at home with Mark night after night, a game of bingo for polos would be exciting. I decided to give it a whirl but kept my excitement under wraps until Tuesday afternoon, when I said, 'Mark I'm just going to have a bath and wash my hair, and I might pop down to see Lynda after work. Is that alright?'

He shrugged and kept his eyes on the television. I washed the dishes from lunch and went upstairs. Knowing I was going to do something Mark would be furious about made my pulse race. I was over-compensating by being nice to him all the time, and felt like I was babbling nonsense when I should have just kept my mouth shut. I was relieved when it was time to pick up the boys from school and I could get out of the house for a short while. After tea I got ready for work, attempting to appear as normal as possible, said goodbye to the boys and reminded Mark, 'Don't forget I'm calling in at Lynda's tonight.'

He gave a silent nod.

'See you all in the morning,' I said cheerfully, turning for the door.

Mark exhaled deeply as if relaxing, and I think he also felt the stress of being together at times like this. He enjoyed being on his own with the boys more, and they always had fun together. I'd asked at work the night before if I could finish early, and watched the clock until 8pm, when I said goodbye to the girls and drove to Lynda's. I knocked on the door and James answered. 'Hello Ann,' he said with a smile. 'Come on in.'

I stepped inside and he said, 'Go upstairs, Lynda's in the big bedroom.'

She was sitting in front of a long mirror dabbing at her eyebrows. 'I told James you were coming here to get ready, just to save time,' she whispered.

'Well I hope it's a damn good night after all this subterfuge,' I whispered back, and we both laughed.

'Do you want to put some make-up on?' she asked.

I didn't usually wear make-up because Mark didn't like me to, but I answered, 'Yeah, why not, I can always wash it off later.'

I was well out of practice and got more mascara in my eyes than on them, but eventually I was changed and ready and off we went. I drove into town and parked the car just off the centre. I couldn't drink because I was driving but that didn't bother me, I'd never been brilliant at handling alcohol so driving was a good excuse not to bother.

'Do you think the place will be busy, Lynda?' I asked as we tottered along the street on our high heels. 'I can't see there being many people out and about on a Tuesday night?'

'We'll soon see,' she smiled.

Gallagher's had three different bars including The Cellar downstairs, hence the name, Gallagher's Bar which was the actual night-club, and another room with a dance area upstairs, where the band was playing. There was hardly anyone in the cellar bar so we went up to Gallagher's, but that was closed. That just left the upstairs bar which is where we headed. Halfway up the stairs the heavy rock music was vibrating the floor and walls. We looked at each other in dismay, and I knew I wouldn't be able to stand that kind of volume for long. Lynda agreed so we went back downstairs and had a few drinks in The Cellar, but went back up after the rock band finished. Disco music had started up and we glided onto the dance-floor. A young bloke came straight over and said something to Lynda, but she wasn't interested so he started talking to me. He was very young, probably early twenties, and said, 'Hi, my name's Patrick.'

'Hello,' I answered politely. 'Mine's Ann.'

Lynda sat down and lit a cigarette, and blew a long stream of smoke out like a 1930s movie star. She looked totally bored. Patrick started dancing around my handbag with me so I just carried on, and chatted to him as we bopped to the music. At the end of the number I said, 'My friend's on her own so I better go now.'

He said, 'Can I and come over and sit with you and your friend?'

'Erm, if you want to, I suppose.'

Lynda was already fed up with the disco, or at least the men present, so we went back downstairs to the Cellar Bar. Patrick followed us and bought her a drink. 'Are you sure you don't want one, Ann?'

'No thanks, I'm driving and there's only so much *Coke* I can take.'

Patrick laughed and I thought he had a nice smile, and we both sat talking to him for the rest of the night.

'Well,' Lynda said as the barman collected glasses. 'Are we going home, Ann?' She'd obviously been bored out of her skull all night.

'Ready when you are,' I replied, pushing my last half bottle of Coke to one side.

'Don't suppose you could give me a lift?' Patrick asked.

Lynda looked at me and I paused for a second.

'I don't live too far away,' he added.

I paused for another second before saying, 'Okay.'

I knew Lynda wanted to get home so took her first, and went inside to change back into my work clothes. I left Patrick in the car but did remember to take the keys with me!

'See you tomorrow Lynda,' I said, slinging my work bag over my shoulder.

'Yeah, goodnight Ann, and don't do anything I wouldn't do.'

I laughed, thinking I'm only giving him a lift, but said, 'You mean there's something you wouldn't do?'

We both laughed as I tiptoed downstairs. I got back in the car and Patrick started chatting straight away. He was easy to talk to, I decided as we drove off, and I quite liked his company. We had to go back through town to get to where Patrick lived, and as we did he said, 'Do you need to go home right now?'

'No not particularly,' I answered, a little intrigued. I never wanted to go home except to see my boys and Tessa.

'Pull over then, and we can talk some more?'

I thought about that, but I did like talking to him and it wasn't what you'd call late. Mark would be snoring his head off by now anyway. I stopped and we got out to sit beside the harbour under a full moon, and chatted. I was talking a bit nervously, can't recall what I was actually saying, when suddenly Patrick leaned forward and kissed me on the lips. I was surprised and put my hands on his shoulders to push him away. He held onto me though and wouldn't let go, and then I did let go. I let it all go and kissed him back. We kissed so passionately that I nearly fell over the wall into the sea. His hands were all over me and my heart was beating so fast I could hardly catch my breath. Soon we were lying on the grass ripping each other's clothes off; one thing led to another and nature took its irresistible course.

Afterwards I was astounded at myself. I couldn't believe I'd let such a thing happen, but would be lying if I said I didn't enjoy it, immensely. I felt genuinely ashamed of myself for giving into raw lust, but couldn't get the vivid memories of it out of my head. How will I cope with this, I wondered. This is something I might have dreamed about but never seriously thought would happen, not to me. What will I do if Mark finds out? The boys will hate me.

'Are you okay?' Patrick said softly.

We were still sitting on the damp grass by the harbour wall.

'Er, yes I am but I must get home right now. Where do you live?'

I pulled up outside Patrick's house and he said, 'Can I see you again?'

'What?' I said with a frown. 'I thought this was just one of those one night stands I've heard so much about?'

'No, I'd like to see you again.'

'Why?'

'Because I really like you. So can I?'

'Well er, alright then,' I replied, not quite believing it was me speaking those words.

'When, and where?'

We arranged to meet the following Tuesday, and I told him I'd pick him up at the garage near his house. He kissed me hard on the mouth one last time, said goodnight and was gone. I felt like a deceitful bitch but knew without doubt that I'd meet him the following Tuesday.

Driving the couple of miles home a bundle of crazy thoughts were racing around in my head, and my heart was still beating like I'd run a 4-minute mile. I sat in the car for a few minutes outside the house, to gather my thoughts and myself before going inside. The door wouldn't open. Mark had locked it so I couldn't sneak in without him knowing. So I knew he'd be awake and it was much later than I normally came home, even if I'd been to Lynda's.

I knocked lightly and after a couple of minutes he opened the door. I smiled unconvincingly and nipped upstairs, feeling his eyes boring into my back and right through to my soul. One glance at his angry face told me he knew what I'd been doing: fucking another man on the ground like a cheap whore. Or were feelings of guilt taking over my mind. Mark's question broke the roaring silence between us, 'Have you been with somebody?'

How he couldn't hear my heart pounding was amazing, because to me it sounded like a big bass drum beating in my chest. I turned and looked down at him. 'Don't be so stupid,' I replied and carried on to the bathroom.

I cleaned my teeth and quickly washed off the makeup that I'd idiotically forgotten about, and went into the bedroom. I put my nightie on and got into bed, said goodnight and turned to the wall.

The next few days were a roller-coaster. My head was in a spin and I felt so guilty, but also like a teenager after her first date. I found myself daydreaming about that first kiss with Patrick, and my heart lurched. I didn't want this to happen, I told myself over and over again, but knew I couldn't stop it.

Patrick was younger than me. I was 32 and he was only 20. I knew he was just a young lad sowing his wild oats, but I found myself longing for Tuesday to come around. I told Lynda what had happened, and also confided in Elizabeth because she was my best friend and I trusted her, but I did not mention it to anyone else, even though sometimes, I secretly wanted to.

Chapter Sixty Three

Benefits of bad behaviour

I knew that what I was doing with Patrick was wrong. He was a young, single lad and I was a married woman with three children, but I couldn't stop. He made me feel fully alive again and being with him was like reliving the lost years after I got married far too young. Why I did that, I still don't know but I think perhaps the fear of being left on the shelf had something to do with it, after being jilted so abruptly by Peter.

I met Patrick once each week but it was like a life tonic. Mark never stopped me going out after the bus episode when Lawrence intervened, so I never had a problem making our dates. Something had changed in Mark now; he knew something was wrong but realised at last that he couldn't fix it by shouting and bullying. Maybe he'd given up on us as well. He enjoyed having the boys all to himself and perhaps that's all he was really interested in? At work I was happy and when Mark wasn't at home, I was happy there too, alone with my sons.

One night at work Susan came through to my department and said, 'Hi Ann, you okay?'

'Yes, I'm fine thank you Susan, everything alright with you?' I replied, slotting a biscuit box neatly onto its allotted shelf.

'Can't complain but listen, Dave and I were wondering if you and Mark and the boys would like to come to *Bultins* for a week with us?'

'Butlins?' I replied, thinking of the bitter-sweet time I'd had there just after Peter dumped me.

'Yes, we've been looking in the brochures at the new caravans they have on site. They look really good and we fancy giving it a try.'

'Oh, I've never seen those.'

'They look really cool and they have plenty of room, and we thought it would be good for you and the kids to get away for a break this summer, if you haven't booked anything yet?'

'No, we haven't. I'll speak to Mark when I go home tonight, and let you know tomorrow?'

As I resumed packing shelves I thought, do I really want another week's holiday with Mark? The answer was no, but at least if we'd be with another couple so might not be tucked up in bed every night at nine o'clock?

Mark had just applied for Invalidity Benefit as he said both knees were now affecting his mobility. Someone down the bookies had told him all about it, but I didn't know how he'd qualify because there wasn't anything wrong with his mobility as far as I could see. He couldn't play football anymore but he could walk farther and faster than I could. I didn't say anything though and hoped that at least it might help with our finances if he was successful. Maybe there were other relevant criteria that I was unaware of?

I was busy daydreaming about my clandestine relationship when Susan dragged me back to reality. 'Ann, are you working overtime tonight?'

I laughed and thought, yeah if I can, as it dawned on me how late it was. I quickly took the spare biscuits back to the warehouse and ran upstairs to get my coat and bag. Ian the manager was waiting patiently at the bottom of the stairs on my way down and smiled, 'You nearly got locked in there, Ann.'

I smiled back and said, 'Well, that wouldn't be such a disaster.'

His smile broadened and he was about to add something, but I nipped through the door and was gone in a flash. I headed straight home for once and when I got there, Mark was watching television as usual but Tessa greeted me and I took time to stroke and pat her. I loved that animal and knew she loved me, and I talked to her a lot. She tried to get up on my lap but she was too big, and I said, 'Tessa darling, you're far too big to sit up there.'

She wagged her tail and licked my face and I'm sure Mark was actually jealous. He said, 'You love that dog more than you love me.'

He was right but I didn't tell him so, and thought what a childish thing to say. Tessa gave each and every one of us in the family her love equally. I nearly said unconditional love but that doesn't exist, as for example: she continued to love me on condition that I fed and cared for her, and didn't hurt her. How very close in temperament all Earth's creatures are. In actuality, Tessa probably favoured me slightly but that was because I was the one who usually fed her.

I said to Mark, 'Susan asked if we fancy going to Butlins with her, Dave and the kids for a week, in one of the new caravans.'

'Yeah?'

'Yeah, what do you think?'

'Suppose it'd be okay.'

'So should I tell her we'll go?'

'Aye, we might as well, I suppose.'

The kids were excited when I told them the next morning, and of course started asking lots of questions.

'I don't know, just yet,' I told them when they asked when we were going. 'It all has to be arranged but I'll get some brochures from the travel agent so you can see what it's like.'

'Ann, I'm going up to my mam's when you come back from school,' Mark told me.

When I got back from taking the boys to school I handed him the car keys and he said, 'The post's here and there's somebody coming next week to assess me for Invalidity Benefit.'

'Really? What will that entail?' I asked, knowing it might involve him being dishonest. Who was I to talk when I was carrying on with Patrick behind his back?

I knew that claiming Benefits falsely was stealing, if that was what my husband intended, but I wasn't sure so there was nothing I could realistically do about it, and told myself it was nothing to do with me. I refused to be directly involved though:

'I won't be here when he comes,' I told Mark.

'Please yourself, I don't need you anyway,' he spat, slamming the door behind him.

How true, I thought, and set about cleaning the house at an accelerated pace. Twenty minutes later there was a knock at the door, which made me jump because of what Mark had said. I hesitated and heard a voice from outside, 'Ann, are you in there?'

It was Brenda and I opened the door. 'Are you going into town today?' she asked.

'I can do but I'll have to wait 'til Mark gets back, he shouldn't be long.'

Ten minutes later he came back in, and I asked his permission as if he was my father when I was a schoolgirl: 'Brenda's asked me to go into town with her, is that okay?'

He didn't answer.

'I could get some brochures from the travel agent for Bultins?'

'Okay, go on then,' he answered.

I made one of his favourites: meat and potato pie, for tea, and peeled some extra spuds to go with it which I left in a pan of water to boil later, so there wasn't much to do when I came back. I made him a sandwich for lunch then washed the dishes.

'I'll be off then,' I said cheerfully.

'Okay, see you later.'

He'd likely go to the bookies while I was out, so wouldn't even miss me and was probably glad I'd gone. Tessa ran to the door to come with me but I said, 'You stay with Daddy, Tess,' and off I went, collecting Brenda along the way.

We always had a good time on our own and were always laughing about something or other, and on our way back we called in for the boys. I served up their tea and then changed for work. I still liked working but did miss the boys when I was there. I wished I could spend more time with them but one of us had to bring some money in, at least some legitimate money.

Susan was watching for me and came over as soon as I arrived at the store. 'We've been looking into Butlins at Skegness, Ann. It looks fab. What do you think?'

'Yeah, sounds great.'

'We'll need a caravan each.'

'Of course.'

'Well how about sometime in July, after the kids break up from school?'

'That sounds great as well. I got some brochures for the boys to look at, so I'll ring and tell them to check Skegness out and see what they think.'

'I'm sure they'll like it.'

'They were excited when I told them about it.'

'Yeah, so were my Emma and little Davey.'

By the next morning we'd all agreed on Skegness and decided to book for the beginning of July, just before the school holidays and only about eight weeks away. I asked my parents to have Tessa again, and they agreed.

'Tessa won't speak to us if we go on holiday,' the boys warned.

'I know,' I said. 'But we're only going for a week and I'll tell her we won't be away long.'

The boys loved Tessa as much as I did and she was great with them, but unfortunately she wasn't as good with other children, and I had to keep an eye on her when their friends came to play. She was very possessive but never looked like biting anyone, though her growl was quite scary if you didn't know her.

The following week, when I knew the person was coming to assess Mark, I went to hide at Brenda's. Someone had lent Mark a walking stick and I watched from Brenda's as he hobbled up and down the steep path under scrutiny. I was so embarrassed and wouldn't let Brenda watch. Mark put in a good performance though, was awarded the Benefit and even got it backdated. The extra money definitely helped, and maybe I was as bad as him for letting him fake it and helping to spend the proceeds? Brenda said, 'Don't worry about it Ann, there're tens of thousands of people doing exactly the same thing, and some of them aren't even British!'

Chapter Sixty Four

Butlins and bitterness

I was still sneaking off to see Patrick every week and even though I knew it would never come to anything, it lifted my spirits immensely. It was my other life, in a different world. Mark's world improved considerably with his invalidity payments, and just before Butlins he took me along to look for a new car. We got a good trade-in deal on a brand new Mini Metro, and collected it a few days before the holiday. It was russet brown in colour and I loved it.

Susan and Dave lived at Bigrigg, just down the 595 towards Egremont, on the site of a 19th century iron mine. We called for them on the big day, and set off in convoy to Skegness, way down on the East Lincolnshire coast. Mark and the boys were in high spirits, and I was driving so my mood was reasonably good too. After my delayed start to driving I now loved it and especially the freedom it gave me, and drove every chance I got. Dave said he'd follow me as he wasn't sure of the route.

'I'm not sure either Dave,' I laughed. 'But I'll give it my best shot.'

I navigated us there safely and soundly after a few little detours which had the boys in hysterics, and we arrived at Skegness in the early afternoon. The caravans were really nice and not too close to each other, which allowed plenty space for the cars and to move around. Some even had picnic tables outside.

We arranged to do something each day and the five children got on like a house on fire. On the second day we took them to the BMX track, where all was going well until Darren came flying off his bike on one of the big ramps. He landed with a thud and the poor lad was dazed, and didn't know where he was. To minimise disruption to the holiday I took him to hospital on my own, while the others stayed at the camp. The hospital found that Darren was concussed and had also broken his arm, which had to be set in plaster, so no more cycling for him that week. He never complained though and made the best of things, and Mark or I took turns sitting by the side of the pool with him so he wouldn't feel too lonely.

We were up and about well before Susan and Dave every morning, so always found something to do on our own. Sometimes we'd end up doing the same thing again with them in the afternoon, but we were all okay with that. We had a good holiday but all too soon time it was time to come home. I always missed being away from home, and have to admit that I missed it more than ever this time - because of Patrick.

Our version of normality kicked straight back in, except that the boys had the rest of the summer holidays to look forward to. Darren had to go to hospital and have his arm re-set as it hadn't been done correctly at Skegness, so he had the plaster on for weeks. The school holidays passed quickly as we went to the beach every day with Tessa, and sometimes even Mark, or with Brenda and all the kids when the weather was especially good. We spent time with Elizabeth and her children, and lazy days at my parents' house being pampered, and also visited Lynda when James was away. I even tried a day at the hound-trails. It wasn't really my thing but we all went as a family, and the boys thought it was great when the hounds were running for the line and everyone was shouting and waving things so the dogs could see their owners. It made them sprint even faster and they looked fabulous.

Although we probably appeared to be quite a normal family, Mark and I were becoming ever more distant, especially in the bedroom. Our love-life, if it could ever be called that, had never been spectacular but now I had to try a little harder to avoid Mark's advances, and in a way that wouldn't make him suspect anything about my affair. I spent hours knitting pullovers for the boys, and would often be up half the night so I didn't go to bed until Mark was fast asleep. Neither of us was happy but I'd convinced myself that staying together for the sake of the children, was the right thing to do.

I wouldn't have blamed Mark at all if he'd looked elsewhere for sexual satisfaction, but instead he started to have intercourse with me when he thought I was asleep. The first time it happened I was pretending to be asleep so I wouldn't have to have sex with him, but he decided otherwise. While he was doing it I lay silently hoping he couldn't hear me sobbing as my tears soaked the pillow. Next day it wasn't even mentioned and we carried on as though it had never happened, but unfortunately it happened regularly after that and each time was as degradingly traumatic for me as the last.

Christmas came around again as it does, and we were invited to Bill and Sylvia's house for the annual Boxing Day get-together. They were always good fun and I felt safe because

Mark's family were there, playing games and all having a good time together. Mark always behaved himself on these occasions, possibly because of the telling-off he got from his cousin Lawrence after the wedding, and also because his parents were present. I played along with the charade and no one knew there was anything wrong between us. It was easy to act normal when there was a crowd around us, and I'm sure we looked as happy as anyone else. Photographs were taken and though it's said that pictures don't lie, ours certainly did, although on some of them I look deathly white and frightened, like a tortured animal. Over the years we'd become experts at fooling people.

I didn't see Patrick over the Christmas holidays, so couldn't wait until the schools re-started and things were back to normal. I started picking Mam up from John Gaskell Court, a retirement home On Sneckyeat Road, near the hospital which could be handy, and not far from the Athletic Club which probably wouldn't. Mam and Dad were moving there shortly though they hadn't been given a date yet, but she went to bingo so she could get to know everyone before they moved in. Unfortunately, bingo was on the same night as I usually met Patrick, so he often had to wait. He always did though, so what we did at our meetings must have been worth waiting for, and I was able to use the bingo pick-up as further cover for our illicit sex.

Chapter Sixty Five

Love and revenge

Mark and I had been to pick the boys up from school and just before passing my parents' house I said, 'Mark, is it okay if we stop to see if my mam's still going to bingo tonight?'

'Sure, no problem.'

The boys wanted to come in and say hello so we jumped out of the car and went inside. 'Hi Mam, I called to her in the kitchen.'

'Hello love, hello boys,' she replied, looking up from cooking tea.

'You still going to bingo tonight?'

'Yes, if that's alright with you?'

'Of course, what time's pickup?'

'Quarter to nine, love, is that okay?'

'Yes, fine. Are you alright, Dad?' I asked, poking my head around the living-room door.

'No, I'm half left actually,' he laughed and the boys giggled.

'We've got our date for moving into John Gaskell,' Mam said.

'Oh good, when is it?'

'It's the Thursday before Good Friday. About six weeks away I think.'

'Well that's not long. I bet you're excited. No more stairs and never being on your own - and bingo thrown in!'

She laughed.

'You'll always feel safe and secure in there, both of you.'

Mam had always hated being on her own which is why Craig stayed over when Dad was on night-shift. I hated being on my own too, most of the time, but with the boys around that was never for long.

'Hope so,' she said.

'Come on boys, best be off or I'll be late for work. Bye Dad, bye Mam, see you at quarter to nine and don't be standing around talking all night,' I smiled.

'I won't, and you won't need to pick me up soon as we'll be living there.'

'Only teasing, Mam,' I reassured her, but was actually thinking about my meeting with Patrick that night.

'Will Mark give us a hand to move?' she asked as I headed for the door. 'Just with some of the smaller things?'

'Yes, I would think so, and the boys will be off school so we can all be here early.'

'Thanks love,' see you all later,' she said, waving to us as we piled back into the car.

It used to be Tuesdays but Wednesdays were now the highlight of my week, and although Patrick and I didn't do a lot together other than rampant sex, I enjoyed every minute with him. After washing the dishes I went upstairs to get ready for work, and Mark followed me. 'So where are you going tonight, after you pick your mother up?' he asked in a flat tone.

'I er, I thought I'd go and see Elizabeth, or Lynda if that's okay?'

He frowned.

'And Mam asked if you could give them a hand when they move?'

'When?'

'It's the Thursday before Good Friday. The boys are off school so we can all help too?'

He nodded.

'I won't be late in tonight.'

I always tried to stick to the same times and not set him off thinking too much. My parents brought us up to always tell the truth and I hated lying to anybody. They'd be so disappointed in me if they knew that my whole life was a web of lies and deceit. Mam always said, 'Telling lies never gets you anywhere. If you tell one lie then you have to tell another and you better have a good memory or you'll be found out every time.'

I was very careful. When I came back downstairs the boys were all watching the television. 'Bye Mam,' they said one by one.

'Bye boys, see you in the morning. Bye Mark, see you later.'

As I drove to work with my music playing, I immediately relaxed and thought what a different person I was away from Mark. Driving always relaxed me and the freedom felt wonderful after the confinements of home. I sang along to my favourite songs and was still humming, when I arrived at work and went into the canteen to say hello to everyone. I never arrived too early and it was only minutes before we all went down onto the shop floor. Susan came over and linked arms and we walked down together, and I felt that I belonged there more than at home.

I was at least more fulfilled in my life outside work now, and that allowed me to enjoy packing shelves more than ever. It wasn't just the packing though, it was being around people with whom I shared a mutual respect, and that created a very pleasant atmosphere. This particular night Les, the under-manager, was on exceptional form with his jokes and antics. We all had a good laugh and everybody had a smile on their face, including me. The shift flew past and it was soon time to collect my mother. I went into the John Gaskell main hall and she was waiting there. 'Hello love,' she said. 'I'm ready.'

I smiled and said, 'Come on then.'

She turned to the lady she'd been talking to and said, 'This is my daughter, Ann.'

She was still proud of me and loved introducing me to her friends. The lady smiled and said, 'Oh Jessie, what a bonny looking girl your daughter is.'

Mam was beaming.

'Thank you,' I replied. 'Come on Mrs Chambers, it's getting late.'

If she only knew what was going on in my head, I thought, she wouldn't think I was so bonny. Or maybe she could see something I couldn't? After living with my husband's insults for so long I thought of myself as fat and ugly, which is what I was told so often, and suddenly I realised something: what I was doing with Patrick wasn't simply for my own pleasure; I was getting my own back on Mark for all he'd put me through over so many years. That realisation gave me even more determination to carry on.

'Did you win anything?' I asked, as we got in the car and set off for the house she'd be leaving for good, shortly.

'Yes, I had a lovely time and won two pounds fifty.'

The amount didn't matter to her, nor whether she won or lost, it was the company and taking part that she loved.

'We only play for coppers you know. Some of the residents don't have much but I won a couple of times.'

'Well I didn't inherit your luck with money, Mam.'

'I know Ann, but you're not doing too badly with new cars and suchlike, and maybe you're lucky in love?'

I smiled and held back a little tear. 'Yeah, you've said that before,' I answered softly, knowing that what I had with either Mark or Patrick, certainly wasn't love.

I used to wonder why I didn't have a loving husband, but knew that I'd never loved him and my loveless situation was partly of my own making. Mam said our lives were mapped out for us before we were even born, but if so I thought that whoever did the mapping needed a damn good slap.

'Night Mam, love you millions,' I said, seeing her through the door and turning back to the car.

'Night night love. Thank you for the lift home again.'

I raced up to meet Patrick and was soon wrapped tightly in his embrace, and also in the feeling of release and being wanted on such a basic level. Our animal instincts were let loose, and it didn't feel like revenge.

Our time together passed quickly as always, too quickly but it cheered me up and made me feel what I interpreted as genuine happiness, though I was no expert on that subject. We talked like true lovers as I took Patrick back to his house, and he kissed me softly when he got out of the car. I never asked much about his domestic situation because I was afraid of discovering something that spoiled what we had. When I got home Mark was in bed so I crept in with him, thinking he was asleep but then he murmured, 'Goodnight.'

Not a bad one, I thought as I lay beside him with my heart racing, hoping he wasn't going to abuse me again. Fortunately he turned over with a grunt and went back to sleep.

Chapter Sixty Six

Losing control

I looked forward to Wednesdays, in fact that one day kept me going through the rest of the week. But I still had to pick Mam up from John Gaskell so when the next one came around, I rushed upstairs after tea, quickly cleaned my teeth, washed my face and brushed my hair. I looked at my reflection in the mirror, winced slightly but thought well, that'll have to do, and came downstairs. I said goodbye to the boys and told Mark I'd see him later. Work passed quickly as always because of the eternal banter between colleagues, and it was soon time to leave.

'Goodnight,' I called to them all. 'See you tomorrow.'

I got in the car, drove quickly up to John Gaskell Court and rang the doorbell. An attendant came to the door and I told her I was there to collect my mother from the bingo. I'd been going for a few weeks by then, so people were getting used to seeing me around and the lady let me through with a smile. I walked around to the bingo room where Mam was waiting for me. She smiled and said, 'Here she is,' to the lady standing beside her. 'This is my youngest daughter, Ann.'

I smiled at the lady as she turned towards me, but she never spoke. Perhaps she could see the strain on my face? Mam was busy talking to everyone as we were leaving, stopping every yard to hug somebody, and I looked at my watch nervously every time she did. I didn't interrupt her though and eventually she said, 'Sorry love, I'm just saying goodnight to all my new friends.'

She could probably also see my impatient irritation and I replied, 'It's alright, Mam, it's just that I'm going to Elizabeth's tonight.'

As I told this lie to my mother, my heart beat a little faster. She hated lies and I hated telling any to her, but she'd hate me even more if she knew the truth. I finally got her strapped into the car and drove home a little too quickly, but she smiled as I dropped her off usual and said, 'Goodnight love, and thank you for picking me up again.'

I loved her so much and would do anything for her, and replied, 'Don't be silly, you don't need to thank me for that.'

'Well, it won't be long now before you never have to collect me again, Ann. Next week will be the last time.'

Her words seemed so sad, maybe because they signalled the end of something good, as well as the start of a new era.

'Goodnight Mam, see you tomorrow,' I said as I shifted into first, and could see her waving in the rear-view as I drove away.

Patrick was waiting patiently as always, and I said, 'Sorry I'm late.'

We talked for a while as usual and he asked, 'Ann, how about us going to the Old Hall disco next week?'

'Disco?' I repeated, already interested.

'Yeah, it's supposed to be pretty good and it doesn't start 'til nine o'clock. At least it'll make a change from just sitting in the car?'

It came as a shock to know that Patrick was already bored with our affair, or at least one aspect of it, and I replied, 'Yeah, I suppose that'll be okay, but I'll be picking my mother up first so it'll be about nine fifteen when I get to you?'

'That's fine, we'll get there just after opening time.'

The few hours we had together always passed quickly, but I was a different person with Patrick and we always enjoyed our meetings. It was nice kissing and cuddling, and snuggling up to each other, which was something Mark and I never did. We never even tried to go through the motions by that point in our relationship.

All too soon it was time to say goodnight and return to our separate homes. I parked the car and went into the house, hoping as always that Mark would be asleep. He never spoke when I slipped in beside him but I knew he wasn't asleep. We never bothered saying goodnight to each other nowadays. I lay awake wondering if it would all be better if I hadn't taken up with Patrick, but knew in my heart and my head that it wouldn't. When I sat at home with Mark six days out of every seven, nothing ever changed, unless it was for the worse.

We'd been married for fourteen years, and I tried to think about the good times we'd had. There were very few of them, all were with the boys but even then, there was always something at the end that spoiled it. Something or someone would upset our unbalanced apple-cart, and I would always get the blame and the blunt end of the punishment stick.

For years I hoped and prayed that we could be a happily married couple, to provide the best situation for our children if for no other reason, but over time too much foul water passed under our bridge, and the current was far too strong to turn back.

Next morning the boys were all up bright and early, and excited as the end of term approached.

'Come on,' I said. 'Stop messing about and get ready for school.'

Breakfast over, pots in the sink, I herded the boys into the car and after stopping to pick Lee up, off we went to get them educated. I dropped Craig off first and then Darren, Wayne and Lee, who all went to the same school. I watched them running to the classrooms, schoolbags flapping, and my love went with them as always.

Next day the boys finished early so I had more time to get ready for work. Lynda asked if we'd like to go to her house the following Monday, so I asked them and two out of the three did. Craig wanted to go hound-trailing with his dad, so I took Darren and Wayne with me. Before leaving I said, 'Mark, we're having lunch at Lynda's, so can you and Craig get something for yourselves?'

'I'm sure we'll manage,' he grumbled.

So we were out all day which pleased me no end, but I had to come home for tea and get changed for work. The boys ate and then went to play with Lee at Brenda's house, and I went off to work. At finishing time I went straight home because I didn't want to push my luck, having been out through the day, and I always tried to keep things as sweet as possible before Wednesdays. If things kicked off and I wasn't able to see Patrick midweek, it would be a disaster for me. Keeping things sweet enough for Mark was becoming increasingly difficult though. He asked about my parents' moving day to John Gaskell Court.

'I told Mam you'd be able to go down to their house early, as the schools are closed?'

'Yeah, that'll be okay.'

'She's very grateful that you're going to help.'

I got my knitting kit out as I saw Mark look repeatedly at the clock.

'I'm going up to bed,' he said, turning to look at me.

'Okay, I'll finish this bit but I won't be long. Goodnight.'

I'd seen something resembling lust on Mark's face so sat up into the early hours, nervously clicking my knitting needles. I did catch a little sleep but it was soon Wednesday, and Brenda and I took the boys out all day for a long walk with Tessa. The weather was fine so we stayed dry, and called by my parents' house on the way back. I waved at Mam who I could see through the window, sitting in her armchair. She jumped up and rushed to the door and said, 'I'm not going to bingo tonight, Ann. There's just too much to do, getting ready for the move.'

'Okay Mam, we'll see you tomorrow then. Mark'll be here straight after breakfast.'

I made tea as usual that afternoon, had a bath as I was still hot from the walk, but knew I couldn't get dressed up too much for the disco, as Mark would suspect something and interrogate me. I put on my black ski pants, and short white boots with matching summer jacket. I felt reasonably attractive and could see Mark secretly watching me, but he never said anything, not even when I dabbed a touch of forbidden make-up around my eyes.

'See you later,' I said when I was ready, after a quick glance in the mirror.

The quarrels and arguments between Mark and I had increased gradually over the past months, and often made me feel ill. I hadn't been eating too well lately as food turned my stomach, and I felt depressed much of the time. I'd lost quite a lot of weight and thought, Oh well, maybe this particular cloud did have a silver lining? I had breakfast that morning though and grabbed a small cheese sandwich before going to work, but that was what I'd eaten all day.

At work the time dragged by, and I wanted it to pass quickly as I was looking forward to going out that night. I looked at the clock every few minutes until it was finally time to pack up and leave. I didn't need to hurry so went to the toilets and combed my hair, and was surprised how slim I looked in the new outfit. Maybe it was down to the mirrors but my reflection certainly cheered me up and gave me some confidence.

I arrived early at our usual pickup point, so just listened to music on the car radio. Patrick soon showed up but had a couple of blokes with him. He opened the car door with a smile and said, 'Hi Ann. These are my marras, Martin and Arthur, do you mind giving them a lift to the disco?'

'No, that's okay. Hi boys,' I said as they all clambered in.

We began chatting like old friends straight away and were soon outside the Old Hall, at Egremont. We parked up and went inside where the music was loud, and I was surprised to see so many people there on a Wednesday night, with most having to be up early for work the next day. Patrick and I started dancing right away and I never once worried who saw us. There could have been any amount of people there who knew me and I think that even then, I might have been pushing the boundaries to hasten an end to my misery at home.

We had a good time but the night soon ended, and I was disappointed when the normal lights came back on and it was time to leave. I'd had a couple of lagers and felt a little giddy, but was sure that was mainly due to not having enough to eat that day. I sat down for a minute as everybody milled around, felt steadier and was sure I was fine to drive home. As I stood up Patrick asked, 'Ann, do you mind giving Martin and Arthur a lift home?'

'Yeah, no problem,' I smiled, feeling as if I knew them now.

As we walked to the car, Martin said, 'I'm starving. Is there a pizza shop nearby?'

'There's one just up the street,' I replied, but it was then 12.30am and as we drove past, it was closed.

'There's a great Chinese carryout at Carlisle,' Arthur said, and we all laughed.

I was still laughing as Patrick said, 'Well give Ann some petrol money and maybe she'll take us there?'

I wasn't quite sure if he was serious or not, but they all coppered up and chipped in, and looked at me. I shook my head, started the engine, and off we went! It just seemed wild and free and wonderful just because of that. We were still laughing and joking which might have distracted me, but the trip went well until we got to Mealsgate, just east of Aspatria and south west of Wigton on the 595.

A sharp bend came at me from nowhere and I took it far too fast. I started to lose control but hoped I could hold on, when Patrick grabbed the wheel and made it impossible. I lost it altogether then as we screeched and swayed and everybody froze into terrified silence. We thumped over the kerb, smashed down a hotel sign, scraped along the wall for a few yards, knocked over a historic milestone and finally crashed into a farm gate on the outskirts of town.

As we bumped over the rutted ground to an eventual halt, the steering wheel bounced up and hit me right in the mouth. We all sat there in silent shock as blood dripped off my chin, until a cloud of steam burst out from under the bonnet. We all got out pretty quick then so I presumed the others only had minor injuries, if any.

'What the fuck happened there?' Patrick said.

'Not quite sure,' I replied. 'Are you alright?'

None of us were seriously hurt but we could hear dogs barking somewhere in the distance, and people shouting. Maybe they thought it was an alien attack, with the noise and steam and headlights flashing all over the place?

I knew there was a breakdown garage just along the road so we headed there, and I knocked on the door to ask if we could use the toilet and a telephone. My mouth was covered in blood and my jaw swollen, and I was shaking uncontrollably. I kept thinking about my poor little car, and that Mark would go totally berserk when he found out.

I rang Lynda who came and collected us, and took the lads home after they assured her that they didn't need any medical attention. She switched her interior light on, squinted at me and said, 'Ann, you should go to hospital.'

'Think so?' I managed to ask, spitting blood onto my sleeve.

'Yes, come on, we're going.'

All the way there my mind was ticking over about the crash and the damage, and the fact that I'd been drinking that night. I was worried about the outcome so at the hospital I lied, and said that I'd been arguing with my partner and we got into a fight. Obviously I didn't give any names other than my own, and I don't think they believed me anyway.

When we came out Lynda said, 'You were on the Carlisle road, Ann. Where on earth were you going?'

'Carlisle,' I answered her, feeling really stupid now I had time to think about our teenage escapade.

'James wasn't happy about me going out in the middle of the night.'

'Sorry Lynda, I didn't know who else to call.'

'It's alright. Do you want me to come in with you and tell Mark you've had a crash?'

'Oh yes please, if you don't mind. He's going to go absolutely crazy.'

'So what will you tell him?'

I thought for a minute then said, 'We've been fighting all the time lately and I've just about had enough, so I'm going to say I was on my way to stay at our Dot's at Carlisle, because I'm fed up with all the rows.'

'Wow, you sure?'

'I think so.'

'Well maybe the crash came at the right time then?'

I thought again. 'You mean like I was supposed to crash?'

She shrugged. 'Stranger things have happened.'

'Wow.'

It was now 2.30 in the morning and I thanked Lynda so much for coming to get me. 'You're a true friend,' I told her with a big hug.

'Or a little crazy?' she suggested.

I smiled. 'Well let's get this over with before James sends a search-party out for you.'

We drove to my house and I could see the downstairs lights on, and knew Mark would be raging. I was never this late so he'd definitely be suspicious about where I'd been. The door was unlocked, which surprised me, and we walked valiantly in to be greeted by Tessa with her tail wagging as usual.

'Hi Mark,' Lynda said straight off without any messing about. 'Ann's been in a crash and the car is a right mess. Maybe even a write-off.'

I stood there like a scolded schoolgirl who'd broken her new scooter. I still had a bloody face and swollen jaw which was now turning purple, and didn't expect much sympathy from Mark, but what he said next shocked Lynda and hurt me because of that. He ignored me, looked at Lynda and said, 'Do you think it'll affect my no-claims bonus?'

I could see the look of horror on my friend's face and for the first time ever, I think I actually despised my husband.

'I'm afraid I really don't know, Mark,' she replied coldly.

He shook his head and looked at the floor. I went into the kitchen in case I cried with embarrassment, but heard Lynda say sarcastically, 'I took Ann to the hospital but don't you worry, she'll be fine.'

I was pouring myself a cup of tea with shaking hands when she called through, 'I'll have to be going, Ann.'

I went back through on legs that didn't belong to me and said, 'Thank you so much for everything, Lynda. I hope James is okay and I'll phone you in the morning if that's alright?'

'Make sure you do,' she said, looking at Mark with utter contempt.

Chapter Sixty Seven

The carnival is over

'**W**hat the hell were you doing on the Carlisle road?' Mark asked me as soon as Lynda was out of sight.

I took a few deep breaths. 'I'm so fed up because all we do is argue all the time, so I was going to stay with our Dot in Carlisle.'

He looked horrified so I continued:

'But I didn't get that far because I crashed the car on a bad bend.'

'So what do we do about helping your parents to move?'

Shit! I'd totally forgotten about that. 'I'll phone in the morning and let them know what's happened.'

'Well I'm going back to bed. Who knows whether we can ever get another car, the insurance will be through the roof.'

'Well it could be worse - I could have died.'

He never answered and didn't even bother to turn around.

The adrenaline finally stopped pumping through my veins and I felt like a junkie going cold-turkey. I also felt bad about everything in my life. I tried to tell myself the crash wasn't all my fault because Patrick grabbed the wheel, but the skid had already started and I was in charge of the car, so it must have been. It certainly brought me back down to earth and it felt like my whole life had crashed. The thought even crossed my mind that maybe it would've been better if I had died, and I sat there after Mark had gone to bed, wiping away the tears that streamed down my battered, unloved face.

If only I had someone to hold me and tell me that everything would be alright, even if it was my fault, and actually care about me. My parents and friends definitely would have, but that's not the same thing as having a husband who loved and protected me.

I sat in the chair for hours feeling totally alone and ashamed of myself, and wondered what life would be like now if I hadn't gone to church that fateful day - the day of our wedding when I hovered on the second step and knew for a certain fact, that I was making a mistake. I think Dad knew as well deep down in his heart, when he told me I didn't have to go through with it. He would've looked after Craig and me but then I remembered Darren and Wayne. I wouldn't have them and I loved them so much and couldn't wish for anything that meant not having them. I was so mixed up and the swerving car kept skidding through my thoughts and crashing into everything in my life, over and over again.

I must have fallen asleep in the chair eventually, as I suddenly woke and realised where I was. I looked at the clock on the wall and it was 5am. I crept up to bed and glanced in the bathroom mirror on the way. My face was a real mess and I thought, you idiot, what were you even thinking about, driving all the way to Carlisle for a takeaway? I dozed off again in bed before I heard Mark and the boys laughing downstairs. I was stiff and sore and almost fell out of bed, put my dressing-gown on and went to phone my mother.

'Hello,' I heard her answer, and wanted so much to tell her the truth. 'Hello Mam,' I replied. 'It's Ann.'

'Oh hello love, what time's Mark coming down?'

'Mam, I er, I crashed the car last night and it might be a write-off.'

'Oh no, are you alright?' she asked and I could hear the genuine concern in her voice.

'Yes, I'm okay, just a bit shaken up but I've been to the hospital and I'm fine.'

'Well make sure you get plenty rest and get over the shock.'

'I will but I'm sorry Mam, Mark can't come to help as we have no car.'

'Don't you worry about that love, as long as you're alright and nobody was hurt?'

'Yes, I'm fine and nobody was. I'm tired though and a bit sore so I'll see you soon.'

'Have you crashed the car?' Darren asked, standing behind me.

'Yes darling, unfortunately I have but don't worry, we can get another.'

'I'm glad you think so,' Mark shouted through.

I put the phone down and went into the kitchen to make myself a drink, and Craig said, 'Mam, I'm going out with Dad.'

'Okay Craig, love you loads and see you later.'

They left and Darren and Wayne asked if they could go play with Lee.

'Yes, that's fine,' I answered as if in a dream. 'Be good lads and don't go away from the house.'

It was nice to be alone with Tessa and my silent thoughts for a while, but the phone rang and it was Lynda, 'Ann, you must call the police and report the accident. I think you have 24 hours and if you don't, it'll be much worse for you.'

'Will it?'

'Yes, it's the law that you have to report an accident and if you don't, they'll think you're trying to get away with something.'

'I am.'

'I know, but they'll think it's because you'd been drinking over the limit, and they could get you on a drink-driving charge.'

'Really?'

'Yes, it's a criminal offence not to report an accident, James reckons, and all those people at the hotel were looking out the windows. Someone's sure to have reported it.'

'Okay, I'll do it now. Thanks for letting me know. I'll come down to see you later?'

'Yes that's fine, let me know what happens. They might want a statement from me.'

'Oh no.'

'Don't worry about it.'

'Okay, thanks again Lynda.'

I found the local number, phoned the police and told them what had happened the night before. They took all the details, thanked me for calling and told me to contact all the people who'd need compensation for the damage I'd caused. There was no mention of drink-driving and I wondered if I'd made a mistake by calling. But it was the right thing to do so I got in touch with the farmer who's gate I'd smashed, the council for the broken milestone, and of course the Pink House Hotel for the damaged wall and flattened sign. It was like a comedy film script, and all for the sake of a takeaway meal that I wasn't bothered about, and didn't get anyway! I reported back to Lynda, who was relieved and picked me up so I could go tell the Co-op I wouldn't be at work for a few days.

The atmosphere at home was worse than ever but I was used to it by now so just carried on regardless. Mark's mother called to ask how I was.

'I'm okay thank you,' I replied politely. 'A bit bruised and battered but I'll be fine.'

At teatime, Mark and I were eating silently when he said, 'I've found out that we can get a new car through my Invalidity Benefit, and that way we won't have to pay a big insurance increase.'

I was puzzled. 'So what does that entail?' I asked with a frown.

'It's called Mobility Component. The garage takes the Benefit, we pick a car and keep it for three years, and they pay the insurance and road tax and they service it as well.'

'You sure?'

'That's what they told me, and after three years we can swap it for another new one.'

It sounded too good to be true but that's what happened. We went to choose another new car and decided on a Ford Escort. It was a silver grey 'Limited Edition' with 25 printed on the side. I never knew what that meant but it was a gorgeous car to look at. Unfortunately, it always played up on cold frosty mornings and coughed like it was already fifty years old.

I was exceptionally lucky that I never heard any more about the crash, and knew I'd never be as lucky again. But I heard plenty about it from Mark over the following months, even though he never asked about my injuries or how I was feeling. I only saw Patrick once more and that was for him to tell me goodbye. He said his mother had found out that he was seeing a married woman in her thirties, with three children, and that she'd crashed her car with him in it while she was drunk at the wheel. Was that really me? *The Carnival Is Over* by The Seekers played on the car radio. He looked at me and said, 'That's how I feel about us, Ann. It's over.'

After the car crash I lost weight as I was very unhappy and not eating properly; even more so without my Wednesday night escapes, and desperately wanted to be out of the relationship that caused me so much stress and unhappiness. I had the confidence to go it alone now, but still hesitated because I was so afraid of hurting so many people, including my sons. I loved them so much but so did their father, and I knew that getting them away from him would be all but impossible. So I decided to push my happiness to one side and carry on for as long as I could.

One of my nieces decided to get married and we were invited to the wedding. My brother Charlie worked for a coach company and he hired a minibus from them to get us there and back. On the morning of the wedding we all lined up in our fineries and I felt proud to be part of the family. I loved these occasions and this one was in honour of one of my sister's daughters, Pauline. I was also her godmother we got on really well. It was a lovely day and we all went back to Dot's house after the reception.

It was one of the rare days that Mark and I didn't fall out over something, and for a few weeks afterwards things were okay. But they were only ever okay, never good, and soon we fell back into the same old rut we'd been trapped in for far too many years. The boys were growing up now and Craig played rugby every weekend. That also took up some of Mark's time, along with the trail-hounds he'd kept in touch with, and Darren and Wayne were always out somewhere or other. I tried to stay home more but the house itself made me miserable, even with faithful Tessa for company. Once the dust settled after the car crash and I knew the cops weren't after me for anything, I started venturing back out to see my old friends, which made life at least a little more bearable.

On the bus to my niece's wedding

Craig with my mother

The boys, my parents and me

Chapter Sixty Eight

A surprise trip to Sunderland

On school days Mark always went out with the hounds again now, and stayed away until tea time. I cleaned the house and in the afternoon I'd visit either my mother, Elizabeth or Lynda, or sometimes all three. When we stayed apart most of the time there was little friction and it was easier to live with each other, and I'm pretty sure Mark preferred that arrangement too.

I actually missed Patrick and often smiled to myself when the carnival song brought back bitter-sweet memories. Being with him had confirmed how little Mark and I had between us. Without the boys we had nothing in common and nothing to keep us together. We lived in the same house and slept in the same bed because there was no other, and I wasn't brave enough to make that stand, but that was it, there was nothing else.

Mark came home from his parents' house one day, and told me there was a full-time job going in the bookmaker's shop at Woodhouse, to the south of Whitehaven. He'd seen an advertisement in the window on his latest visit, though he said he was putting bets on for his dad, and had the affront to bring me an application form! So why don't you apply for it? I thought. You know the routine way better than me!

'You'll be good at it, Ann. Dealing with people and working with figures.'

'Yes, you're probably right,' I said, taking the course of least resistance.

At first I was going to forget about it and suggest he found himself a job instead, but the more I thought about it, the more I liked the idea. It would be five full days and I suspected Mark's motivation was that I'd be at work all day, so wouldn't be able to get out with my friends as much. But neither would I have him watching me all morning. I filled in the application and sent it off.

Leaving the house for work I felt unusually happy, and for the first time in months sang along with the car radio all the way there. The only thing that spoilt the morning was thinking about the boys. It wasn't their fault that I was unhappy with their father; they loved him equally as much as they loved me, and were now the biggest part of his life by far.

Tessa met me at the door when I got home after work and I said, 'Hello Tessa, are the boys okay?'

Mark snapped, 'Yes, they're all tucked up in bed and they're fine, why wouldn't they be?'

'Just joking,' I said, shrugging my shoulders en-route to the kitchen, where I put the kettle on the hob.

'Do you want a drink?' I called through to him.

'No, I'm off to bed.'

'Okay, goodnight.'

I got my knitting out and sat downstairs for hours, clicking away and hoping Mark would be fast asleep when I went to bed. Luckily he was.

Next morning he took the boys to school while I cleaned the house. I was all done and dusted when he came back, but I knew by his expression that something was bothering him.

'Have we any spare money?' he asked, looking around him as if a stray tenner might have floated in through the window.

'What for?' I replied with trepidation.

'There's a horse running today and it's a sure thing to win.'

'Oh, well, no not really.'

We had a nice house, a car, the children were always smart and we had decent food to eat, but we never had spare cash. It often caused friction and because of Mark's gambling and petty theft in the past, I still kept a sharp eye on what was in my purse. It was needed for various things; car fuel being one of them, and I could account for every penny. I carried on with the housework but when I checked later, I knew for sure that money was missing from my purse.

When I came home from picking up the boys, Mark was in a much better mood. 'Hello boys,' he said cheerfully.

'Hi Dad,' they replied in unison.

He'd been out, and come back with packets of sweets for the boys.

'Don't eat those until after your tea,' I warned them.

'Okay Mam, we won't,' they giggled, sneaking a few into their pockets.

'I thought you had no money?' I said quietly to Mark in the kitchen.

'I found a betting-slip in my jeans and there was some money left on it, so I put it on the horse I was telling you about.'

'And it won, right?' I said sarcastically, knowing he was lying to my face.

But at least he was in a better mood, until his next visit to the bookies which wouldn't be very long. We didn't have much money, and though I could put up with him spending some of it at the bookies if it kept him happy, he lost too often and it always put him in a temper.

I was off work for a few days that week and Mark decided he needed the car, and would collect the boys from school. Lynda took me into town as I needed a break from the house. She pulled up outside the Three Tuns pub, on the corner of Duke Street and I asked, 'Are we going in there?'

'Yeah I've arranged to see Brian. You ok with that?'

I shrugged and got out the car.

The Three Tuns, named after the three ancient towns, or settlements, which originally occupied the area, was reputedly where all the local hippies congregated, though my brother spent time there and he wasn't particularly a flower-power kind of guy. It was a dark, dismal sort of place when we went inside but Lynda saw Brian right away. She walked straight over and sat beside him, and I followed. Lynda was always confident with men and immediately started chatting away to him, so I thought they must have met previously. He was with another bloke I'd seen around town a couple of times.

'This is Alan,' Brian said to me, nodding at his pal.

'And this is Ann,' Lynda added.

So of course he started talking to me. I couldn't believe I was sitting in a pub in the middle of a weekday afternoon. What would my parents think? Suddenly Lynda said, 'Are you coming to Sunderland with us then?'

'What? Are you joking?'

'No, I'm not, Alan lives there knows a good nightclub.'

'All the way to Sunderland for a nightclub? It's the other side of the country!'

'Oh, don't be an old stick-in-the-mud,' she said to me. 'Are you coming or not?'

'What will you tell James?' I asked.

'I'll tell him you and I are going to visit my mother. He often says I should go see her more, and he'll look after the kids.'

'But Mark would want to know every detail.'

'Well just don't go home and tell him tomorrow,' she giggled.

I laughed at the absurdity of it all but then said, 'I haven't got any clothes with me.'

'Well we'll go and buy some,' she said, grabbing me by the hand and hauling me out into the street.

Lynda always had lots of money, and I followed her like a little lamb as she paid for new clothes, underwear and some makeup. I had a sickly feeling in my stomach and wasn't sure if it was excitement or fear, or maybe a bit of both. She phoned Brian to say we'd be back in an hour, then we drove back to tell her husband we were going to visit his mother-in-law, who'd just been taken ill.

'You are totally crazy,' I told her, and then told myself I was crazy too for being so easily led.

'It'll be a laugh Ann, and I can tell you like Alan,' she smiled.

I didn't even know Alan and even if I did like him, that wouldn't mean I wanted to go to Sunderland with him! I continued to follow though as she packed a case and said goodbye to James and the children, and we trotted back down the path to the car. I got in the passenger seat telling myself I'd get out at the first bus stop, but all too soon we were back at The Three Tuns. Brian and Alan saw us pull up, came straight out, dived straight in and off we sped onto the 595, heading north east.

Just after the crossroads near Brigham, Brian said, 'Let's stop at Cockermouth for a drink,' so we parked up and went into the Black Bull. I didn't have anything as I was wary of the long journey ahead, but Lynda bought a big bottle of red wine to take with us. As soon as we set off again they started drinking and smoking, and I sat there laughing along with them but thinking: what the hell am I doing here? It was crazy and Lynda was more of a wild-child than I ever imagined.

After about an hour Alan asked Lynda to pull over for a toilet stop, and she turned into the next pub we came across. Again they ordered drinks but I declined. Lynda looked at me and said, 'Live a little, Ann, you're a long time dead.'

'I'm scared of getting car-sick,' I replied. 'I'm not a very good traveller.'

We stayed for half an hour and then resumed our trip, up towards junction 44 on the M6 near Carlisle. I hoped Lynda was alright to drive after drinking, but she seemed okay and I didn't have the courage to criticise her, not with my recent driving record. She turned to say something to Brian when suddenly there was a loud thump. We'd hit something but Lynda carried on driving and didn't even slow down.

'What was that?' I asked.

'Not sure,' she giggled.

'Do you think I should drive, Lynda?'

'Yeah, I could do with a break,' she said, and pulled over again.

I drove onto the A689, then onto the 69 at Brampton, and due east to Newcastle. On the outskirts of the city I took a right onto the A1 to Washington, then across to Sunderland on the 1231. We found a multi-storey park near a nightclub they knew

398

and left the car there, but they wouldn't let the lads into the club as they were wearing jeans. Brian was quite drunk by that time and had been smoking pot, and looked a bit worse for wear. He was going to argue with the doormen when Lynda said, 'You and me should go in Ann; see what the talent's like inside.'

I laughed and thought, I don't even know what the hell I'm doing here: It's late; I have no money, and no idea where I'm going to sleep tonight if we're not going home, and I feel like a real fool. Lynda was now talking to the head bouncer, who was at least a yard wide across the shoulders, and I asked her, 'So what are the plans for tonight, Lynda?'

'Plans?' she said with the hint of a slur. 'I don't have any plans.'

'So where are we sleeping tonight? Are we sharing a room somewhere or do I have to drive us all the way back home?'

'No,' she laughed. 'Don't be daft. I'm sleeping with Brian and you're with Alan. Or we can swap if you'd prefer?'

'What?' I said. 'Are you serious?'

'Yes, very. The hotel's just down the road.'

'Lynda, I've only just met the guy. No way I'm sleeping with him.'

'Well get a twin room then,' she laughed.

I couldn't do much else but laugh along with her, as I wondered what I was going to do, but then Alan gave me a nudge and said, 'Come on Ann, let's get some sleep, you've a long drive back home tomorrow morning.'

I wished I was home already, as Lynda and Brian disappeared into the lift.

'Don't worry, I've booked a twin,' Alan said, and with no other realistic option, I followed him to our room for the night.

Next morning we met Brian and Lynda for breakfast before setting off home. Brian looked awful and was actually shaking. Lynda whispered to me, 'Did you have a good night?'

'Erm, it was okay.'

'Bloody Brian fell asleep two minutes after getting into bed, and I haven't slept all night worrying about what we hit back there on the road.'

'What do you think it was?'

'No idea but I hope it wasn't a person,' she giggled nervously.

We were soon back on the road to Cumbria but had to stop at another pub so Brian could use the toilet. When he'd finished he ordered a beer so Lynda and I had soft drinks while we waited for him. He was shaking so much he could hardly hold his glass, and Lynda was visibly embarrassed.

'Your friend has a problem,' I said, going outside to phone home.

'Don't I know it,' she replied.

Mark answered my call and asked me where the hell I was.

'Lynda had to rush down to Bolton to see her mum. It was an emergency and she asked me to go with her for support.'

He was silent but I could hear him breathing into the phone like an angry bull.

'We'll be home later today,' I offered.

'You have an interview today, for the job at the bookies.'

'Oh no, I didn't know. Give me the number and I'll phone to apologise.'

I rang and gave them an excuse, and they arranged another interview for the following week. Mark was raging with me when I got home and I didn't blame him. I knew what I'd done was unforgivable, but I didn't want his forgiveness and as always, the more we argued the more determined I was to stand up to him. The boys were delighted to see me though and asked where I'd been. I hated telling them lies and decided I had to find a final solution to the problem.

I went for the interview the following Tuesday and got the job. I was sad to leave the Co-op and all my friends there, but I loved working at the bookmakers immediately and met some new colleagues. My ability with numbers was a real bonus, and it was the first job I'd had where I used my brain instead of physical labour.

I watched all sorts of people coming in and losing lots of money in short periods of time. Sometimes they won but the bookmaker never lost in the long run. The little shop I worked in was a real goldmine, but I felt sorry for those unfortunates who lost their cash there time after time. They reminded me of Mark and the distress his gambling caused, and I wanted to shout at them, 'Why on earth do you keep doing it. When will you learn?'

I knew it was a very bad habit that was hard for a lot of men to shake off, and knew what their wives must be suffering. I felt sad as I knew the feeling and the desperation that caused so many fights between Mark and I, and thought how strange that I should now be actually working in a gambling-den, and enjoying it. Gambling really can be an illness, I felt sure.

I worked every Saturday, which was usually the busiest day of the week, but had Sundays off and a day during the week, plus every evening which I was unused to. I wondered what surprises and opportunities my new job might bring along with it, and looked forward as always, to finding out.

Chapter Sixty Nine

An old flame

I saw Alan around town a couple more times after the Sunderland escapade. He was a young, good-looking bloke who was also a gentleman, and must have had women falling at his feet all over the place. Lynda and I started going out whenever James was home and could look after the kids. He had leave every six weeks and stayed for a fortnight, so we'd go out both Thursday nights around the pubs in town. James didn't seem to mind and at first I wished Mark was the same, but considering what Lynda got up to, I wondered if it was really a good thing to be so uncritical?

One of the pubs had a disco until midnight and we usually finished up there. Lynda was asked to dance as soon as we went in one night, so I stood watching, sipping from my glass when a young man came over and asked straight out, 'Are you married?'

'Yes I am,' I answered. 'And I have three children.'

'Mm, I don't usually bother with married women,' he said, unperturbed. 'But I can talk to you?'

He seemed reasonably intelligent and I liked his forthrightness, so replied, 'If you want to, I'm not going anywhere.'

'Well my name's Bob.'

'Hello Bob, I'm Ann.'

'Do you come here often, Ann?' He laughed.

'That's a bit of a cliché but yes, my friend and I come about once a month,' I answered, nodding at Lynda, still moving on the dance-floor. 'When her husband's home from the rigs to watch the kids.'

He got the message but just laughed, appeared harmless and we talked most of the night. By the end of it we were chatting like old friends at a school reunion, not that I've ever been to one but can imagine...! He smiled a lot, touched my arm once or twice and his eye-contact never wavered, and as the DJ was winding up, Bob asked me if I'd go out for a meal with him.

We were getting along well together, so I agreed to meet him strictly as platonic friends. We met a few times over about six months, but then he tried it on with a hand under the table and I knocked him back. We kept in touch by telephone until he told me he was going on holiday to Thailand, and I knew why men went there so severed our contact straight away. It was sad really, as before that I'd found him really sensible and interesting to talk to. Obviously I wasn't meeting all his needs and nor did I want to. I was pursued by another handsome young man called Martin, but he had more baggage than me and I chose not to take on any extra.

Life at home was still the same, and we did have some good times when out with the boys and Tessa. Mark and I could still laugh and joke and I'm sure that to most observers, everything seemed as it should be in a happy marriage. For me though, nothing was and it felt like I was balanced on a knife's edge.

Things could fall either way at any given moment and because of that, the stress of uncertainty ate away at me constantly. Life was always so up and down, and I'd come to the conclusion that it would be easier to deal with it either one way or the other - even if that way was down.

One night Mark and I went out with Elizabeth and John to a local darts league competition. I'd always liked watching darts and would've loved to play for one of the pub teams, and not just as a reason to get me out of the house every week. In West Cumbria however, I didn't know of any women's teams. I think we were supposed to stay home and watch the kids but this particular night, my parents agreed to do that for us.

I enjoyed the matches and having a night out with Elizabeth, but Mark got so drunk he became an embarrassment yet again. We'd had words about what I was wearing before leaving home, just to get the night off to a good start, which obviously put Mark in one of his aggressive moods. So when he went to the toilets and never came back, I thought what the hell, he's off on one of his tantrums again.

After a while John followed Mark into the toilets to see if he was alright, but came back after a few minutes and said one of the cubicle doors was locked, so Mark must be in there.

'Maybe he's not feeling too well,' I suggested to contain my mortification, before trying to change the subject.

'Probably,' John said. 'Maybe he had a bad pint.'

'Just the one?' I asked sarcastically.

John laughed and said, 'I'll pop back in there later if he doesn't show up soon.'

He didn't show up, and John discovered that the door was locked because the toilet was out of order. I told him not to worry and whispered to Elizabeth, 'He'll have gone home sulking.'

'What about?' she asked as we got up to dance.

'He doesn't need a reason.'

At the end of the night I took Elizabeth and John back to their house, before driving home to mine. When I went in Mam said, 'Hello love, where's Mark?'

'Isn't he here?'

'No.'

'Well he's not with me. He got drunk and disappeared halfway through the night, and I've not seen him since. I thought he'd be here by now.'

'Where could he have gone?'

'God only knows. He was in a right mood with himself. John had to climb over the toilet door looking for him but he wasn't there.'

Dad said, 'Does nobody care where the lad is at this time of night?'

Mam and I looked at each other.

'Somebody needs to find out where he is,' Dad continued. 'Anything could have happened if he wasn't feeling right.'

Mam said, 'Chuck, I need to go home if you're going to look for Mark. Can Ann run me home first?'

'Aye, go on then, and be quick.'

I took Mam home and when I came back, Dad had Tessa on the lead and went out like a search-party looking for Mark. He was gone over an hour and wasn't happy when he returned.

'Did something happen tonight?' he asked.

'No, Dad, it's just Mark.'

'What do you mean, it's just Mark?'

'It's how he is. If he doesn't get his own way he runs off and sulks. He'll have gone somewhere to chill out.'

'But what if he's in some sort of trouble?'

'He'll turn up soon, Dad, he always does. I'll phone you when he comes back.'

'Alright, but make sure you do. I'm still worried about the lad.'

I gave him a kiss and said goodnight, and he walked home so I could stay with the boys, who were still asleep in bed. I was sitting in the armchair telling Tessa all about my troubles again, when I heard a loud thud in the hallway. Tessa barked and we went to see what had caused the noise, only to find Mark lying on the floor with the front door wide open. Obviously he'd fallen straight in while trying to open it, and lay there laughing.

'Are you alright?' I asked him as I noticed a terrible stench coming off his damp clothes.

'I don't know,' he giggled. 'How do I look?'

'Not so good and you smell even worse.'

'Yeah, sorry about that, I fell in a ditch outside the club and it was full of dog shite.'

'Right, and now so is our hallway.'

'I'll give you a hand cleaning up,' he slurred.

It was just then that I realised I had actually been worried about him, and burst into tears of rage, frustration and desperation at my predicament. I cried and screamed and told him he was a fucking idiot, and that I hated him so much and why he didn't just go away and leave me and the boys to live a normal life. He went quiet, then rolled over to look up at me - and carried on laughing.

I eventually got him undressed and scrubbed down, put him to bed and dumped his stinking clothes in the washer. I then phoned my dad to tell him Mark was home safe, but still drunk and covered in dog crap.

'Oh well that's a relief,' he said.

'Really!? Anyway no need to worry now so you can go to bed. Thank you for looking after the kids and sending out the search-party for Mark.'

He laughed. 'Night-night, love.'

'Night, Dad.'

Next day at work I was watching the world go by, waiting for the first punters of the day and thinking that every time Mark and I went anywhere together, it always ended up in disaster. Suddenly the door opened and in walked Peter. I hadn't seen him for years but my heart still missed a beat, and I fought to concentrate on the figures I was totalling. I stayed right where I was, looking at the numbers but not seeing them. He came straight over, passed me a betting slip and said, 'Hello, Ann, how you doing?'

'Fine, thank you,' I answered as nonchalantly as I could, keeping my eyes on the slips.

I felt my face flush and my heart was beating fast, because I'd never known him to be interested in horse-racing, and I remembered how he'd sauntered into Woolworths that day years before, just like he had here, today. I gave him his receipt and when he left one of the other girls asked, 'Who was that, Ann? You're still blushing.'

'Oh, I used to go out with him, years ago.'

The way I felt about Peter had never changed, and I was hoping he didn't always use this bookie's shop, because it would be torture seeing him every week.

Lynda and I were going out the following week and as usual, I got changed at her place. It was a Thursday night so we decided to go to Gallagher's, and when we walked in the first person I saw was Peter. Again my heart lurched as Lynda, who'd been his long-time, high-school sweetheart, said hello to him. I smiled nervously as Lynda stopped to talk with his friend, and Peter shuffled over to me.

'Hello again, Ann,' he said. 'I've never seen you in here before.'

'Oh, I've been a few times. I do get out now and again.'

I was being quite cool but he looked right into my eyes and flashed me one of his devastating smiles, and before I could stop myself I said, 'The last time I saw you, Peter - you broke my heart.'

Lynda finished her conversation and said, 'Come on Ann, let's get a drink.'

I don't know whether she still had feelings for Peter but if so, she never let them surface in an obvious way. I often wondered what exactly she was searching for in life, despite being married with a family, and concluded that her search must be very similar to mine. I was more understanding of her after that night. I followed her to the bar but could feel Peter's eyes all over us. After a few minutes he came over and asked me, 'What did you mean, before?'

'Just what I said - you broke my heart.'

'Well I can try to fix it now. Can I buy you a drink?'

'I'm driving so I'm okay, thank you.'

'Well if you're driving, can you give me a lift home?'

My heart thudded like a machine gun and all the old feelings came flooding back. I knew I'd always loved him and probably always would.

'Mm, possibly, but I have to take Lynda home,' I replied, nodding at her as she swirled around the dancefloor.

'If you drop me off last we could maybe have a chat about old times?'

'Mm, maybe,' I answered. 'Don't you want to talk to Lynda?'

'Not really. That all died a long time ago.'

When we got out of the car at Lynda's so I could collect my things, she said, 'You're asking for trouble there, Ann.'

'No I'm not, he just wants to talk and I'd love to hear his apologies.'

'He'll hurt you all over again.'

'I'll be fine,' I shrugged. 'See you tomorrow.'

'Be it on your own head,' she said, weaving up the drive.

I drove Peter home and we sat at the end of his street talking, until suddenly I was aware of the time.

'I'll have to go now, Peter,' I said.

'Okay,' he said. 'Can I see you tomorrow?'

'Oh er, I'm not sure about that. Why would you want to?' I asked, worrying about ructions at home and fiddling with the car keys.

'Because I just can't forget you.'

'You know I'm married with three kids, right?'

'Right, so can you pick me up at the Pelican Garage at half past seven?'

I turned to face him and asked, 'You sure about this?'

He leaned over and kissed me on the lips, just like he did all those years back, and it felt like I was back in my own little heaven.

'Never been so sure of anything in my life,' he answered.

Had I finally found that elusive silver lining to the grey cloud of my life?

Chapter Seventy

The caravan

The next day was just the same as any other and I went about my work with a smile as always, and was hoping Peter wouldn't come into the shop and make me blush again. Thankfully he didn't but the day dragged and for once, I couldn't wait for it to end. When I got home the boys were down at Brenda's and Mark was sitting watching television as usual. I made tea and phoned Brenda to send the boys home. After we'd all eaten I washed the dishes and went upstairs to get ready. Lynda rang and asked what the latest news was, and I told her I'd see her later. As I put the phone down Mark said, 'Are you going to Lynda's again tonight?'

'Yes, if that's okay? She's still not coping too well,' I lied.

'Okay,' he said, turning away abruptly.

I felt like a deceitful bitch but knew we coped better the less time we spent together, and that Mark was happy being at home with the boys. If he'd said, 'No, I don't want you to go,' I probably wouldn't have, and maybe even respected him a bit more than I did. But I knew that in the long run it wouldn't make the slightest difference to the final outcome, because whatever that might be it definitely wasn't a happy future together.

I felt nervous and irritable, and a vision kept flashing up in my imagination: Lynda hurtling towards Sunderland in her car and suddenly a face appearing in the glare of the headlights. It was a man standing in the middle of the road with a terrible look on his face - a condemning, accusing expression that lingered in my mind. Then there was an awful thudding noise and the sound of Lynda's laughter. Or was it me laughing? I wasn't sure but I knew that the face in the road, blocking my progress to wherever I was going, was that of my husband.

I'd just finished knitting a pullover for myself, and tried it on in front of the bedroom mirror. It looked nice and I added a mini-skirt that showed my long legs and slim figure off to their best. Something was missing though so I pulled on black tights and white boots, and concluded that I was still reasonably attractive. That thought cheered me up immensely and I held onto it tightly.

Lee came down to play with Darren and Wayne and I stood watching them with a smile on my face. Craig was maturing fast and had gone to a friend's house to do grown-up stuff like listening to music. I leant against the door jamb, feeling the tight clothes hugging the curves of my body, and thought about my own life. I regretted much about my past but remained optimistic about a better future with my children, then I said goodbye to Darren and Wayne. They looked at me with confused expressions and I said, 'Love you both lots and I'll see you in the morning.'

They smiled and I kissed them both on their heads. They didn't like me kissing them now they were big tough boys, and especially when Lee was there.

411

I drove straight to the Pelican Garage and bought some cigarettes and chewing gum, and turned on the radio. It was quite nice sitting in the shadows, smoking and listening to music. I didn't remember Peter being as tall as he was, striding down the lane towards the garage. I hoped he couldn't see me smiling or hear my heart beating so fast.

'Hello Ann,' he said. 'You look nice.'

'Thank you,' I replied as a little voice in the back of my head suggested that looks were all he was ever interested in.

'I was worried that you wouldn't turn up,' he added.

'Mm, I had my doubts about you, as well.'

'Well here I am,' he smiled.

I smiled back and he kissed me passionately on the mouth, and all the magical memories and feelings flooded back from when Puppy Love was number one in the charts, and I was so much in love with the man sitting right next to me. I discarded all thoughts about the hurt that followed back then, and felt like that teenager in love all over again.

We drove to St Bees and walked along the promenade and listened to the waves crashing, and when Peter saw me shivering as the day drew to a close, he put his arms around me and held me close to him. I wanted that moment to last forever. I was in the middle of a wonderful dream and didn't want it to end.

We walked back to the car and watched the sun setting on the horizon, far out on the Irish Sea. We saw its dying light as it slowly dipped out of sight, just like it was drowning in the still water. It made me think about how all things die, including love, but I knew that very same sun would rise again the following day, and hoped that's what had happened to the love between Peter and I.

I snuggled up to him in the car and felt safer than I ever had. It felt like he'd come home and nothing could ever part us again. We talked about life, and our lives, and every now and again he tilted my head up to kiss me softly. The time just evaporated and eventually I whispered, 'I'll have to go now, Peter. Should I drive you home?'

'Yes, suppose it is getting late,' he said and kissed me again.

When I stopped the car at the end of his street I said, 'I really must go now Peter, it's very late.'

'Okay, but can I see you again?'

I paused for a moment. 'Are you sure you really want to?'

'Yes, of course.'

'Well, okay then, if you're sure.'

'So when's best for you?'

I knew I could meet him most nights instead of going to Lynda's or Elizabeth's, so said, 'Your choice.'

It was Tuesday at the time, and when he said Thursday I was delighted that he wanted to see me again so soon. At that moment my world seemed to be taking a big turn for the better.

'Goodnight Ann, see you Thursday, and remember we were very young all those years ago, but I did love you back then.'

I thought my heart was going to burst out of my chest. 'Goodnight Peter,' I croaked, holding back tears of sheer joy. 'See you Thursday.'

I watched him walk up the road until he was out of sight before I drove away. He never even tried to have sex with me, I thought to myself. Maybe he was behaving himself and being a gentleman, or maybe he doesn't fancy me now and is just being kind; making up for breaking my heart when I was young and madly in love with him? I still loved him as much as ever which meant that he could destroy me again, I reminded myself as I remembered Lynda's warning. But I pushed those thoughts to the back of my mind and relived the last few hours I'd spent with the love of my life.

Tessa came to greet me when I got home and I whispered, 'Hello girl,' before creeping up to bed.

Mark was still awake and when he looked at me, it felt like he could see right into my brain and read my thoughts. The burden of my guilt hung heavy.

'My mam and dad bought a holiday caravan today, Ann,' Mark said brightly in the darkness. 'It's up at Allonby near the beach, and they wondered if we'd like to go and see it on Sunday?'

'Oh, yes that'll be fine, Mark. The boys will enjoy that,' I replied, turning away. 'Goodnight.'

I pretended to go to asleep and prayed that Mark wouldn't do or say anything to spoil my fantasy. I know I was being selfish but re-connecting with Peter was very important to me, and I at least wanted to hold onto my dream for a little while longer. Nothing more was said and eventually we both fell asleep.

The boys were excited next morning when Mark told them about the caravan. 'Can we take Tessa, Dad?' they asked.

'Yes, I don't see why not. We can take her for a walk along the beach at Allonby Bay. The caravan site's just across the road.'

'Yippee,' the boys chorused.

I decided not to go to Lynda's or Elizabeth's that day, and phoned to let them both know.

'Is everything alright?' Lynda asked.

'Yes, fine, I'm just a bit tired.'

'Oh yes? So how did the big date go?'

I couldn't say too much over the phone, but let her know that all was well.

I was enjoying my work at the bookies and evidently had a few admirers. One bloke said to Colin, the manager, 'What's a good-looking lass like Ann doing, working in this place?'

Colin just smiled and I blushed as usual when I received any attention, but was always cheerful and smiled at everyone throughout the day. At home I tried my best to keep the peace between Mark and me, and when we fought, which was more often than ever, I escaped by walking out the door.

On Thursday evening I sat in the car wondering if Peter would show up again, but smiled when I saw him walking down the path. We drove to the outskirts of Workington and went to a pub, which was a change from just sitting in the car. I wanted to snuggle up to him like I had on Tuesday, but just being with him was more than enough for me. We hugged and kissed later but again didn't take things any further, and eventually we parted and went back to our separate homes and lives. We arranged to meet again the following Tuesday.

On Sunday, Mark, me, Tessa and the kids followed Mary and Billy up onto the B5300, and through to the caravan site. The sun was shining and glinting off the rippling Solway Firth, and everybody was in high spirits. Even Tessa barked with excitement when she saw the sea crashing onto the shore, and dashed down the beach to chase the waves back. Wayne caught her and said, 'Don't worry, Tess, we'll go for a nice walk soon.'

The caravan was roomy and really nice, and Mary made a pot of tea, with juice for the boys. Billy was very respectful towards me, and had apparently changed his mind since suggesting Mark should take me down some backstreet to get married. Now he always insisted I was 'far too good' for Mark. It wasn't nice and I was never too good for Mark or anybody else, especially not now when I was repeatedly cheating behind his back. It was probably the other way around nowadays.

I often wondered if Mary knew what was going on, as she was friendly with women who would have known about the crash I had with Patrick in the car. In fact she probably knew Patrick's mother, but if she did know, she never said a single word about it and I never detected anything in her manner towards me.

As we sat gazing out across the Solway towards Scotland, Mary said, 'There's another tourer for sale on site, Mark, it's a four-berth and we were wondering if you and Ann would like us to buy it, so you can be here with us and help me out with your dad?'

'That would be great,' Darren said and everybody looked at me.

'Can we, Mam?' Wayne asked with a pleading smile.

'Well, if you're sure?' I asked Mary, thinking how on earth could I deprive my family of such a generous offer.

'Yes, of course we are,' she answered.

I looked at Mark and he nodded.

'Alright, thank you both, that's really nice of you.'

'You can have a week here in the summer holidays, Ann,' Mary continued.

'Or maybe two weeks?' Mark said, smiling at me.

'I might not be able to get two weeks off together,' I said, hoping not to burst the little bubble of family joy. 'There're other people at the office who also have children, so the school holiday weeks are booked up very quickly.'

'Oh, that's a shame.'

'But a week shouldn't be a problem and there are always weekends,' I offered, hoping nobody would take me up on the weekends.

'Shall we go and have a look, Ann?' Mary asked me, already rising from her nicely cushioned seat.

'Yes, okay,' I replied politely, and everybody except Billy trooped off to have a look at the caravan for sale.

It was very clean and tidy if a little small compared to Mary's six-berther, but we could always eat in their van if they were there at the same time. The boys loved it so Mark and I agreed, thanked Mary and Billy for their kind gesture, and they bought it for us to use.

All the way home the boys chatted about the caravan and Tessa barked every now and again, to show she was pleased when Wayne told her she could come on holiday with us now.

I'd been seeing Peter for a few weeks and still he was being the perfect gentleman, and hadn't tried to have sex with me. Mark and I had a particularly bad argument one morning before I went to work, and the sourness stayed with me all day. It was about the money he wasted betting on the horses as usual, and I was furious that he still stole from my purse.

I was meeting Peter that night and when I got home the boys had already had their tea. Mark tried to make amends. I didn't speak to him though, made my own meal and went upstairs to get changed. I always felt unclean at work because just about all the customers puffed away nervously on cigarettes. The ban on smoking in public places hadn't yet been introduced.

I spoke to Tessa and the boys and told them I was going to Lynda's. Mark watched and listened but didn't say anything. As I left I turned and said, 'See you later, Mark.'

He didn't answer or even look in my direction, and in temper I grabbed the caravan key as well as the car keys. I looked at him again with my heart pounding, but he just sat in the chair with his eyes glued to the television. I went to pick

Peter up and asked him straight out if he'd like to see our caravan. He said, 'Yeah, sure.'

We drove through to Allonby Bay and I made coffee in the caravan, and we sat chatting and listening to some music tapes Peter brought with him. They were songs from various artists and the first one was *It Started With A Kiss*, by Hot Chocolate. We listened for a while and then he said, 'This is the one that always reminds me of you.'

I felt tears in my eyes and then he kissed me, on the lips first, then my neck, and my breasts after he pulled open my blouse, and then everywhere. He caressed me gently and asked if I was sure I wanted this to happen, and although I desperately wanted it to, I knew it was so wrong and sat up, pulling my clothes around me. He was breathing hard but stopped, respected my decision and relaxed.

We lay together for a long time, on the narrow bed in the caravan that my husband's parents had bought for us, and he asked if I was alright.

'I'm fine Peter, are you?'

'Well, kind of,' he replied.

I smiled and kissed him on the cheek.

We never went to the caravan again and I wished we hadn't done so even that once. I always felt so guilty when I thought about it, usually sitting in the same van with Mark and the boys, as it was bought by Mary & Bill and not mine to abuse.

Peter and I still met for coffee every week and because of what he told me, I really believed he was seriously unhappy with his life, and that my boys and I might eventually live with him. I dreamed about it all the time but after a while, Peter never actually spoke about it. I assumed he felt guilty about what he was going to do and convinced myself that it was bound to happen, because we both loved each other so much.

When I thought deeply about the situation, I remembered a saying my mother often repeated: 'Never count your chickens before they're hatched.'

Chapter Seventy One

Pain and passion

Despite both being married to other people, Peter and I acted like a couple; an item, when we were together, and nothing seemed to rock our little boat. But it was still rough water out there and I looked forward to the nights we met. On the other days I visited Lynda or Elizabeth, and looked in on Brenda regularly too. She was evidently clear of cancer and feeling very positive. I saw my parents every Sunday without fail, sometimes with the boys or on my own if they were out walking with Colin.

During the school holidays we took a trip to the caravan, and I tried to enjoy it as best I could for the sake of the boys. It was difficult being cooped up in the little van with no escape from Mark, acting like a normal family, but the scenery around the bay and the Solway Coast was magnificent, and went a little way to keeping me cheerful.

One afternoon when we returned to the site after a day out, our van had been broken into it and most of our belongings stolen. It was never the same after that, we couldn't leave anything there or relax even when we were at the beach, just across the road. Mark was very wary and even the boys' enthusiasm waned, so the van was hardly ever used after that and only then for day trips. Not long afterwards we suggested that Mary put it back on sale, and everybody was pleased when it sold quite quickly. I was particularly relieved as the temptation to take Peter there, especially when it was cold at night, was compelling but I did always resist.

I was knitting and daydreaming one drizzly, Sunday afternoon, as the boys played around the house with Lee, and a couple of other friends. I hadn't been back long from visiting my parents, and was just beginning to relax when the telephone rang. I got up again and answered it, just as Mark came through the door after walking the hounds.

'Can I speak to Ann Murdock?' the female caller asked politely.

'This is Ann Murdock,' I replied.

'Are you going out with Peter Andrews?'

'What? What has that got to do with you?' I answered abruptly.

'Well it has a lot to do with his wife, so just leave my brother alone or you'll regret it.'

I quickly hung up the phone with my heart racing, and went to sit back down in the living room.

'Who was that?' Mark asked with a puzzled frown.

'Oh, it was just a wrong number,' I quickly replied, knowing my face was bright red with guilt and embarrassment. 'Would you like a drink?' I asked him with a false smile, heading for the kitchen.

Mark never said anymore about the telephone call, and I hoped that she didn't ring back.

Peter and I had been seeing each other for over a year, and I couldn't believe it had passed so quickly. After the call from his sister though, I suspected that his wife had found out. It would be surprising if she hadn't by then, as we were sometimes out late after falling asleep in each other's arms, in the back of the car. I knew we were both skating on thin ice, but I was so in love with Peter that I'd risk just about anything to be with him, and didn't know how I'd cope if it all had to end.

I wasn't even sure if he'd turn up on the next Tuesday night, but he did and although I didn't want to tell him about his sister's call, thought it best to say something. So after we'd chatted for a while I lied about the caller, 'Peter, I got a phone call on Sunday from Lynda, and she told me to leave you alone.'

Although it was dark in the car I saw the colour drain from his face. 'Are you sure it was Lynda?' he croaked.

'Well it sounded like her, although we haven't spoken for quite a while.'

'Strange,' he said and we carried on talking, but he was very distracted and I knew he was worried.

So perhaps he wasn't as ready to ditch his current life as I'd thought? That realisation disturbed me and I wondered if I was heading straight into another dead-end.

'Are you alright?' I asked him.

'I'm okay,' he answered, but not very convincingly.

I half-wished I hadn't mentioned the phantom phone call at all, but couldn't take it back. It was nearly 11.30pm and I said, 'Do you want to go home?'

He nodded and I was disappointed, but I turned on the ignition and set off to his house. I dropped him at the end of the street and he kissed me briefly as he got out. He seemed so worried that I really thought I might never see him again, but the next time we met he was in much better spirits. I asked what had happened and he said, 'Janet never mentioned any phone call, so she obviously doesn't know anything about it.'

'Oh, right,' I said, a little puzzled.

'So I don't know what your pal Lynda knows, but maybe you should find out?'

'Yeah, okay, I'll ask her.'

We carried on as normal until one night after we'd stayed at the beach a little longer than usual, and it was nearly 2am when I arrived back home. As I drove towards the house I saw that the living-room light was on, and noticed Mary's car in our parking space. Oh shit, I thought, what's going on?

When I walked in, Tessa greeted me as always but Mary wasn't there, so I knew Mark had borrowed her car to look for me. He got straight up with a strange expression on his deathly white face, and his eyes bored right into me as he asked, 'Where have you been, Ann?'

'I...I've been to Elizabeth's.'

'No you haven't. I went looking for you and your car wasn't there.'

'No, no but I was there earlier and then went to Lynda's.'

'So why wasn't the car there either, when I called round that way?'

Shit, I thought, my mind whirring. 'I hid it around the corner in case you were looking for me,' I blurted the most stupid excuse ever.

He shouted, 'You are fucking lying, Ann. Are you having an affair?'

I was so fed up with all the lies and deceit and wanted it all to be over, so as tears welled in my eyes, I looked straight at him and said, 'Yes Mark, I am.'

He let out a little gasp and looked like a wounded dog, and asked, 'Do you love him?'

'Well, yes, I do,' I replied cruelly but honestly.

'And does he love you?'

'Yes, I think so.'

He looked at me and said, 'Who the fuck could love you, you conniving bitch?'

'I know I've not been a very good wife to you, Mark, so you'll be better off without me, because I love him even if he doesn't love me.'

'Who is it?' he asked.

'It's nobody you know.'

I couldn't tell him who it was as for years he'd told me that I should have married Peter. He knew I'd always loved him and I knew it would hurt him more than anything to think Peter had won in the end.

He got up and went to bed and left me alone with my thoughts, and the tears that streamed down my face. I didn't want to hurt him in that way and it crushed me when I had to. I eventually went to bed and when Mark thought I was sleep, he forced himself inside me and carried out an act of abuse that again ensured I could never ever love or respect him.

When I came home from work the following day, the boys were out walking with Colin and Mark was calmly watching television. I finished my tea and washed the dishes, and sat in the living-room with Tessa at my feet. She kept doing the canine play-bow and looking towards her ball, wanting me to throw it for her. She loved playing games, especially hide & seek when I put her out of the room and hid one of her toys, then let her back in to find it. She was so clever and always remembered the place I'd hidden it the previous time. I was mustering up the energy to play with her, when she put her head on my knee and looked into my eyes. She always knew my mood, and especially when I was upset or worried. One day when Mark and I had been arguing, I lay on the dining-room floor crying, and unbelievably, she lay down beside me and howled just like she was crying too.

Mark often hurt me with his hateful words but the pain was never plain to see. There were no physical bruises or broken limbs, just a bruised heart and a broken spirit. When Mark shouted at me Tessa would hide away from him, and he would often scream at her too. Later, when we were together I'd joke with her, saying, 'You should look after me and bark at him when he's shouting.'

She would always wag her tail and lick my face. She was devoted to me and the kids but knew not to upset Mark, and always obeyed him with her tail between her legs. Suddenly my doggy daydream was shattered by Mark's booming voice: 'Do you want a divorce?'

The question brought me crashing back to reality and I said, 'Er, yes please, I'll look for somewhere to live with the boys.'

'It's alright, I'll move out,' he offered, and I knew he could live with his parents, whereas my parents were now in a retirement home.

'Thank you.'

'I'll get the papers and we can sort it out,' he said.

He seems keen to get it over with, I thought, which is for the best but I was dreading having to explain to the kids, why Daddy wasn't living with us anymore. That night the time dragged slowly and I was pleased when Mark went to bed. As far as I knew neither of us had mentioned anything to the boys, but I'd no idea what he might have told them when I wasn't there. I sat for hours staring into space, feeling frightened and alone. I knew my parents would stand by me but what could they do? The unknown was frightening.

Eventually I fell asleep on the sofa, and woke when the light of dawn filtered through the window onto my tear-stained face. It was 5.30am and the ticking of the clock was so loud in the silence, as I made myself a drink and went upstairs to have a bath. Soon the boys were awake and I got them ready for school, and then I got dressed for work. I was so pleased that I had a full day's work to go to, and try to forget about our family nightmare for a while. How Mark coped with not going to work was beyond me, but I suppose it had advantages when the sun was shining. When I got home the boys were all in the living-room and asked if I was okay.

'Yes, I'm fine,' I said, watching them watching me and wondering what they knew.

I didn't want to put them on the spot though, particularly with Mark lurking in the background, and hoped that they were just concerned because they'd heard all the shouting and screaming the night before. I got changed and said, 'I'm just popping out to see Elizabeth.'

Mark probably knew I was lying again but I didn't care about that anymore, and off I went to meet Peter, telling the boys I'd see them in the morning.

Peter was smiling as he got into the car and I said, 'Hello, are you okay?'

'I'm fine,' he replied, and we drove to Workington where we had a drink in the corner of a quiet little pub.

'Peter,' I said after he kissed me the fourth time. 'Mark and I are getting divorced.'

'Honestly?' he asked with wide eyes.

'Yeah, he knows I'm seeing someone but doesn't know who.'

His demeanour changed immediately and he sat there fidgeting, and looking very concerned.

'It's alright though,' I tried to reassure him. 'I'll never say it's you.'

He didn't look reassured though and decided it was time to go. I was concerned that his mood could change so quickly and dramatically, and as we left he looked seriously worried. We didn't discuss the matter on the way home and I parked near the beach to ask if he was alright. He kissed me again and smiled, but something was definitely missing and it upset me.

'I'll have to go, Peter,' I said without looking at him. 'I've rocked the boat enough in the last few days; I don't want to sink it completely just yet.'

He smiled strangely as he got out of the car and unusually, we never arranged our next date. The house was in darkness when I got home but I knew Mark would still be awake. I braced myself to blank out the abuse that would probably ensue when I got into bed, but Mark said, 'I got a phone call before, from a guy who asked if I knew where my wife was.'

My heart instantly beat faster and I felt panic churning my stomach. 'What did you say?' I managed to ask.

'I told him it had nothing to do with him, whether I knew where my wife was or not.'

I looked at him hopefully.

'Then he told me he knew where you were, and that you were with his brother-in-law, Peter Andrews.'

I lay there feeling mortified and genuinely afraid of what would happen next. I knew this information would hurt Mark more than anything else, and possibly to the point of revengeful violence. I lay there in absolute silence, not daring to speak or even knowing what to say.

'I always knew you loved him,' Mark said calmly.

He was right, I always had, but I'd tried so hard to love Mark and in the early days thought I did. I'd ended up doing this terrible thing to my husband but surely, surely that was partly because of all the terrible things he did to me?

Chapter Seventy Two

Separation or surrender?

When I got home from work next day, Mark told me he was divorcing me and naming Peter as the main Respondent. It sounded awful and I knew we'd have talk to the boys sometime soon. So after tea when we were all in the living-room, I told them we were splitting up. Craig went straight to his room and slammed the door angrily. Darren and Wayne listened but probably didn't understand what was happening. I told them I'd be staying with them, and that Mark still loved them even though he wouldn't be living with us. Then I went upstairs to talk with Craig. He was lying on the bed with his face in the pillow, and I knew he was crying. 'Craig,' I whispered. 'Mam and Dad still both love you all very much.'

He turned over and looked at me with hatred in his eyes and snarled, 'I want to live with Dad.'

My heart was breaking. I never wanted my children to suffer this and hated myself for causing it. Craig was fifteen now and old enough to understand more than his brothers.

'Are you sure?' I asked him.

'Yes I am, because Dad has nobody but you'll have someone else next week, he says.'

My son's words pierced my heart like a knife and I was unable to speak. My legs went weak and tears fell like raindrops onto my chest. I put a hand on the wall to steady myself and whispered, 'It's alright if you want to live with your dad, Craig but please remember that I love you and I always will.'

He threw his arms around my neck and I could feel his tears on my cheek. 'I love you too, Mam,' he said. 'But Dad will be lonely on his own with nobody to love him or look after him.'

I couldn't say anymore and felt like I was about to collapse. I kissed my boy and went into the living-room, where I fell onto the sofa and sobbed like a baby, hating myself for allowing this happen. Darren came and sat with me and said, 'I'll live with you, Mam.'

My heart lurched into my mouth and I hugged him to me, still unable to speak. Then little Wayne said, 'I love you both so I don't mind who I live with.'

A little flutter of nervous laughter found its way out of my mouth and I said, 'So will you stay with Mammy?'

He smiled and replied 'Okay then.'

Those minutes were by far the most emotional experience of my whole life, and they left me completely stunned, shocked and unable to function normally. All previous plans were out of the window; totally scrapped and after the boys went to bed I said to Mark, 'I'm so sorry for all this, Mark. Our boys are the most important people in my life and I don't want them to be separated or unhappy in any way. I'll finish with Peter and maybe we could try again to make it all work for us?'

He didn't answer.

'If it doesn't work I'll move out on my own and leave you all in peace?'

Mark still didn't say anything but he must have been thinking it over, because he ripped up the divorce papers and threw them in the kitchen bin. I realise how much he must love me to do that, and wished I could love him even half as much. We decided to try and lead a normal family life, and I prayed that he'd stop doing all those stupid things that had previously made it impossible.

I purposely didn't see Peter for a few weeks, then waited to catch him after work one day so I could explain the situation to him. He saw me but walked straight past without another glance in my direction. I was hurt but determined, and drove after him. He carried on walking and I called out, 'Peter, have you got a minute?'

He stopped and asked, 'What?'

'Mark and I aren't getting divorced now. I've told him we can try again because he was going to name you as Respondent, and I don't want your family going through the same thing as mine – it's been horrendous.'

He said, 'Yeah, okay,' and walked away again.

I didn't expect a medal or anything, for trying to protect him and save both our families from misery at the same time, but a simple 'thank you' would've gone a long way. I couldn't decide whether he was seriously annoyed that I'd cut short our last date and never arranged another one, and hadn't been in contact since, or just decided he didn't want to know me anymore. Whatever it was, Lynda was right that I was asking for trouble getting involved with him again, and now my whole world including my family, was falling apart as a result. Or were we falling apart anyway? I found it difficult to think straight and much easier not to think at all.

Life at home improved a little bit and surprisingly, I didn't miss Peter as much as I thought I would. Not yet anyway. Darren and Wayne seemed happy but Craig was very quiet and introspective, so I didn't know really how he was feeling. He continued to do well at rugby though, and Mark still went with him to every match. Craig was often mentioned in the local news, as a young star who played for the Hensingham under-19 team, and I also made time to watch him play a few times. He's my son so I was biased, and I'm certainly not an expert on rugby, but it was obvious even to me that he was a very good player. I was so proud of him and it was easy to be happy when I was with the boys, or even with colleagues at work. I loved my sons and I loved my job, and those were the things in my life that I concentrated on.

I was transferred to another betting-shop at Woodhouse, to the south of Whitehaven, where I worked with Frances, Pat, and the manager, Madeline. They all knew Mark and were friendly and supportive from the start. I'd been asked to train as Office Manager, which absorbed me and took my mind off family problems. I hated gambling but loved the financial side of it: working out all the figures and amounts, and profits and losses, and I learned all the procedures very quickly. Soon I was looking after all the offices on the managers' days off, so got to know all the different areas and staff. I preferred Woodhouse overall, Frances and Pat had worked there for years and we got on really well, and I didn't let my promotion interfere with that.

Christmas came and went but it didn't bring its usual magic for me, though as always I felt a little disappointed when the festive season was over and the boys were back at school. Just afterwards we received news that a team including the Chief Executive was coming through from head office at Barry

Island, South Wales, to investigate some 'financial irregularities'. Some of the staff looked at me strangely and I wondered what was going on, so I telephoned to find out and was told, 'Someone is stealing money from the Woodhouse branch and we're going to find out exactly who it is.'

Oh my God, I thought, I hope they don't think it's me. I was bound to be a suspect with the theft occurring so soon after I'd been given access to the accounts, and the following days were stressful. I carried on with my work as normal and one morning received a telephone call to attend the Woodhouse office at 9am prompt. The CEO wanted a word with me. I couldn't believe it. I'd just settled into a job that I loved more than any I'd ever had, and now I was going to lose it and be accused of stealing!

I was a nervous wreck on my way to the office that morning, and kept rehearsing in my head what I was going to say to defend myself and my professional reputation. I was told to wait outside the office and sat there wringing my hands for twenty minutes, before being called in. I tottered through and sat where I was told, in front of three big-shots behind Madeline's desk. I tensed in preparation for the interrogation, and the man in the middle of the three, who I found out later was the CEO, said to me, 'Do you like working here, Ann?'

I was wary of what was coming but answered, 'Yes, I do. I like it very much.'

'Good,' he said. 'I'm glad to hear it.'

He was staring right at me and not knowing what else to do, I smiled at him. To my surprise he smiled back and said, 'What I'm going to tell you is classified information and you must not repeat it outside this room. Do you understand?'

I nodded.

'Madeline has been suspended from work with this company as of today, until further notice pending investigations, possibly by the police'

I gulped but said nothing.

'Regarding yourself,' he continued, looking me straight in the eye and pausing.

I gulped again and fought to keep my fidgeting hands still.

'We've had nothing but excellent reports about you and your work, and we'd like you to operate as manager here until further notice.'

I was stunned, and relieved, and almost broke out into a nervous release of laughter.

'Do you accept?' he continued.

'Yes, yes I do and thank you very much.'

A few weeks down the line we heard that Madeline had been sacked for stealing money by putting on false bets, and also found guilty in court. After a few months I was offered the manager's job permanently, and was stationed at Woodhouse full time. I took to my new role with renewed enthusiasm, and with Frances and Pat fully on board, we made a good team.

Things at home didn't go as well though and I still hated finishing time at work. By the time I got back to the house the boys were often out, and Craig was always playing rugby or training or socialising with his team-mates, which meant Mark and I were alone a lot of the time. I tried making conversation but the scars were still raw in Mark's mind, so it never went very far.

I started going to Elizabeth's house again because Mark trusted her, and never worried much when I was there. After a while I started popping into Lynda's on the way home but didn't tell Mark. He blamed Lynda for my affair, which let me off the hook a little, but she never held a gun to my head. He insulted her to me often and I always wanted to say, I'm the one who's responsible and you caused me to be. If only you could've treated me like your wife and not a possession, and if you hadn't been so insanely jealous we might have fallen in love instead of out of love. I never put a foot wrong in our marriage for years, and I took all the cruel shit you dished out when you were lazing at home, because you wouldn't go to work. Why was everything left to me and why did you steal money from your family to waste at the betting-shop? Marriage is supposed to be a partnership but you only ever thought of yourself. The memories still made me angry and tragically, we were trying to resurrect a marriage which died a painful death years ago. My son said he hated me and thought I was a slut because of what you told him behind my back, and everything was just a total mess which could never be fixed. I hated myself for what I'd done but if I'm completely honest, given the same circumstances - I don't think I was strong enough to do anything differently.

Chapter Seventy Three

The hardest decision of my life

Every day that passed told me that Mark and I weren't going to survive as a couple. If anything had changed it was that he was now more emboldened, after my failure to leave when the door was wide open right in front of me. One morning on my day off work, he returned from visiting his parents' after taking the boys to school, and was in one of his sulky moods. I couldn't stand another conflict so early on my rest day, so said I was going to see my mam and dad. I telephoned Mam and she was really busy, but I needed someone to talk to and didn't want to risk a trip to Lynda's. I told her I was fed up but she said, 'You'll be alright, love. I'll see you later.'

I tried Elizabeth but she too was busy, so in desperation I finally called Lynda, and she didn't have time for me either! Maybe they all knew something I didn't? Although none of them really knew what I was suffering, and thought that I was now committed to my previously failing marriage, it felt like no-one cared. I was empty and alone and had nobody to turn to in my hour of need. Eventually I got in the car and drove into town, and parked opposite Peter's workplace. I could see someone through the big windows, going in and out of the office, but it wasn't him.

A high spring tide was in and the big, ancient harbour where thousands of African slaves had first set foot in England, was full to the brim. I was parked near a ramp which small fishing boats used to enter the dock, and the turbulent sea was lapping up and over the top of the harbour wall. I sat there watching the waves trying to escape their confines, and knew just how pointless their efforts were. I imagined myself leaping in to join them, so they might drown me and all my sorrows.

The tears dripped off the end of my chin onto my blouse, and I thought that if I really tried to drown myself, it would probably go wrong like everything else in my life. And it would be so selfish, I told myself, remembering how much pain I'd already caused my sons, even though they'd probably be better off without me. Some hope must have still flickered in my heart though, because I turned away, started up the engine and drove off.

I called in to see my parents and Mam said, as she so often did, 'Hello love, is everything alright?'

'Yes,' I lied, not wanting to worry her.

'Sit down then and I'll put the kettle on.'

I wanted her to hug me and tell me everything would be alright like when I was a child, and get me out of the big mess I'd created. But how could I tell her when I felt so ashamed of myself and what I'd done?

We sipped tea and chatted, and after an hour or so I felt a little better. I went to visit Elizabeth, and telephoned Mark to tell him I'd collect the boys from school. I never told him, Elizabeth or anyone else how low I felt that day, and when I picked up the boys, I was pleased that I didn't have the courage to throw myself over the harbour wall.

Work was a refuge and a lifeline and I was always happiest there. Frances was a real tonic and made us all laugh. One day I noticed a new customer who'd started coming into the shop very regularly. He was young and stocky with black hair and obviously knew Frances and Pat quite well, as he was always laughing and joking with them. He stood at the back of the shop studying form in the newspapers, and chewing on one of our pens. Frances saw me watching him one afternoon and said, 'His name's Bill and he goes through at least three pens a week.'

I laughed and commented, 'You know him then?'

'Yes, he's really nice. He's married and has two lovely little girls.'

'Oh yes?'

'Yes, he sometimes brings them in with him.'

I smiled and turned back to my work, but maybe Bill noticed us talking about him because he came up to the counter and asked, 'Who's the new girl then, Frances?'

'Her name's Ann and she's the manager,' Frances smiled at me. 'And she's married with a husband and three lovely sons.'

I smiled back at Frances, wondering why on earth she'd said all that, then nodded to Bill and sat down to do my job.

A couple of weeks later Lynda and I were in town for a secret night out, and just as we were leaving the last pub to go home, who came in through the door, but Bill. He'd obviously had a drink or two, said hello and the next thing I knew he was kissing me. I pushed him off and said sternly, 'Excuse me!'

He smiled.

'And you're married.'

'No I'm not,' he said. 'Take no notice of Frances.'

'And she's mistaken about your two little girls as well, is she?' I said sarcastically, brushing past him.

'No she's not,' he replied, grabbing my arm. 'I do have two daughters but I'm not married.'

Lynda had stopped by the exit and was busy talking to someone she knew, so I moved to the side and Bill followed. I called out, 'Lynda, are you ready?'

'Oh, yes,' she answered and turned for the door.

'Can I share your taxi?' Bill asked.

'We haven't got a taxi,' I replied without looking back.

'Are you walking?' he persisted, setting off after us.

'No, she's driving,' Lynda informed him.

'Well can you give me a lift?' he pleaded, grabbing my arm again.

Lynda and I both turned towards him and he gave us a big, puppy-dog smile.

'Oh give him a lift,' Lynda said. 'Or we'll never get home.'

'Come on then,' I said, thinking it couldn't do any harm with her there. 'Where do you live?'

'Where do you live?' he asked.

Lynda told him her address and he said, 'Oh, I live really close by,' so I drove towards her house.

When we got there however, he said, 'Oh no, I must've got mixed up, I don't live anywhere near here.'

'You should stick to fizzy pop,' Lynda said, getting out of the car and leaving me alone, with Bill in the back seat.

Neat move Bill, I thought with a wry smile, but I actually felt quite relaxed with him. He gave me his real address and on the way there we chatted about life in general. When we arrived he said, 'I hope you didn't mind me kissing you earlier?'

I didn't answer.

439

'Couldn't help it,' he continued. 'I've been wanting to since I first saw you.'

'Well thank you for the compliment Bill, but I must go home now.'

'Do you fancy meeting up again, Ann? Just to talk like we've done tonight. I don't often get the chance to talk like that with anybody.'

'Really?' I asked, a little intrigued.

'Really,' he confirmed.

'Tell you what, ask me again when you're sober and I'll see if I can find some chat time.'

He asked again at work, and as I was so lonely and unhappy, and because it was close to finishing time and I didn't want to go home, I agreed because I also enjoyed his company.

We talked about everything under the sun, and it was such a relief to share my problems with a sympathetic listener. After we'd discussed all our problems to death I agreed to meet him again on the same footing. Mark guessed right away that something was going on, probably because I was a little more cheerful, and asked me, 'Are you seeing Peter again?'

I didn't want to open up a whole new chapter so said, 'Well, yes, I've been seeing Peter but just because we both need to talk about the past, so we can put it all to sleep for good.'

He seemed to accept that and actually said, 'Look Ann, I didn't mind you having an affair as long as you're discreet about it.'

'Honestly?' I asked in surprise. 'Are you sure?'

'Yes, I've thought about it and I don't want to lose you, Ann. I want our family to stay together for the sake of the boys, so if that's what it takes – that's what it'll have to be.'

I was amazed but what he didn't add, was that he thought he was entitled to have his share of me all the more now. His night-time abuse continued and one evening when I was ready to go out, he came upstairs and looked in through the bedroom door.

'You look really nice,' he said, eyeing me up and down.

I said nothing and kept my eyes on the floor.

'Look at you, now you've lost weight, you look gorgeous.'

'Mark, look…' I began, eyes still on the carpet.

'How could you do this to me?'

I looked in the mirror and saw an aggressive scowl on his face behind me. Our eyes met and then he grabbed my collar, flung me onto the bed and as I tried to push him off, he raped me. When he'd finished he got up, grunted as he re-fastened his belt, and went back downstairs without another word.

I lay there crying and thinking that I could not allow him to treat me like a piece of meat ever again. I knew without doubt at that moment, that I would have to leave this increasingly abusive relationship if I wanted to even survive as a human being.

I got up off the bed I never wanted to see again, went to the bathroom to clean myself up and pull myself together mentally, and went out. After a phone call I met Bill and told him I never wanted to go back home. Bill got a key from a mate whose caravan we stayed in that night.

By morning I'd calmed down and knew I'd have to go back to make sure the boys went to school, and to collect some things including my work clothes. Mark was already up and as soon as I walked in, he started shouting. I argued back and he grabbed me by the neck, and pinned me against the kitchen door.

'You fucking slut,' he screamed. 'You're making a bloody fool of me.'

He had me by the throat and I couldn't speak, Tessa was barking frantically and I heard Craig shout, 'What the fuck is wrong with you two? I wish you'd grow the fuck up, the pair of you.'

Mark let go and I ran upstairs into the bedroom and pushed the bed against the door. I heard him go out and slam the front door, so went back downstairs just as Bill phoned, to ask if everything was okay when I'd returned home? I was still in a state of panic and told him about the screaming argument, and Mark grabbing me by the throat. He went very quiet, and said he might see me later.

I bathed and got changed and went to Lynda's, and I was telling her the news when my mobile rang. It was Darren crying, 'Mammy we're frightened, there's a man banging on the door and Daddy's shouting at him to go away.'

Oh no, I knew it must be Bill and felt awful about what I was doing to my children. I couldn't live like this anymore, I knew for a certain fact, and had to leave as soon as possible as I was wrecking their young lives. I decided to go home and make arrangements to sort things out as quickly as possible, and told Mark I'd leave the house but he had to leave me alone until I could arrange things. He nodded his agreement and next morning I took the boys to school as normal, and then went to work. When I came home everything seemed calm and after tea when the boys were all out, Mark said, 'I saw your Albert today, and asked if you can live with him.'

'Oh right, what did he say?'

'He said it would probably be okay and you just have to go see him about it.'

I spoke to Albert and he said moving in was fine. I'd booked a week's holiday for September 14th and I said I would move in

442

that day. That morning I got up early and said to Mark, 'Have you told the boys I'm going to live with uncle Albert yet?'

'No, I haven't.'

'Okay, thanks. I want to tell them that I love them all dearly, and explain to them that it's you I'm leaving and not them.'

He said, 'Look Ann, I don't want you to upset them before they go to school.'

'But I have to speak to them before I leave.'

'Ann, you made the decision to leave, so just fuck off.'

I was too frightened of his violent temper to go against his wishes, and knew he could tell the boys anything he liked once I was gone. I tried to argue but was emotionally distressed and hated myself for not being stronger. I hung around as long as possible though and all my sons said goodbye before going to school, but they didn't know that when they came home – their mother wouldn't be there anymore. I stayed silent and listened to the door close behind them, and watched them through the window as they walked down the path.

When Mark came back from school he drove me to my brothers and left me there in a flood of tears. The only things I took from our home were a chest of draws for my clothes, and a school photograph of each of my sons. I stood the pictures on the chest, and lay on the little single bed weeping as I have never wept before or since, as their three beautiful faces smiled down at me.

We were apart now because I truly believed that was the best option for them, but we would not be apart forever and I would dedicate my life to staying in contact with them.

I thought of you today,
But that's nothing new.
I thought about you yesterday,
And every other day too.

I think of you in silence,
I often speak your names,
But all I have are memories,
And your pictures, in frames.

My memories are treasures,
From which I'll never part,
I can't hold you in my arms,
But I keep you in my heart.

Ann Murdock

***

Me with Mam and a snowman

Me with Dad

Poet bound for USA

A WHITEHAVEN poet is bound for America after being nominated as the International Poets Society Poet of the Year 2000.

Ann Murdock, of Fleswick Avenue, Woodhouse, is now jetting off to Washington for a glittering awards ceremony in August.

The mother-of-three will join 110 other finalists competing for the $5000 prize money and publishing contract.

The inspiration behind the winning poem was Ann's mother, Jessie Chambers, who lost her brave fight against liver cancer earlier this year.

"I wrote the poem for her in Christmas 1998 - three months after the cancer was discovered," said Ann. "When I found out my Mam was poorly, I wanted to express how much I really loved her."

She entered her poem after spotting an advert for the International Society of Poets in a magazine. "It is quite an achievement to get this far.

"I only sent it away on thought nothing ventured, nothing gained."

Ann is travelling to the three-day convention with her brother, Albert Chambers, from

On the night, all finalists receive a bronze medallion and commemorative plaque and then read out their poem in front of the audience

USA BOUND: Ann Murdock

The poetry competition

447

About the author

Ann Murdock was born in Whitehaven, West Cumberland; a small fishing port which used to be one of the largest slave-trading ports in the world, and the main landing point for early American trade. Her mother came from Blackburn, Lancashire, an industrial manufacturing hub in the north of England, and her father worked at the infamous Sellafield nuclear reprocessing plant. Ann grew up with three brothers and a sister, and a staunch work-ethic on the far northwest coast, looking out over the Solway Firth to southern Scotland. She also grew up with idyllic aspirations to a perfect love affair and marriage such as that of her parents, and fell deeply in love as an attractive 16 year-old who worked long hours stacking shelves in a Woolworth's store. Unfortunately the dream turned sour and her young heart was broken forever. She ended up in a tragic marriage which for decades included mental and sexual abuse, but also produced 3 children. It became her mission to escape the abuse and find the life she'd always dreamed of, without destroying the lives of those children. Could she do it? Would she ever be free? She had major decisions to make and years of suffering to endure first.

Ann's maiden voyage

The boat was off and sailing,
And I was all aboard,
But the vessel was already failing,
And the crew were in discord.

We steamed along, straight ahead,
On a course I didn't know,
I'd no idea where it led,
Or how far, we had to go.

I saw my true destination,
Across a turbulent sea,
And used my aspiration,
To claim back my life, for me.

The captain didn't like it,
When I abandoned the trip,
But I preferred to hike it,
Than go down with his ship.

A cloud, black as a raven,
Hovered over me like a beast,
So I left dear old Whitehaven,
And headed east.

Rob MacGowan 2017

The sequel to this book, titled 'Still Searching' will be released in 2018 and available on Amazon, and all major online retailers. Keep in touch with the author and buy your personalised, signed copy: annq.murdock@sky.com

23009636R00256

Printed in Great Britain
by Amazon